A MORMON

— *in the* —

WHITE HOUSE?

A MORMON

—— *in the* ——

WHITE HOUSE?

10 THINGS EVERY AMERICAN
SHOULD KNOW ABOUT MITT ROMNEY

HUGH HEWITT

Since 1947
REGNERY
PUBLISHING, INC.
An Eagle Publishing Company • Washington, DC

Published in association with Yates & Yates, LLP, Attorneys and Counselors, Orange, California

Library of Congress Cataloging-in-Publication Data

Hewitt, Hugh, 1956–

A Mormon in the White House?: 10 things every American should know about Mitt Romney / by Hugh Hewitt.
    p. cm.
    Includes index.
    ISBN 978-1-59698-502-5

    1. Romney, Mitt. 2. Romney, Mitt—Political and social views. 3. Presidential candidates—United States—Biography. 4. Mormons—United States—Biography. 5. Mormonism—Political aspects—United States. 6. Presidents—United States—Election—2008. I. Title.
    E840.8.R598H48 2007
    974.4'044092—dc22
    [B]

                           2006103328

Published in the United States by
Regnery Publishing, Inc.
One Massachusetts Avenue, NW
Washington, DC 20001

www.regnery.com
Distributed to the trade by
National Book Network
Lanham, MD 20706

Manufactured in the United States of America

10 9 8 7 6 5 4 3 2 1

Books are available in quantity for promotional or premium use. Write to Director of Special Sales, Regnery Publishing, Inc., One Massachusetts Avenue NW, Washington, DC 20001, for information on discounts and terms or call (202) 216-0600.

FOR MY FAMILY

Contents

INTRODUCTION 1

SECTION I: Who Is Mitt Romney? 19

CHAPTER 1:   This Isn't Mitt Romney's First Presidential Race:
                  The Romney Legacy 21

CHAPTER 2:   "Bain Washed" not "Brain Washed" 45

CHAPTER 3:   A Gold Medal Performance 63

CHAPTER 4:   A Christmas Card Family 73

SECTION II: What He Believes and What He Has Done 99

CHAPTER 5:   Mitt Romney Is Pro-Life 101

CHAPTER 6:   Mitt Romney Defends Traditional Marriage . . 119

CHAPTER 7:   Under the Golden Dome:
                  Romney's Governorship 145

SECTION III: The Campaign Ahead 161

CHAPTER 8:   Mitt Romney's Advantages 163

CHAPTER 9:   The Attack: The "Too Perfect"
                  Critique—Envy as an Attack Ad 195

CHAPTER 10:   Mitt Romney's Got a Mormon Problem
                  (and So Does a Lot of the Country) 205

CONCLUSION 249

APPENDIX: Interview with John Mark Reynolds
                  and Craig Hazen, October 2006 271

ACKNOWLEDGMENTS 289

INDEX 293

Introduction

At about 9:20, the telephone rang in the hall. Dean Acheson was calling from his country house in Maryland.

"Mr. President," he said, "I have very serious news. The North Koreans have invaded South Korea."

FROM *Truman*, BY DAVID MCCULLOUGH

It is with evenings like that one of June 24, 1947, in mind that Americans ought to cast their primary and general election votes for presidents. When devastating surprises arrive, whether on December 7, 1941, September 11, 2001, or any such future day— and there will be many—our country's survival depends upon the man or woman in the Oval Office.

The first duty of American conservatives is to use their talents, time, and treasure to conserve America. And not just any sort of America, but one in which all men and women are understood to have been created equal and endowed by their Creator with "certain unalienable rights," rights which are best protected through the institutions created by the Constitution and operated under that Constitution's design of mediated majoritarianism.

Conservatives understand the value of life, including the life of the unborn; the deep and enduring benefits of freedom of religion and of the press; the absolute necessity of the right to hold property free of excessive governmental intrusion; the joy, efficiency, and breathtaking productivity of free markets and free minds; the necessity of an uncorrupt judiciary fairly dealing out justice under a rule of law and the dangers of unelected judges asserting for themselves roles and claiming for themselves powers outside their constitutional duties.

Conservatives also understand clearly the war in which the West finds itself. Serious conservatives know as well that the war can be lost and the world engulfed in a barbaric darkness, one suddenly brought about through the release of the awful powers of nuclear weaponry or through contagions manufactured for the purpose of spreading disease and death.

Conservatives are deeply uneasy as the nation moves toward the end of the Bush presidency. We know that there is not a single serious contender for the Democratic nomination who has evidenced anything resembling seriousness about the war. A Democratic Congress cannot lose the war although it will make victory much more difficult. But a Democratic president can indeed lose the war and unleash through weakness, incompetence, and blindness awful forces as Jimmy Carter did when he failed to prevent the installation of a revolutionary Islamic Republic in Iran, and as Bill Clinton did when he did not move decisively against the nuclear ambitions of North Korea or the menace of an al Qaeda nested in a barbaric, Taliban-led Afghanistan.

Many conservatives do not see a standard-bearer in the field, or at least one with a prayer of success.

Senator John McCain is a nationalist, and a man of unquestioned courage and resolve with regard to the war. He reminds many of Douglas MacArthur. But he is no conservative.

Senator McCain allowed his fear of money to trump his faith in free speech, and sacrificed the latter in a—vain—redesign of the First Amendment via the McCain-Feingold campaign finance fiasco.

Senator McCain later chose the rituals and privileges of the Senate and his love for the spotlight over the Constitution's clear design when it came to the nomination and confirmation of judges. His Gang of 14 backroom deal undercut the vast majority of his GOP colleagues, his president, and his party, and did not even in its second year of operation gain for judicial nominees the up-or-down floor votes promised them.

Senator McCain also chose to trust Senator Kennedy and not his own party on the issue of border security. Then, as the elections of 2006 approached, he engaged in a dramatic demand that the Supreme Court–mandated and Bush administration–designed law governing the trials and treatment of War on Terror detainees be redone according to his own vision of the good. It was a train wreck–causing public relations stunt that led to cosmetic changes in the law and the loss of crucial legislative weeks. With those lost weeks came the loss of crucial legislation and nominations, and quite likely many seats in both the House and Senate.

Conservatives do not trust Senator McCain. It is difficult to believe that even the best campaign by him will erase that distrust.

Conservatives admire Rudy Giuliani, the mayor who strode towards the Towers, and whose reputation for toughness and clear-eyed understanding of the enemy is the equal of McCain's.

But Mayor Giuliani will not change his long-held views on abortion rights, including partial birth abortion—he believes in *Roe* v. *Wade* and its even more extreme progeny. Like Senator McCain, Mayor Giuliani is simply not upset by the assault on marriage by arrogant judges. For many conservatives, Rudy Giuliani would make a superb Secretary of Defense. But president?

Florida's Jeb Bush is sidelined by his name, even though in any other year he might be the one conservative who could rally the party. But not this year when everyone knows the GOP nominee must in many ways be the anti-Bush: not from Texas, not given to malapropisms, not a late bloomer, not connected to the perceived mismanagement of post-Saddam Iraq, and definitely not named Bush.

Enter Mitt Romney, the former governor of Massachusetts, former leader of the Salt Lake City Olympics, a billionaire venture capitalist who blazed his way through Harvard's Business and Law

Schools and then built a reputation as one of the country's most brilliant and successful entrepreneurs. The eloquent, funny, self-deprecating father of five sons and grandfather to eleven grandchildren has been married to Ann Romney for more than three and a half decades. He is pro-life, pro-marriage, and pro–Second Amendment. He understands economic growth and the world economy as only wildly successful international businessmen do.

Romney grew up in politics with a father who was a three-term governor of Michigan (and a one time front-runner for the 1968 GOP presidential nomination), and later a member of Richard Nixon's cabinet.

And Romney knows the war. He has worked to learn its complexities and the nature of our diverse enemies, constantly reading the sorts of books that must be absorbed. He has made journeys to places like Afghanistan, Iraq, Beijing, Tokyo, and the border between the Koreas to gather the sorts of facts that cannot be found in books. When Iran's former president—a terrorist himself complicit in a regime devoted to terrorism—was inexplicably granted a visa to the United States and extended an invitation to Harvard, Romney denounced both decisions and refused him the courtesies normally extended the former leaders of foreign countries.

The preceding suggests what has long been known to America's political obsessives: Mitt Romney is unique. He has a talent for politics and leadership that is extraordinary amongst the ranks of professional politicians. What's more, his record of accomplishment in both the private and public spheres is remarkable. If Mitt Romney's personal characteristics and record of achievement didn't clearly qualify him for the presidency, there would be no discussion about his faith. But he is a serious candidate for president; a very serious candidate.

Indeed, it is no wonder that Romney had the best 2006 of all the Republicans. He was the best prepared. In a year that destroyed first the ambitions of George Allen and then those of Bill Frist, Romney soared in the speculations of the political class as he raised more money for the GOP than John McCain and Rudy Giuliani combined. When the James Baker–led Iraq Study Group issued its report urging engagement with Iran and Syria, Romney—as did McCain—rejected the idea as the absurd neoappeasement it was. The *Boston Globe* attempted to discredit Romney for his strong stance on border security and the fencing mandated by Congress with a story breathlessly reporting that the landscaping company that trimmed his Belmont, Massachusetts, home's hedges had employed illegal aliens. Instead of having its desired effect, the story triggered laughter directed at the *Globe*—not criticism of the candidate. A short while later, concerned opponents dug into the 1994 files of Romney's unsuccessful run against Ted Kennedy and locked onto statements from that campaign to disingenuously charge that Romney was not really pro-life in 2007, only to discover that most Republicans are more impressed by his steadfast defense of marriage and his strong pro-life stands as governor than by accusations of what he believed or didn't believe fourteen years earlier as a rookie candidate.

Even Romney's long and strongly held beliefs on the necessity of treating gay and lesbian Americans with the dignity and respect that is owed all our fellow citizens—thought by his opponents to be a certain momentum killer—turned out to mirror the feelings of most conservatives regarding the appropriate approach to take towards the private lives of all Americans. Romney's long-standing and consistent record of acceptance for gay Americans made his vigorous fight to preserve the traditional definition of marriage all the more credible as a defense of constitutional majoritarianism rather than bigotry.

"Mitt Romney possesses a combination of intellect and warmth that is very rare in politics," Congressman John Campbell told me in an assessment of Romney that echoed sentiments I have heard repeatedly from individuals who, like Campbell, have had success both in politics and business and who have only recently met Romney.

Campbell was elected to Congress in the fall of 2005 in a special election. He arrived in D.C. after five years in Sacramento as a state representative, a senator, a couple of turns as Arnold's debate prep partner, and a shining career in business that made him not only wealthy, but also an admirer of financial and management talent.

"During my political career," Campbell continued about Romney, "I have never seen anyone so equally gifted in an interview or debate, in a one-on-one conversation and speaking to a thousand people. He has all the raw materials to be a great candidate and a great president."

Reviews like Campbell's have accumulated, contributions have flowed, and Romney's star has unquestionably risen. As Campaign 2008 got off to its unprecedented very early start, conservatives began to see in Romney what they needed: a national security conservative who also brought along a set of shared values on other crucial issues and about whom there was no doubt as to incredible intelligence, energy, eloquence, and, crucially, integrity.

With the higher profile have come the inevitable and necessary questions—questions this book will answer: What role did his father's political career and failed presidential campaign play in shaping Romney? What is the "Bain Way," and what's that got to do with Romney? Does leadership of the Olympic Games really matter in politics—and if so, why?

And what about his family—his wife and kids and grandkids? Was he a success as governor of Massachusetts? Is he really pro-life? Did he fight the good fight on marriage? What are his advantages as the campaign for the presidency begins? What are the handicaps?

Those are the first nine questions, and then there is the tenth question: "What about the Mormon problem?"

As the buzz on Romney has increased, so too has the murmuring about his religion. Many among the political elite began to say, "Romney is a Mormon, and a Mormon cannot win the nomination, much less the presidency."

Bret Stephens is the extremely talented member of the *Wall Street Journal* editorial board who was previously the editor-in-chief of the *Jerusalem Post*. Early in 2006, I asked him about Romney's Latter-day

Saints (LDS) beliefs. "It's out there that it's a 150-year-old version of Scientology," Stephens said. A moment later he caught himself and asked if this was an on-the-record conversation, and I assured him it was. "The Scientology comparison is a keeper," I replied, but I also assured him that it would be accurately reported not as what he believed but what he has heard among the sippers in the reporters' bar and the gluttons at the press room buffet. (When I quoted Stephens to Romney and asked for a response, the governor responded immediately, emphatically, and with a look of genuine offense written across his face. "It's not." How would he explain the difference? "I'll leave that to the Church authorities," he prudently replied, avoiding any potentially controversial comments on either Scientology or the LDS theology, much in the manner that Catholic politicians beg off at having to defend this or that position of Rome, past or present.)

Though Stephens was careful to distance himself from an endorsement of the comparison, by the close of 2006, less responsible journalists were ready to adopt the "150-year-old version of Scientology" charge as conventional wisdom.

Jacob Weisberg is the editor of *Slate*, the online magazine now owned by the Washington Post Company. Weisberg is a talented writer, a columnist for the *Financial Times*, an alum of *The New Republic*. He is a Yalie and a Rhodes Scholar.

He is also, most surprisingly, a bigot, and an unashamed one.

In a December 20, 2006, column for *Slate*, "Romney's Religion: A Mormon President? No Way," Weisberg declared bluntly that if Romney "gets anywhere in the primaries, Romney's religion will become an issue with moderate and secular voters—and rightly so."

"Objecting to someone because of his religious beliefs is not the same thing as prejudice based on religious heritage, race, or gender," Weisberg declared in a bold break with American political tradition.

Weisberg went on to detail the expansiveness of his religious bigotry, but returned to Mormonism's founder, Joseph Smith, declaring him "an obvious con man," and adding "Romney has every right to believe in con men, but I want to know if he does, and if so, I don't want him running the country."

Such overt bigotry, directed at, say, a Muslim or a Catholic would ignite a storm of justified outrage from the guardians of those groups' public profiles. Weisberg is not so bold as to slam Islam or its prophet, but he was quick to make clear the slope on top of which he stands: "Perhaps Christianity and Judaism are merely more venerable and poetic versions of the same [fraud]," Weisberg sums up. "But a few eons make a big difference. The world's greater religions have had time to splinter, moderate, and turn their myths into metaphor."

And there you have it: The Left will relish the assault on Romney's faith, treating it as the soft underbelly of a more generalized assault on the idea of religious belief leading, they hope, to the routine dismissal from the public's consideration as leaders any man or woman who believes in revelation as well as reason. Everyone whose beliefs make their faith more than a matter of fondness for "myths" and "metaphors" will be vulnerable under the Weisberg formulation.

"The religious right has been enormously successful at convincing journalists not to raise questions about the political implications of a candidate's religious beliefs," Damon Linker wrote in the cover story on Romney for *The New Republic* two weeks after Weisberg's column appeared. "This is unfortunate," he concluded, as he launched into a lengthy inquisition about the Church of Jesus Christ of Latter-day Saints and the dark potential of a Mormon in the White House.

It did not take long for wise political observers to sniff out the raised stakes illuminated by Weisberg's robust bigotry.

One of the wisest, Father Richard John Neuhaus, wrote a "response to Jacob Weisberg and others who would use religion to oppose a candidate for the presidency in a manner not substantively different from their use of religion in opposing the present incumbent of the White House."

"One need only recall the innumerable rants against a president who is born again, prays daily, thinks he has a hotline to God, and is bent upon replacing our constitutional order with a theocracy," Neuhaus noted. "In the game book of unbridled partisanship, any stick will do for beating up on the opposition."

Neuhaus had arrived exactly where I had journeyed after a year exploring the subject. On the evening of my first extensive interview with Governor Romney in his Massachusetts State House office, I had dinner in Harvard Square with an old classmate, Joe Downing, who asked me why I was writing this particular book. Although this is my eighth book, none of my earlier efforts had been biographical even in part, nor have I written extensively on the issues presented by a Mormon candidate for president.

I responded to Joe's question of why I was writing on this topic by saying, "Because Mitt Romney ought not *not* be president because of his religious beliefs."

"That's a very American view," Joe replied.

Joe was correct, but given the Weisberg column—and many others of similar tone and substance that preceded it and that will follow—I have to wonder if my belief in our "civic religion's" commitment to abhorrence of religious bigotry remains steadfast. The civic religion is the accumulation of principles, traditions, and institutional practices that over time come to define a country. Only some of the civic religion makes it into law, but the most important aspects do find some expression in our founding documents. Our nation's abhorrence of religious bigotry was embodied in Article VI of the Constitution, which prohibits "religious tests" for office.

"Not applying a religious test for public office," Weisberg asserted without any evidence or argument, "means that people of all faiths are allowed to run, not that views about God, creation, and the moral order are inadmissible for political debate."

When Weisberg declares, "I won't vote for someone who truly believed in the founding whoppers of Mormonism," he is imposing a personal religious test. It is true that Article VI no more prohibits Weisberg's bigotry than the Fourteenth Amendment prohibits racial bigotry on the part of Klansmen. But Article VI embodies the civic religion's ideal, and it is that ideal that Weisberg and others are trashing, and the danger is general to all people of faith, not just Mormons.

"Everyone has skin in this game," Dean Barnett wrote me after reading this manuscript. Dean is my co-blogger at HughHewitt.com, a longtime friend of Romney's, and a keen editor who worked on the final drafts of this book as long and as hard as I did.

"If it becomes permissible to question the tenets of Romney's faith, all religious people will be vulnerable," Dean argued. "All religions require a faith in the fantastic and a belief in the unbelievable. If Romney's belief in the Book of Mormon is used as evidence that he is a fool, a new kind of political attack will be legitimized. Christians who believe in the Assumption of the Virgin Mary and the literal truths of Communion will be dismissed out of hand.

"It almost goes without saying that certain secularists already hold such views. But if members of other religious communities support the attacks on Romney's faith because of some animus towards Mormonism, the weapon they legitimize will in short order be turned against them."

If any significant number of voters disqualify Romney from their consideration because of his faith, it will be a disheartening breach of the Framers' contract with themselves and their political heirs on the subject of religion's place within the American Republic. The concern is more than academic. An astonishing 43 percent of 1,000 people polled by Rasmussen Reports in mid-November of 2006 told the pollsters that they would not even consider voting for a Mormon, a higher negative response than atheists or Muslims received, and double the number saying they would not vote for a Mormon in polls taken in the late '90s. More than half of self-identified "evangelicals" told Rasmussen that voting for a Mormon was out of the question.

If this general objection becomes a concrete prejudice in the presidential campaign of 2008, it will prove a disastrous turning point for all people of faith in public life. If much of the campaign of 2007 and 2008 is spent exploring, evaluating, debating, and mocking the Mormon faith, expect the very arguments used to diminish Romney's qualifications in this regard to return in the future against devout evangelicals or orthodox Catholics. Once a long-closed door to a religious test is opened, it will not be easily closed again.

Will the Jacob Weisbergs have their way? Will Romney's faith in fact be a problem for him? I asked America's most comfortable, telegenic, and never-at-a-loss-for-words politician, Arnold Schwarzenegger, the latter question.

I have interviewed, introduced, and dined with Arnold many times. I have never seen him nonplussed or even remotely so.

But this simple question stopped the Terminator cold. He hemmed, fumbled, and at last replied tersely. "I really don't know," he said with some hesitation. "I mean, it could be, but I really don't know." Arnold added, "I think that his talent speaks for itself."

I asked the obvious follow up: "Why might it be a problem?"

"I have no idea," Arnold responded.

I tried again, asking if he thought evangelicals were comfortable with Mormons.

"I have no idea," a suddenly testy Arnold replied. "I am more concerned about California issues than worrying about what would be a problem for Romney when he runs. I don't even know if he's running or not."

And so we moved on to Arnold's re-election campaign.

Arnold's ordinarily unflappable demeanor and perfect timing hit the wall because he was not expecting the question and he had not encountered it before on the record. But he knew what everyone knows: An American's religious beliefs are not supposed to impact his or her electability. To vote on the basis of disdain for or approval of a candidate's creed is antithetical to our "civic religion" and violates the spirit of our Constitution's Article VI. So deep is the commitment to this egalitarian embrace of religious pluralism that Arnold knew he could not say "Yes, Romney's faith will be an issue," without an explanation. That explanation would have taken him very close to the edge and perhaps into the abyss of candor. "No" would have been a display of naiveté that no politician—and especially not The Governator—could indulge.

So Arnold offered a hedge. That too is a problematic pose, and not just for Arnold but for every politician who responds to the question in that manner. How can any moderately savvy pol not know that Romney's Mormonism will be a problem for his presidential run? When George Herbert Walker Bush was quizzed on the price of milk and came up short, he was lambasted for being out of touch with the concerns of ordinary Americans. Arnold's hedge—and I have heard it from a lot of people, again and again in preparing this book—is not credible, and if it were, it would be an admission of cluelessness far worse than Bush 41's lack of experience with the ten items or less lane.

If the recently retired governor of Massachusetts is rejected by Republican primary voters because they have weighed his universal medical insurance plan and believe, along with the libertarian Cato Institute, that it is "big government" or in some other way wanting, then Romney's exit will be the result of a combination of bad policy and bad marketing. And thoroughly unremarkable in the long and richly entertaining history of presidential ambitions smashed.

If Romney cries on the back of a truck, pronounces an enslaved country free, doesn't know how to react to a hypothetical about his wife being raped, wears funny hats, falls off a stage, sweats profusely during a debate, runs into a right hook before a national audience—"There you go again," or "I knew Jack Kennedy, Jack Kennedy was a friend of mine..."—or, to mention the obvious, pronounces himself brainwashed on any subject at all, he will join a long line of could-have-been contenders and become another familiar and beloved tale for analysts to recall and embellish and weigh and analogize to for decades to come.

If Romney looks at his watch in a debate, tries to cut off a microphone someone else has paid for, announces a global test, outs a daughter of an opponent in a debate, or shows up as three different people on three different debate nights promoting Dingells and lockboxes, he'll be just another footnote in the long history of bumbling candidates and fumbled opportunities.

But if Romney is attacked—openly or sub rosa—for the particulars of his faith, and those attacks, alone or in dominant combination with some other assault, keep him from the Oval Office and he was the man who ought to have been there, then the country will have walked out on one of our most vital founding principles. This problem—a core problem, a fundamental problem—is what inspired this book, though my examination of Mitt Romney's life and career has raised other questions unique in the history of presidential campaigns. Should we welcome or fear the role of the MBA class/venture capital/über-business consultant on the national and international stage? Is the country really going to accept a billionaire as president?

Serious historians have already rejected the idea of the sort of inquisition that Weisberg (and others) propose to conduct. "I'd like to believe it's not going to be a problem," Doris Kearns Goodwin told me.

"I think what [Romney] needs to say is that which Lincoln was able to say," she continued, "which is, 'if you want to judge me by whether or not I belong to an organized church, or if I go every Sunday to some sort of religious service, that's one thing. But if you want to judge me by the way I deal with people, my ethical foundations, that's what really matters.'"

"What Romney needs to do," she concluded, "is just to say that his religion is a part of his life, it always has been, and he believes that America is a place that was founded on religious freedom, and he can quote from John Kennedy from that Houston speech."

Will that in fact be enough?

This book is in essence an inquiry into Mitt Romney's candidacy for the presidency. As such, it must necessarily tackle two main questions: 1) Does this still relatively obscure blue-state governor have the "right stuff" to be president; and 2) If the answer to the first question is yes and most Republicans believe that answer is yes, will Mitt Romney's faith nevertheless disqualify him from being the Republican nominee for president?

Now for some disclosures.

I am not now, nor have I ever been, a Mormon. No member of my family is or has been a Mormon. My wife had a first cousin who converted to the LDS faith. She died a few years ago and we never had the occasion to discuss her conversion with her.

That said, I love Mormons and count many among my friends. In 1996 I conceived and hosted a national series on religion in America for PBS, *Searching for God in America*, which took me into the history of the Saints and to Brigham Young's Beehive House in Salt Lake City for many hours of interviews with Apostle Neal Maxwell, at that time one of the most senior leaders of the denomination that numbers ten million. I returned to Utah a few years later at Elder Maxwell's request to conduct another lengthy bit of taped questioning for another PBS series, this one for Utah viewers only. Elder Maxwell became a friend, one with whom I had the chance to talk politics both in person and via the phone from that time until his death in 2005.

I also have a friend in Dr. Jim Davies, a brother-in-law to Mitt Romney, an accomplished eye surgeon, and a convert to the LDS faith, as is his sister, Ann Romney, Mitt Romney's wife. Jim's an extraordinary fellow, so giving that he has donated a part of his own lung to a young lady with cystic fibrosis. Jim is also passionate booster of his brother-in-law.

Many friends of mine in evangelical, Catholic, and Jewish circles of Massachusetts are admirers of Mitt Romney. I have been hearing great things about him from them since he gained the Commonwealth's statehouse in 2002.

All of which goes to the issue of whether I can be fair in analyzing Mitt Romney's candidacy and the impact on it of his faith.

I will leave that to the reader to decide, but note only that I wouldn't promote my best friend's candidacy if I thought his background—including his religious beliefs—would result in massive Republican-base defections because of some personal characteristic. I have no interest in winning arguments and losing elections. The times in which we live don't allow for quixotic stands that end up with the nomination of a candidate who cannot win.

By the same token, though, if the best candidate who could undoubtedly win the general election is denied the nomination and as a result the White House is lost to a Democratic Party currently constituted as being against serious prosecution of the war against Islamist fascists, then a deep and potentially fatal error will have been made.

The war against Islamist fascism can be lost. Devastating blows far beyond even the horrors of 9/11 can be delivered. Mushroom clouds or rapidly spreading diseases can appear in America. We have been well protected and well led since 9/11—and lucky.

The Democrats do not believe this. They will return us to the 1990s, to the years that followed the first World Trade Center bombing, to the era of Khobar Towers, the African embassy bombings, the attack on the *Cole*. They will return us to a course of inaction, of fecklessness, to desperate attempts to maintain the appearance of peace while ignoring the reality of a growing menace.

If the nomination of Mitt Romney would lead to his election and continued GOP stewardship of our national security, Republicans would have cause to cheer and the nation would benefit. But if, because of his faith, he lost in the Republican primaries to a less able candidate and that in turn led to the election of Hillary, the defeat of Romney on the grounds of his religious beliefs would be a national tragedy.

Thus this book. In the book's first part, I'll try to help the reader get to know Mitt Romney as I've come to know him through many interviews with him, his family, friends, and associates that I conducted for the specific purpose of preparing this book. After Part I, hopefully you'll share my conclusion that Mitt Romney is qualified to be president. Perhaps even over-qualified.

And then we'll move on to Part II, a review of Romney's political positions of special concern to conservatives. Part III is a discussion of the strengths and weaknesses of the Romney candidacy at the start of the campaign, and concludes with an examination of Romney's Mormon faith and what it should mean and, perhaps more importantly, should not mean to Romney's fellow Republicans and fellow Americans.

Before introducing you to the Mitt Romney I've come to know, I think one more word regarding the preparation of this book is in order. While the governor cooperated with this endeavor, this is not an "authorized" biography. The conclusions I've reached are my own. Mitt Romney will only come to know them in the same way you will—by reading this book.

I have not endorsed Governor Romney and will not do so until a moment comes when I have to decide whom to vote for in California's Republican primary. The next year will tell us many things about all the candidates, and no voter should be unwilling to absorb the twists and turns and revelations about the men and woman running to replace George W. Bush.

But in fairness to the reader, I do have to disclose that if the California primary were held tomorrow, I would indeed vote for Mitt Romney. I have been around American politics for a long time, beginning with work on a congressional campaign in Massachusetts in 1974, the year of the post-Watergate deluge. I was a Ford man in the '76 primaries, and led the "Youth for Ford" campaign in Massachusetts as a Harvard junior. Seven years later, after a ghost-writing career with Richard Nixon that began at America's Elba, San Clemente, and continued after RN's move to New York and three years at the University of Michigan Law School, I went to work for Ronald Reagan, first at the Department of Justice as a special assistant to William French Smith and then Ed Meese, and then in the White House Counsel's office before moving to the agencies. Since beginning my teaching and broadcast career, I have studied and repeatedly interviewed the most senior officials of government and in politics during more than seventeen years behind microphones and in front of cameras.

I have never met a more intellectually gifted, curious, good humored, broadly read, and energetic official than Mitt Romney. Whether he can convey these gifts to the electorate and thereby earn their support is another question entirely. Like every other reporter and most other voters, I'll be watching to see if that is the case.

But even at this early stage I am certain about one thing: bigotry about Romney's faith ought not to be a legitimate part of this campaign, or any future campaign for the presidency.

Who Is Mitt Romney?

Chapter One

This Isn't Mitt Romney's First Presidential Race: The Romney Legacy

M itt Romney's presidential bid is not the first time a Mormon has sought the presidency—it is the fifth such try. And it really isn't Mitt Romney's first presidential campaign. It's his third.

The founding prophet of the Mormon Church, Joseph Smith, declared his candidacy for the presidency in 1844. "Smith embarked on an astonishing round of political activity in early 1844," Richard and Joan Ostling recount in their superb 1999 book, *Mormon America*. "With the backing of the Quorum of the Twelve Apostles, he declared himself an independent candidate for the U.S. presidency on January 29, running on a progressive platform of religious rights, purchase of freedom for slaves, emptying of the jails, and overhaul of the economy in a populist mode. In February he organized the apostles and hundreds of other missionaries to fan out across the country in support of his candidacy."

Smith's candidacy was quickly eclipsed by the crisis engulfing his young church then planted in Nauvoo, Illinois. The wanderings of Smith's followers are well documented elsewhere, but wherever the Church of Jesus Christ of Latter-day Saints traveled, persecution and violence followed. The Mormons developed a private militia of more than 3,000 men, and after their expulsion from Missouri in 1838, the refugees gathered under Smith's leadership in southern Illinois. Their persecution in Missouri had been severe, with Governor Lilburn Boggs declaring in an October 27, 1838, letter that the Mormons "must be treated as enemies and must be exterminated or driven from the state, if necessary, for the public good."

The settlement in Nauvoo had prospered for a time, but the Mormon's uniqueness rekindled fear and hatred. Smith had been charged as an accessory to the attempted murder of Governor Boggs, and political tensions grew in Illinois with a vigorous anti-Mormon campaign fanned by splits among the Saints, lurid headlines about the church, and Smith's erratic behavior. After Mormons destroyed the press of a Nauvoo newspaper that was critical of Smith, press hysteria bloomed in surrounding towns, and Smith declared martial law in Nauvoo. "Non-Mormons pressured Governor Thomas Ford to mobilize the state militia," the Ostlings recount. "Everyone had good reason to be afraid; civil war was a very real possibility."

Smith disarmed the Mormon militia at Ford's request, then fled to Iowa, only to return to face charges in Carthage when given Ford's promise of safety. Smith was jailed in Carthage on June 24, and three days later was assassinated by a mob. The Mormons' attempts to live among their fellow citizens had failed dramatically, and Brigham Young led the vast majority of Saints to their new sanctuary in Utah and commenced the building of Salt Lake City. No Mormon would seriously contend for the presidency for more than 120 years.

Mitt Romney's father, Michigan governor George Romney, ran a full-scale campaign for the presidency in 1967–68, which ended after a blowout loss in the New Hampshire primary. Three years earlier, George Romney had briefly considered a "Stop Goldwater" bid. At the 1964 Republican Convention he was nominated as a "favorite son" from Michigan, with his teenage son Mitt on the floor supporting him at San Francisco's Cow Palace. (Though, by the time of the convention, any opportunity to block Goldwater had passed.)

Arizona congressman Mo Udall, a Mormon, made a run for the 1976 Democratic nomination which never got out of the gates, though Udall was a beloved figure on Capitol Hill, a man of great good humor.

Utah senator Orrin Hatch, another Mormon, threw his hat into the ring against the Bush machine and the McCain insurgency in 2000. Though a conservative and highly respected senator in 2000, Hatch did not make the first cut.

In only one of these races did the Mormon candidate come close to the nomination—George Romney's run in 1968.

Romney was actually the GOP front-runner for most of 1967, and with that status, his faith became a topic for a delicate sort of scrutiny. (It was such a non-issue in 1964, journalist Theodore White did not even mention it in his book, *The Making of the President, 1964.*)

That scrutiny arrived, somewhat gently, in David Broder and Stephen Hess's book, *The Republican Establishment*. Written in 1967, Broder and Hess looked hard at front-runner George Romney, which meant they had to try to explain the LDS to the American public. The authors made four points about the LDS faith they thought were significant to the upcoming election:

1. Mormonism is an American religion.
2. Mormonism is rooted in the American West.
3. Mormonism believes in self-deification through effort.
4. Mormonism encourages definite personality traits.

Each of these points remains relevant in 2007, but especially the first and last.

"More than being merely American," Broder and Hess concluded, "Mormon doctrine is patriotically American, reflecting a kind of romantic nationalism peculiar to the nineteenth century.... These people whose beliefs and practices are so idiosyncratic, and who actually took arms against the United States government, are also as hyper-American as a rodeo or county fair."

The "definite practices" they referred to remain hallmarks of the Mormon faith, and the Broder/Hess analysis of the effects of George Romney's faith on him—both benefits and burdens—remains very relevant to the son's campaign.

"The Mormons are a homogeneous group of predominantly Anglo-Scandinavian ancestry," the two authors wrote. "They neither smoke nor drink, not even tea or coffee. They tithe, that is, give 10 percent of their gross income to the church." They continued, as though explaining a tribe apart from America:

> They do not curse. Romney says "gosh," "by golly," and an occasional "aw, nuts." When *Newsweek* in 1967 attributed to him the improbable quote, "I call my best friends sons of bitches," Romney fired off an anguished letter to the editor denying he had said any such thing. Carefully avoiding any repetition of the offensive "vulgarism," as he called it, he said, "The quotation is particularly repugnant to my character. . . . Use of such a phrase is contrary to my belief and my nature."
>
> Physical fitness is as integral a part of their applied Christianity as moral purity, since Mormons believe that "The body is the temple of the spirit." Romney plays a sort of "Compact golf" in the early mornings before going to work. By using four balls at the same time, he can play the equivalent of thirty-six holes in about one hour and fifteen minutes. "I play golf for exercise and humility," he says. "And on that basis I never lose, you see, because the more exercise, the more humility." (This is a set line and he always laughs after he has delivered it.)
>
> Mormons, despite rigid convictions, are not a dour or antisocial people. They encouraged dancing, for instance, at a time when such frivolity was generally frowned upon in church circles.

The Romneys have made some adaptations to the customs of the business and political world. At a party, they may hold a "consommé on the rocks" to assure that their drinking guests are not self-conscious. They began serving liquor in their home after learning, through sad experience, that guests confronting a dry evening often fortified themselves too well in advance.

But Mormons are not conditioned to take a passive attitude toward the non-Mormon or "Gentile" World, as Saints call all outsiders. Instead, they are trained to feel that "theirs is still the task of carrying the option of redemption and salvation to all men," writes Robert Mullen, the author of a highly laudatory book on the Latter-day Saints. It is a proselytizing and a missionary church, in which Romney and most other men serve their two-year turns as missionaries.

This proselytizing urge may give Mormons a tendency to be argumentative and long-winded. A close political associate of Romney's observed that during the 1962 debates with Governor John Swainson it was almost impossible for Romney to keep his remarks within the allotted time segments. Reporter Julius Duscha wrote in the *Washington Post*, "He is the kind of man who can make a political cliché . . . sound like a sentence from the Sermon on the Mount." More succinctly, a one-time (and now disenchanted) adviser described Romney as a speaker in three words: "A dynamic bore."

The dangers of carrying a strong sense of one's own virtue and a missionary zeal into the political arena are many. The Book of Mormon can be read as a story of "good guys" and "bad guys." Romney has been accused by his critics of applying these same simple standards to politics and politicians.

Whether it is more of a handicap than a help may be argued. John F. Kennedy, who laughed off Richard M. Nixon's clumsy effort during their television debates to make a moral issue of President Truman's salty language, apparently did not take Romney's moralism as a joke. According to the late president's friend, Paul Fay, Kennedy once said, "The one fellow I don't want to run against [in 1964] is Romney.... No vice whatsoever, no smoking, no drinking. Imagine someone we know going off for 24 or 48 hours to fast and meditate, awaiting a message from the Lord on whether to run or not to run. Does that sound like one of the old gang?"

Kennedy was referring to Romney's much-publicized day-long fast before announcing his candidacy for governor in 1962. Mrs. Romney once said that "fasting is basic to our worship, and prayer on appropriate occasions is to us like breathing." But to some the pre-announced fast was more sanctimonious than pious. Said August (Gus) Scholle, the president of Michigan AFL-CIO, "The big clown. He thinks he has a private pipeline to god." Romney replied that "the same pipeline is available to Mr. Scholle, if he cares to take advantage of it."

Broder and Hess quoted a *Harper's* magazine writer as saying that "Romney is so clean-cut he makes your teeth ache," and warned that "Romney's conspicuous purity makes other Republicans squirm." The Beltway-bound Broder and Hess saw a "holier-than-thou attitude" and asserted that when Romney was considering a run in 1964, the "joke among unamused politicians at the time was that Romney, if nominated, would be the first presidential candidate without a running mate, because he could find nobody who was worthy of the honor."

The Broder/Hess analysis foreshadowed the difficulties George Romney encountered in his run for the presidency in 1967 and 1968. It is worth retelling the story of that campaign in some detail—using the work of the best of the chroniclers of presidential campaigns, Theodore White—because of its certain impact on Mitt Romney.

Most veterans of presidential politics can quickly tell you how many campaigns they have "been on," in the manner of a seasoned traveler counting cruises, or a golf addict toting up Tiger's majors. A presidential campaign is such an all-consuming effort, even in 1964 and 1968, that many more people than the candidate "run" for the office. Certainly the would-be first family is swept along, and in the process internalizes many, many lessons that never fade even if they are concealed.

George Romney made a lot of mistakes in 1967 and 1968, even as he had in 1964. In '64, he simply dithered and then dissented, refusing to endorse Barry Goldwater, citing concerns over the father of modern conservative politics' ambiguous commitment to civil rights, for which Romney had tirelessly worked in racially divided Michigan. Romney possibly could have given Goldwater a real contest after New York governor Nelson Rockefeller's withdrawal, as he would have had strong support from the Republican governors who feared the Arizona conservative would lead the party over the cliff. But when those governors met in Cleveland that summer on the weekend of June 6 and 7, with Richard Nixon in attendance and encouraged by Ike to consider all options, the governors, including George Romney, demurred.

Forty-four years later, Mitt Romney has shown no such hesitation in his bid for the nomination.

Almost as soon as the GOP wreckage in 1964 was surveyed and totaled, George Romney began running for the presidency. Romney had survived the political ruin of the GOP, and won re-election as governor in that deadly year for Republicans, earning him early "front-runner" status. It didn't take long for the bloom to fade, and Theodore White's account from the classic *The Making of the President, 1968* tells the story best and should be read again and again by any student of the younger Romney's presidential ambitions:

> Governor James Rhodes of Ohio was later quoted with the cruelest epitaph on the Romney campaign. "Watching George Romney run for the presidency," he said, "was like watching a duck try to make love to a football."

Yet there was nothing comic in the performance itself—only in the mirror of the media and the press through which the nation saw the performance. And the story of the Romney campaign is less one of politics than of the influence of the media in modern America.

Of this changing media environment in the past decade of American life there will be much more to say later in this book. The American journalists who represent the media and report for its press, to whose brotherhood I have belonged for thirty years, are the most efficient, honest and accurate press corps, taken as a whole, in the world. Yet since time on air is always limited and space in print is always tight, all reporting must be the snatching of fragments of a continuum, chosen by each reporter's own inner judgment of which fragments reveal or symbolize a larger general truth. Reporters and media thus sit in judgment on candidates. But the media-men themselves are judged by critics in the thought-climate of New York and Washington who can make or break reporters' reputations, advance or destroy their careers by extraneous judgments on their culture of style, manners and elegant aesthetic cruelty has grown up which removes people like George Romney—and to a lesser extent Richard M. Nixon—as far from judicial consideration as a rabbi in Nazi Germany. In the new culture of American criticism, to be kind, soft or tolerant in judgment is to be labeled "square." Copy must have bite; TV shows must "march"; by these standards reporters themselves are judged.

The media, White argued, was much more the enemy and the opponent of George Romney than Nixon ever would become.

Somewhere out beyond the Alleghenies the old culture of America still persists—people who think Boy Scouts are good, who believe that divorce is bad, who teach Bible classes on Sunday, enjoy church suppers, wash their children's mouths with soap to purge dirty words, who regard homosexuals as wicked, whose throat chokes up when the American flag is marched on the Fourth of July. In its extravagant and hyperbolic form—as in Barry Goldwater's cosmology of demons—the old culture sees the Atlantic Seaboard, particularly the Boston-New York-Washington belt, as the locus of a vast and sinister intellectual conspiracy, a combination of capital and decadence, corrupting the moral fiber and legendary decencies of an earlier America.

The new culture, of which we shall talk later, is the child of prosperity and the past decade. Characterized by an exuberance of color, style, fashion, art and expression flowing from the enormous excess energies of American life, it defines itself best not by what it seeks but by its contempt and scorn of what the past has taught. Its thrust lies in the direction of liberties and freedom, but with an exaggerated quality of aggressive infantilism. In its exploration of the limits of sensibility, all laws, manners, mores, institutions which restrict such areas of individual expression as drugs, sex, obscenities and mob violence are generally held to be oppressive; and the greatest agent of oppression in the twentieth century is generally held to be the United States government. As parochial as the old culture, the new expressionist culture is as sure of its own moral superiority over the old as the old culture is of its superiority over the new; and in its extreme and paranoid form the new culture is as convinced of the conspiracy of a military-industrial complex pushing America to war and ruin as, say, the John Birch Society is convinced of a Communist conspiracy pushing America to slavery.

In the operational climate of American politics, the critical difference between the two cultures is that the new culture dominates the heights of national communications, subtly but profoundly influences those who sit astride the daily news flow in New York and Washington, and thus stains, increasingly, the prisms of reporting through which the nation as a whole must see itself.

George Romney of Michigan, despite the fact that he is a shrewd, efficient, hard-driving business and government executive, is, by style, a man of the old culture.

The clash between what White describes as the "new" and "old" cultures of America has never been resolved and has in fact intensified, as any student of red and blue America will acknowledge. The first Romney, in part because of the deep traditional patriotism that is part of the Mormon faith, was deeply rooted in the "old" culture and fundamentally unprepared for the scorn of its competitor:

In a state like Michigan, as in many other states of the Midwest, West and South, a man of the old culture campaigning on a state level, through state media, dealing with statehouse reporters who understand the idiom of the homefolk, can and frequently does win out. But when a man like George Romney ventures out on the national scene, he must operate in a totally different environment—the environment of the national press and media. In a Presidential campaign there is no such thing as an Off-Broadway production; wherever a microphone is held to his lips, or camera crew assigned to him by the great national networks, a Presidential candidate is on Broadway; and the performance expected of him is entirely different from the quality of a performance in Grand Rapids, Michigan. There is a natural timberline in national politics beyond which certain kinds of men cannot thrive. Once George Romney began to press into the stratospheric environment of national media and attention, his Presidential image was to wither; and this withering was to be shown as a matter of cruel amusement to the nation.

The "not-ready-for-prime-time" aspects of the George Romney campaign had many explanations, but one crucial moment combined with one crucial betrayal undid Romney. The crucial moment was the famous "brainwashing" episode. The crucial betrayal came as a stab in the back from his biggest supporter: Nelson Rockefeller.

George Romney's "brainwashing" statement, if remembered at all, will be remembered as a tiny episode in the pre-campaign of 1968; but it was huge in public thinking at the time and will illustrate as well as any other episode the relation between the reality of politics and its distorted reflection in the media. For what-is-it-that-makes-news is not taught in any course on politics as presented in schools. Not only did millions of Americans know that George Romney stated he had been brainwashed; millions of them saw him say it on their home TV screens. It is so difficult to deny the episode as fact that it is well, for the purposes of demonstration, to show how a slip of the tongue is inflated to a major statement of policy.

The actual story went this way:

Several weeks prior to the supposed "statement," Mr. Romney had been approached by a broadcaster in Detroit called Lou Gordon. Lou Gordon had previously been a Midwest garment-manufacturer's representative, a Midwest leg-man for the Drew Pearson column, but in an expression of his own identity he was a radio-TV personality in the Detroit area. As a master of a "tele-phone-in" question-and-answer show on the radio, he had major local prominence—for Michigan politicians he was a man who could give away air time free by exposure on his show. Gordon has supported Romney with friendly air time in campaigns of the past. Romney had actually filled in as guest-host on the show on one occasion when Gordon was off on vacation.

But now Gordon's career was moving forward; he wanted to become a national TV personality, a Midwestern Mike Wallace. He was to launch, right after Labor Day, a new television question and answer show which would be exposed at various times later, not only in Detroit but in Philadelphia and Boston. He needed a headliner for the launching of the show, and Romney was both a friend and a headliner. For Romney, a generous man, consent to the invitation was a simple response to another old friend—and also, since the show was aired in Boston two weeks later, it was a free opportunity to reach voters in New Hampshire, where he was entered in the primary.

Thus innocently and out-of-the-blue arrived one of the pivotal moments in American political history, one of the first significant episodes of "gotcha" journalism where a single answer, gesture, or hesitation is suddenly assigned an importance far beyond merit, and attributed symbolism—by the media and political opponents— replaces the actual statement or facts.

On the day set for the taping, August 31, 1967, Romney had visited the Michigan State Fair outside Detroit, when one of his grandchildren went missing. Frantic state troopers, fearing the worst, scoured the fairgrounds until they found the child riding the Ferris wheel.

"Upset and very late for the scheduled taping of the television show," White recounts, "Romney dashed into Detroit with, as one witness said, 'cowflop and dirt from the State Fair still sticking to his shoes.'" White continued:

> Composing himself, his handsome Presidential face earnest and serious as always, deprived of Cross's wise counsel, bereft of any aides or briefing, Romney swung into the question-and-answer session and, a few minutes later, still pulling himself together, responded to a question by Mr. Gordon thus:
>
> Question: (on Vietnam) "Isn't your position a bit inconsistent with what it was, and what do you propose we do now?"
>
> Answer: "Well, you know when I came back from Vietnam, I just had the greatest brainwashing that anybody can get when you go over to Vietnam. Not only by the Generals, but also by the

diplomatic corps over there, and they do a very thorough job. And since returning from Vietnam, I've gone into the history of Vietnam, all the way back into World War II and before. And, as a result, I have changed my mind . . . in that particular. I no longer believe that it was necessary for us to get involved in South Vietnam to stop Communist aggression. . . . "

It was, said one of those present, a "tossaway line," and nobody thought it important. Romney himself did not even want to hear the playback, being already late and tightly scheduled to sweep back from Detroit immediately after the television show to a state budget session in Lansing. Indeed, when the machinery of publicity cranked into action for the mini-build-up of the mini-show, the covering press release announced only that George Romney had said "he would not be interested in accepting the Vice Presidential spot on the Republican ticket."

The blossoming of "brainwashing" in the next ten days is a perfect illustration of the mechanics of public relations, media, publicity and politics. Mr. Gordon read the full transcript of his show Sunday, three days later. He decided then that "brainwashing" was more important than anything else in his show for attention-catching purposes. He telephoned the *New York Times* man in Detroit (Jerry Flint) to that effect, giving him a full transcript. Flint, four days after the actual taping of the show, reported the story to his desk, burying "brainwashing" down in his text. The man on his desk caught the "brainwashing" quote. On Tuesday, September 5th, the day after the telecast, on page 28 of the *New York Times*, a full five days after the blurt-out, the story came to national attention: ROMNEY ASSERTS HE UNDERWENT "BRAINWASHING" ON VIETNAM TRIP. The *New York Times* is the bulletin board of the great TV companies; its news reports are the alert signal for the national evening news shows, and thus by Tuesday night the nation could see the thirty-second clip, requested from Gordon by the networks, in its homes.

Shorn of background and circumstances, Romney was saying exactly what he was quoted as saying—the part presented as the whole, the fragment presented as reality.

Within the next day or two, happy Democrats of the administration made of the statement national controversy. John Bailey, Democratic national Chairman, first saw the opportunity and declared that Romney's statement had "insulted the integrity" of "two dedicated and honorable men"—General Westmoreland and Ambassador Lodge, who had briefed Romney in Vietnam. Robert McNamara weighed in with "I don't think Governor Romney can recognize the truth when he sees it or hears it." The Detroit newspapers, which had up until then ignored the tiny newsslip, weighed in with local pride; and the *Detroit News* prepared for its Sunday editorial pages a denunciation of George Romney, a demand that he quit the race as an incompetent, and a declaration that only Nelson Rockefeller could save the Republican Party.

It would have been well—but probably already too late—for Romney to have ignored the matter. But his pride was involved and he felt he was being abused. Wherever he went, thus, he must for the next six weeks, against all advice and pleading and urging of his staff, reply to the charge of innocence. And no one wanted an innocent for president.

Romney, perhaps, was the first to know that his hopes were over. He had planned to attend the floating gathering of the National Governors' Conference of 1967 on their autumn shipboard journey to the Virgin Islands. He appeared on the boat to join his basic constituents, the governors, like one of the walking wounded, pale, exhausted and dragging of foot. As the boat took off, a copy of *Time* magazine was placed under every door with a joint cover-picture story on Rockefeller and Reagan, writing Romney off as a fool unqualified for high office. Three times on board the boat, closeted with Rockefeller in Rockefeller's cabin on the sun-deck, he pleaded with New York's governor to let him off the hook. He was through, Romney insisted; Nelson must run for President. But Rockefeller would not—the plan was for Romney to run as the governor's candidate. He must go on with it.

This is the often forgotten bit of drama from the turbulent campaign of '67–'68: New York governor Nelson Rockefeller, the powerful, driven, enormously talented, and endlessly ambitious (but never loved by his party's base) Nelson Rockefeller was Romney's biggest backer. George Romney had given Rockefeller a pledge to run, and so run he would.

On and on the good man went for the next few hopeless months, embrangling himself further with the press, whom he now regarded as a native American Viet Cong. He flew to Paris to polish his image as a foreign-affairs expert, at least on European affairs—and fell into additional befoulment with the press as he claimed that reported had misquoted him and their little portable tape-recorders proved they had not. He flew on to Vietnam, and the dispatches from Vietnam portrayed him as a blunt, crude, unfeeling politician campaigning for office in a land where men were dying. Romney could not win with the press.

Meanwhile, the New Hampshire primary of 1968 was approaching, and Rockefeller had put up one final installment of money to sound out the sentiment of New Hampshire voters. Three days after Christmas Romney lieutenants secretly rendezvoused at the Port Authority Conference Room of the LaGuardia airport in New York to receive the results of the poll. Only one voter in eight among New Hampshire Republicans, said the private poll, picked Romney to be President. As a matter of cold figures, Richard Nixon, without having spoken on Vietnam, was the choice of New Hampshire Republicans by 64.2 to 12.0 for George Romney—a five-to-one preference, a disaster.

Further analyzing the secret polling results and weighing the volunteered comments of the sample, one of these present summarized the impression that George Romney had made. "I guess the poll shows," he said, "that New Hampshire Republicans think George Romney is too dumb to be President of the United States."

As Romney struggled, Rockefeller's ambitions reignited, and when he let it be known he'd be available for a draft at the convention, he effectively gutted Romney from behind. The backstab came on February 24, 1968, after Rocky had addressed a Detroit fundraising luncheon for Romney. After first declaring his support for Romney, the press pressed: would he be available for a draft? Rockefeller said "Yes," and that signaled the end of the Romney campaign. A few days later, George Romney withdrew from the race.

I asked Mitt Romney about the '68 campaign and the lessons, if any, he took away from it.

"[My father] wrote me lengthy letters when I was in my Mission about what was going on and what his experience was," Romney recalled about his dad. "He had made a commitment to the Republican governors that he would be the standard bearer for the non-Nixon wing of the party but if it didn't look like he could get the job done, he would withdraw. He concluded that following the brainwashing statement, the decline in the polls, and the rush of his key people to Rockefeller that his commitment to the other Republican governors was such that he needed to step aside."

"He did not want to step aside," Romney continued about his father's defeat. "He wanted to keep fighting. He thought he could go forward and ultimately overcome the challenge, but he had made a commitment and felt that he needed to honor that commitment and give the Republican governors a chance to pick someone else. That was the way he described it to me in the letters."

Was Romney senior bitter over Rockefeller's gambit?

"I think Dad was disappointed in Rockefeller," Romney answered. "I think Rockefeller tried to sail a little too close to the wind and justified reversing his commitment. And he did it in a way that wouldn't look like he was reversing his commitment, that he was forced into the race."

George Romney's wife, Lenore, was more than disappointed.

"I know that my mother was very direct with Rockefeller," Romney recounted, smiling.

"They saw each after [Rockefeller] began saying he wouldn't rule out a run for the presidency, [that] he'd be open to a draft and my mother saw him and he said, 'Oh Lenore, how are you? I'm so sorry to hear that George has withdrawn,' and she said something to the effect that 'You are the cause of it, and you know you caused it.'"

A lesson in Rocky's reversal for the younger Romney? None that he would voice.

"You recognize in politics there are some people you can count on. There are some people, if they give you their word will not vary from it. And those are the people that have real potential and a future in politics. I think long-term that people who have character and stick by their word are the ones who are successful."

I also asked Romney a softball question, but he added a twist to the easy answer.

Would his dad have made a good president?

"A fabulous president," Romney replied with enthusiasm, "because in my view one of the greatest and most important contributions a president makes is to demonstrate to the nation an example of character. My dad is someone who had faith, who loved his wife, who loved his children, who loved his country, who would do whatever he thought was best for the country. He was true blue through and through. He was as American as they come."

Romney then riffed a bit on the presidents he admires.

"I look back at the great presidents—and I have done a lot of reading about Teddy Roosevelt, for instance—[and] what stands out is that Teddy Roosevelt was of extraordinary character and his love for the land, his conservation—the fact that he hated the concentrations of economic power and the trusts. These things and his character are what stand out. Dwight Eisenhower, too, it is his character."

The flip side of this issue (and of course a blast in the general direction of his likely general election opponent if Romney gets that far): "For me, the biggest failure of the Clinton administration was the failure of character," he volunteered. "He did some pretty good things from a policy standpoint. He did some that I really disagree with.... But it was the failure of character that I think has had the most lasting impact on America and is the most detrimental aspect of his presidency."

Back to his father: "Dad was a man of unquestionable character and when he passed away.... The *Detroit News* and *Detroit Free Press* were on strike at the time he passed away. They came back as papers and wrote an edition about him and his passing.

"He truly was an extraordinary person and he had an enormous impact on the people who knew him in Michigan, Republican and Democrat, public and private. He would have had that kind of impact on the nation."

Character matters to Romney, a lot, and that will no doubt be a theme of his campaign.

But in holding up his father as a man of great character, he is also making the point that character is not enough to win the presidency, as it clearly didn't carry Romney senior even as far as the 1968 GOP convention.

Others have wondered whether the collapse of George Romney's campaign has already affected Mitt Romney's plans, and more crucially, his personality.

"Forty years after the father's birth, the son was born. Forty years after the father became a governor, the son won his own governorship," Neil Swidey wrote in an August 13, 2006, article for the *Boston Globe* magazine, "The Lessons of the Father." "And forty years after the father's presidential dream was dashed, along comes the son cue-

ing up to make his own run." The comparisons are obvious, as are
the differences:

> On the surface, the two men are near clones. Same business-
> world pedigree. Same storybook marriage to his high school
> sweetheart. Same square jaw and large forehead, made larger
> when he flashes that bright white smile and his eyes recede under
> a heavy brow. Same central-casting sweep of black hair with a
> dose of distinguished white at the temples. (Sure, it's talked about
> entirely too much, but, good Lord, is that a nice head of hair.)
>   Beneath the surface, however, Romney version 2.0 runs on a
> different operating system. Whereas George Romney was often
> zestful, impulsive, hot-tempered, Mitt is analytical, cautious,
> even-keeled. Michigan reporters loved to cover George because
> they knew they could always get him worked up enough to
> deliver a headline. You never hear Beacon Hill reporters talk
> about Mitt like that.

Speculating about what he terms an "emotional deficit" in the
public face of Mitt Romney, Swidey asked: "Is it possible that Mitt
Romney learned the lessons of his father too well?"

Swidey missed the two most obvious differences between father
and son.

He ignored an aspect of George Romney's career, one that Broder
and Hess recognized and noted, and which White's chronicle
detailed. George Romney was not from America's political elite. The
Michigan governor was of the mountain states and Midwest, from the
car business, and began his adult life with almost nothing economi-
cally, although he made a fine upper-middle-class living as he
climbed the rungs of postwar America.

George Romney never got close to a college degree. He was a
stranger in a strange land when forced onto the turf of the Beltway
and Manhattan media.

Mitt Romney, after Stanford, after thirty months in France including long stints in the City of Light, stormed BYU and emerged as its top student and then blitzed Cambridge, Massachusetts. At Harvard Business School and Harvard Law he succeeded again.

Once among the elites, he stayed in their company, and, in fact, rose to the top of an East Coast financial community—the new class of investment bankers and consultants. Over and over again from 1978 through his founding of Bain Capital, and then again—after a short and brutal course in politics and media in the '94 run against Kennedy—Romney took up buying and improving and selling corporations before crashing the international gates of the IOC with all of its incredible haughtiness and hierarchy.

In the eyes of many, the son had surpassed the father's achievements even before becoming governor of Massachusetts. Mitt had executed tasks and deals far more difficult than the cluttered obstacle course of the '67–'68 Republican presidential nomination race.

Perhaps the more important difference between George and Mitt is the political genes Mitt inherited from his mother. Lenore Romney was also a formidable political force, one who ran and lost a United States Senate campaign. She was always at her husband's side and frequently the brighter of the two in small settings.

Broder and Hess followed the Romneys on a campaign swing to Alaska in February 1967. On Sunday morning the pair attended the Mormon services in Anchorage, Alaska, which that morning swelled to about 850 members, a fifth of all Mormons in the state. "Lenore stepped to the rostrum, slim, pretty, and amazingly youthful looking for a fifty-seven-year-old grandmother of nine, and said, with perfect assurance, 'Good morning, brothers and sisters.'"

The authors continued:

She spoke for only six minutes, but the reporters were left with mouths agape. This was no shy and stumbling candidate's wife, nor one who would confine herself to platitudes. She was a witty, dramatic and highly professional platform performer in her own right, as becomes one who had taken a flier at an acting career in Hollywood before her marriage. She was obviously to be reckoned into any calculation of Romney's assets for the presidential campaign, and when she referred to the "four years we have been in state government," it was surely no slip of the tongue.

Broder and Hess go on to describe Lenore Romney's passionate talk on civil rights and the good fight waged by her husband. It was, they concluded, "an intense and emotional talk," which she ended with a quip: "I've always had a lot to say, but nobody seemed to care until George became governor."

"In the stunned silence," they continued, "Romney began by making the only sensible remark possible on the occasion: 'You have just heard,' he said, 'the one person who can beat me in Michigan.'"

This small glimpse of Lenore ought to inform the write-ups of Mitt Romney that will flow between now and the conclusion of his campaign for the presidency. There's a lot of George in the son, but a lot of Lenore as well.

"My mom had an extraordinary ability to connect with audiences," Romney told me when I asked about Lenore's impact on him. "She spoke from her heart and she spoke with great passion and sympathy with the audience she spoke to."

"I learned a lot from her about connecting with individuals person to person," he continued, "My dad was better standing up in front of a podium you know, pounding his fist and saying how things ought to be. My mom was best in a small group talking to people one on one in some cases or hearing the sentiment of an audience and responding to it. She was very sensitive in that regard. In my better self, in my better moments, I try and capture a bit of both of them. Frankly, I'm just as comfortable standing behind a podium as I am in a room of five or six people having a discussion about something that matters to them."

The ability to connect to small groups is a crucial advantage in the early caucus and primary states of Iowa and New Hampshire, where "retail" politics matters more than the "wholesale" approach of television ads and robocalls. Will Lenore's political genes help him in these states?

"Well, you'd have to ask them first of all," Romney replied, "but Iowa and New Hampshire—you're right, it is all retail, at this stage, and probably always will be. That's frankly what I like about Iowa and New Hampshire being the first among the sweepstakes states, is that [the campaigning] is done retail. People actually get to know who might be their president and make a decision about them. I think that's why Howard Dean was not as successful as people anticipated him being going into Iowa. . . . He was not as effective on a person-to-person basis as he was behind the podium. I can't tell you how people respond to me, but I've gotten good support from those I've met with in that kind of setting."

Mitt Romney is a blend of his parents with a great deal of Harvard and Boston meritocracy layered on top of that significant political legacy. And he has been through the presidential campaign grinder before, if only from a distance.

Everyone who follows Romney is probably sentenced to read scores of comparison pieces between '68 and '08, but the premise is absurd, even as the comparisons between the 1992 and 2000 presidential campaigns of Bush 41 and Bush 43 are absurd—and those were only eight years apart.

There are a couple of lessons in George Romney's campaign, but none unique to it: Gaffes can kill campaigns. Allies can switch sides. Difficult wars make for difficult interviews.

What George Romney's campaign didn't have to deal with, though, was religious bigotry. The elder Romney just didn't last long enough to see anyone try to raise a "Mormon objection" to his qualifications.

One veteran of the George Romney effort sent Mitt Romney an analysis of why George's campaign floundered—an assessment that the younger Romney recalled "had twenty reasons why he lost."

"One of them was *not* because he was Mormon or people didn't understand the Mormon Church or whatever," Romney underscored to me. "He had all the reasons on why he thought he lost and it was pretty well researched and because he was part of the campaign he had an inside view."

Mitt Romney wondered out loud to me whether his LDS faith will influence the votes of "some tiny slice of people for whom that's a major issue." "Of course," he said, answering his own question. "It may be an issue for some, but it's not a factor in the final analysis."

It certainly wasn't in 1967 and 1968. Which is why it is crucial to note that Mitt Romney has watched the presidential process from box seats as both a young man and as a governor with a choice speaking spot at the 2004 national convention.

The 2008 presidential campaign is in many respects unprecedented. Neither party has as a candidate a serving president or vice president, the first time such a circumstance has occurred since 1952 pitted Ike against Adlai Stevenson. As a result the field is wide open and as the spectacular debut of Senator Barack Obama has demonstrated, not even Hillary has a free ride through the primaries.

It is not the first election post–9/11 of course, but it is the first in which the vast benefits of incumbency are unavailable to either side, and of course the cost of the war and its mind-boggling complexity will dominate the campaign.

It also appears, likely, though sadly, to almost certainly be the first race since 1960 where religious bigotry plays a role.

And it is most certainly the first time that the "Bain way" will be applied to presidential politics.

Chapter Two

"Bain Washed" not "Brain Washed"

When he returned from his thirty-month LDS mission—after narrowly surviving a head-on car crash that gravely injured him, killed the passenger seated next to him, and led to his parents being notified of his death—Mitt Romney did not go back to Stanford, where he had enrolled and spent his freshman year prior to the start of his mission, but instead transferred to Brigham Young University (BYU), the church's lighthouse educational institution, where he graduated from the College of Humanities in 1971. Romney delivered two commencement addresses at BYU, one to the College of Humanities and another to the entire graduating class. Romney is careful to point out that he never claims to have been the valedictorian or to have had his graduating class's highest GPA, as has often been reported. "I had the highest BYU GPA in the College of Humanities," he notes, but "if you blended in my first year at Stanford, it wouldn't have been the highest."

(Romney told me he has often been introduced as the valedictorian, or as number one in his class. "I've never said that, but somebody keeps passing it along," he says. His care about such a small detail reflects a recognition—present in all of our interviews

45

and in my interviews with his family, staff, and friends—that precision matters a great deal in campaigns, as it does generally for public figures.)

Romney entered the joint MBA/JD program at Harvard in the fall of 1971, and while he did well at the law school, where he graduated cum laude—or somewhere in the top third of his class—he was a much better Harvard Business School student than law student, graduating from the famed HBS as a Baker Scholar—a designation awarded only to the top 5 percent of each entering class of approximately five hundred students.

"They used to say," Romney recalled, "I think appropriately, that you could tell the law students from the business students. The law school students had furrowed brows and the business school students had bags under their eyes. The law school cases were intellectually challenging. You wondered what you were trying to draw out of the case. It was always a puzzle as to what was more important from the case. Business school, you had a lot of reading and you drew much more on human experience. The extensive reading was tiring but perhaps not as intellectually demanding as law school."

Romney's Harvard Law education included some of the most famous names in legal education. He took Contracts from Philip Areeda, who, if not the model for John Houseman's Professor Kingsfield character in *The Paper Chase*, was a master of the Socratic Method. Romney learned his antitrust from now Associate Justice of the United States Supreme Court Stephen Breyer. (Breyer was "very engaged with his students, and enjoyed the give and take.") Though the joint degree requires only roughly two-thirds the number of law school courses as the three year J.D., the four years at both HBS and Harvard Law provided Romney with a graduate education second to none in the United States.

From there, it was on to Bain & Company.

Each year more than ten thousand of America's smartest college seniors apply for the entry-level jobs at Bain & Company—jobs open to a select few of America's graduating classes from elite universities. Bain & Company is the Boston-based consulting firm whose name has become synonymous with excellence in the consulting field.

"Bain is very selective," one Bain partner told The Vault, an online resource for job seekers. "Recruiting is primarily from top Ivy League institutions. Our interviews are tough and if you don't get through the cases, you won't get an offer, no matter how impressive your resume might be. Some firms make their interview processes easier or harder depending on the caliber of the candidate. We are a complete meritocracy, for better or worse."

This "complete meritocracy" formed Mitt Romney, for better, or worse. Not only did Romney get through all "the cases," the currency of Harvard Business School, he has since created the raw material for scores more. HBS explains the case method on its website this way:

> When students are presented with a case, they place themselves in the role of the decision-maker as they read through the situation and identify the problem they are faced with. The next step is to perform the necessary analysis—examining the causes, considering alternative courses of actions—to come to a set of recommendations.
>
> To get the most out of cases, students read and reflect on the case and then often meet in small study groups before class to "warm up" and discuss their findings with other classmates. In class—under the questioning and guidance of the professor—students probe underlying issues, compare different alternatives, and finally, suggest courses of action in light of the company's objectives.
>
> As a case study unfolds in class, students do 85% of the talking, as the professor steers the conversation by making occasional observations and asking questions. This classroom interaction is enriched by the 80–90 individuals from diverse industries, functions, countries, and experiences.

During their time at Harvard Business School, students study and prepare over 500 cases—a transforming experience that helps them to recognize the unique aspects of different situations, define problems, suggest further avenues of analysis, and devise and implement action plans. Once they finish the program, HBS graduates have the confidence they need to go off and tackle the many business challenges they will face in their careers.

The "case method" formed Mitt Romney's approach to business, catapulted him to the top of two professions—consulting and investment—and earned him the reputation as a gifted turnaround artist. This reputation led him to be summoned to save the Olympics and to right the upside-down Massachusetts state budget. It may yet cause Republicans to call on him to reverse the disastrous results of the 2006 elections which left the GOP a double minority in Congress for the first time since 1993.

"Bainiacs," as they are called, are driven to succeed, are a dogged group of Type AAAs who have brought enormous energy and insight—and, most importantly, increased profitability—to the more than 3,300 companies that have hired Bain to "consult" with them on their company's fortunes and futures since its founding more than three decades ago. With thirty-two offices in twenty countries, the partnership that runs Bain & Company employs more than 2,400 consultants. What do these consultants do? The firm's slogan explains it: "Helping make companies more valuable." The promise is profits. The promise is usually kept.

Bain & Company was born in 1973, when Bill Bain, then a vice president at the Boston Consulting Group, left that partnership with a half dozen others to found the company that still bears his name. Though Bill Bain exited the company in 1991, the year that saw Mitt Romney lead a turnaround that saved it, Bill Bain is still a revered figure there and in the world of consulting. The mythology around the founding of the firm is that Bill Bain wanted to move beyond the traditional approach of consulting firms which would dispatch teams to clients, which would in short order arrive, review, report, and retreat. Bill Bain, it is said, wanted to *change* companies.

Bain believed in having his teams stick around even after they issued their last report in order to implement the changes they recommended and to achieve the results they predicted would follow.

Whether Bain & Company really did do things differently than other top-tier consulting firms such as McKinsey & Company was beside the point. In any event, Corporate America responded to the message (and to the guarantee that Bain & Company would take only one client from each business sector), and Bain & Company took off like a rocket. It quickly became the hottest place for top college grads aspiring to MBAs (and especially those seeking admission to Harvard Business School after a couple of years in the workplace), as well as one of the most sought-after landing zones for the HBS best and brightest.

Bain was "it." The most ambitious graduates sought Bain because Bain mattered. Bain changed things.

"The idea that consultancies should not measure themselves by the thickness of their reports, or even the elegance of their writing, but rather by whether or not the report was effectively implemented was an inflection point in the history of consulting," Mitt Romney told *Consulting* magazine. Every Bain & Company alumnus I have spoken with conveys the same message.

In late 2006, the website of the company (www.bain.com) prominently featured a *USA Today* quotation: "Bain delivers results, not theory." This is a superb pitch to make to a CEO in need of quick help from a name that the board of directors will recognize and in which they will have confidence.

What, exactly, does Bain & Company do? A college roommate of mine went off to Bain after our graduation in 1978. Paul visited me in San Clemente, California, while on a business trip in 1979. Bain had dispatched him to the Orange County fairgrounds to see if Shakley

Products were being sold illegally at places like the fairgrounds' massive weekly flea market. Paul was collecting *data*, the coin of the realm at Bain. Of such mundane tasks, married to the high purpose of increasing efficiency and profitability, are the researches and recommendations of Bain & Company made.

Of course Bain & Company consultants also troll for takeover targets, push technology deep into an old corporate culture, or help engineer corporate change.

They do, in short, whatever really, really, really needs to get done.

How do they do it?

They begin by hiring the right people.

"I like smart people," Mitt Romney wrote in his memoir of his Olympics experience, *Turnaround*. "Bill Bain, my old boss, used to joke that most things can be fixed, but smart—or dumb—is forever." Romney then details how it was the people he brought to the Olympics that made the team that saved those Games (more on that in the next chapter).

This is one of the crucial lessons that Romney absorbed first at Bain & Company, where Bill Bain recruited him in 1978: everything begins with smart people.

Romney would learn that principle as an associate and then a young partner at Bain & Company, and then put it into practice at Bain Capital, a firm he founded in 1984.

With a group of Bain & Company partners, Romney's new firm set out to raise money and then use that money to buy or invest in companies to which the Bain & Company approach for strategic improvement could be applied.

Company legend has it that when Romney posted a notice on a Bain & Company bulletin board that he was headed off to form Bain Capital and asked for sign-ups from employees willing to go with him, every single employee signed up.

Though Bain & Company and Bain Capital were completely separate firms doing different things, both had the same approach. Bainiacs at both firms knew that if they could get enough data, they could save failing companies and turn good companies into great ones. At the consulting firm, the wonder workers were paid fees to do this, but they did not have an ownership stake in the companies that employed them. At Bain Capital, the partners would either buy outright or invest significantly in the company to be turned around, and after the hard work was done and the company's profits and operations were improving (or soaring), the company would be sold and the investors in Bain Capital would reap huge financial rewards. The approach worked, and names like Staples and Domino's lead the list of companies that have benefited from Bain Capital investments and leadership.

From a first fund of approximately $30 million, Bain Capital is now on its ninth fund, and actively manages $9 billion in investors' money. The way of the Bainiacs worked when applied to private equity financing.

I asked one of Romney's colleagues for the single best example of Romney's turnaround talents from the business world. Without a doubt, he said, it was the rescue mission Romney performed for his own original firm, Bain & Company.

In early 1991 Romney was summoned back to Bain & Company, as the original partnership neared the rocks. Romney rescued the ship by again focusing on keeping the right people. Of all the partners he needed to retain to resuscitate the then struggling firm, Romney lost only one. "You have to understand how hard that was to accomplish," a colleague from those days told me. There was an enormous amount of debt, which meant "by definition, these professionals were making less than they could have on the open market because revenues had to first go to pay off the debt." The details are below, but Romney pulled it off and then returned to Bain Capital in December 1992. Bain & Company has prospered ever since his intervention.

At both Bains, Romney grew attached to the "strategic audit" and to the key concept that data and analysis are the two secrets to any exercise in problem-solving. At the beginning of any complex task, the strategic audit is undertaken to provide a detailed, completely accurate picture of the situation at hand: how strong are the assets; how weak the break points? The audit identifies the crucial data, and then the analysis begins and doesn't stop until the plan of action is conceived. A lot of this is numbers, and a lot of it is complicated prose. Romney's Harvard MBA helps with the former, his Harvard JD with the latter. But his real talent according to former partners is a relentless curiosity and an endless capacity for spirited argument and disagreement combined with a clear commitment to fairness.

One of the smart people Romney likes to have at hand is Bob White. White is a longtime business partner and friend of Romney, whom Romney recruited to join Bain & Company out of Harvard Business School. White played key roles in the start-up of Bain Capital, the rescue of both Bain & Company and the Olympics as well as the organization of the governor's early days at the helm of Massachusetts. He remains a close associate though White has returned to a leadership position at Bain Capital. Some folks describe White as Romney's right arm, but I think that understates the depth of their decades-old partnership.

White says Bain's approach depends on bringing the smartest people you can find into an environment where they can share their data-driven opinions. Where did Bain & Company and Bain Capital find these smart people? The nation's elite business schools, of course. For many years, Bain & Company sent Romney to find them. This headhunting background has helped him staff complex organizations including the Salt Lake City Olympics and of course Massachusetts's state government.

Once assembled and the data collected, the strategic audit gets under way. Here's Romney's own description of what that means:

In business turnaround settings, the first thing we had learned is that you should begin with a strategic audit. In a large business, the process could last as long as three months or more.

Our strategic audit took us to customers, to board members, to Wall Street analysts, to bankers, to suppliers, to former employees, and where possible, to competitors. We also got copies of every report that the company produced. We analyzed the numbers according to the tools that that had been proven to work before in other diagnostics. Every conceivable way of interpreting market shares, segmentation, business differentiation, cash flow, investment policy, competitive position, product quality, customer satisfaction, technology position, and countless other measures were employed. At the end of the strategic audit, we had a pretty good map of what was right and wrong in the business, of what had to be fixed, and which things were urgent and which were long term. We had hypotheses on which actions would have the greatest impact.

Is Romney accomplished at the practice of "the Bain way"? As noted above, when the founder of the firm and its struggling partnership needed a turnaround specialist to do for them what they had been doing for decades for others, they turned to Romney. Examining the story of Romney's return to Bain & Company in 1991 reveals not only Romney's business skills, but also the esteem with which his peers regarded him then—and now.

"I had some partners at Bain & Company while I was at Bain Capital," and here he digressed in carefully diplomatic aside to tutor me, a lawyer-journalist who might not know better. "You know the difference between the two? I call them 'Bain Consulting' and 'Bain Investing.'" Lesson gently delivered and learned, he moved on. "I had some of the Bain Consulting guys come to me—some of the partners—and say, 'Look we're going over a cliff and we need you to come in and run the organization. We'd like you to go see Bill Bain and talk to him about making that change.'"

That was step one: an appeal and an invitation from friends. There was a huge step two, though. Romney's mentor and friend, Bill Bain, was still in the captain's chair at Bain & Company.

"I went to see Bill Bain and I said, 'I've been approached by some of the partners thinking that I could make a difference,'" Romney recounted, "and that I would be willing to do so."

Romney discovered that Bain already "was planning on stepping aside saying that it was time for new leadership."

"He said, 'Would you be willing to do it?'" Romney stressed that he was not part of a coup against his mentor. "I didn't come in and say, 'Hey, I want it, give it to me.' I said that it had been recommended and that I would consider it. My perception is he was taken with the idea." Although difficult for anyone outside the private equities/consulting world to grasp and for many to even believe, there was little if any self-interest motivating Romney at this juncture. He had his private equity fund, and his fortunes were not in any way tied to the rejuvenation of Bain & Company. So why did Romney dive in?

"There was no upside," he assured me. "There was no particular reason to do it other than a sense of obligation and duty to an organization that had done great things for me and which employed 1,000 people. If it disappeared, it would mean 1,000 people out of work at a very difficult time. America was in a recession. There were 1,000 people that I cared about, some very good friends," he continued.

"I'd worked there—how many years? I don't know, eight years or something. A very good relationship. I loved the people there, and they felt I was needed. As I looked at it, I concluded that in fact the skills developed in my new life at Bain Capital as a financial manager and as a turnaround specialist could really be helpful and were really exactly what the doctor ordered."

Upon taking the assignment, he applied the Bain way to Bain & Company, by beginning with a message to the partners: stay put, do what you do best, and we will turn this around.

"I met with the partners," Romney told me, "and said, 'Look, I'm willing to leave Bain Capital and become the chief executive officer…but there are a couple of conditions and you know what the conditions [are]. One is: you have to unanimously want it because if somebody wants a different path, be my guest. Number two: you have to agree to stay. Barring some very unusual circumstance, you must stay for at least a year to get us back on track.' I pointed out that if they begin to go, the whole firm obviously implodes."

The risk in this approach, Romney explained, was that "all those partners could get a job within six months. The thousand or so in the rest of the firm would really be out of luck because it was a tough economic time."

"We really had a responsibility and a duty as partners of that firm," Romney continued, "to maintain the enterprise for the benefit of the thousand or so people who wouldn't be able to get jobs. To a person they made that commitment. Only one individual moved on, and I understood. He was really anticipating becoming the CEO himself, and so it made sense."

The first order of business was business. Romney ordered that big-picture deliberations on the future of the company and the complicated details of its work-out be limited to Saturdays.

"We had work to do for our clients during the weekdays, and I didn't want everybody in the halls constantly wondering what the future was going to be and what was going to happen internally and the politics of the survival of our enterprise. So we had our partner meetings on Saturday when we could devote our full attention to the affairs of the consulting firm rather than the affairs of our clients."

Was it a close-run thing?

"There were some really frightening months there when we wondered if we could make it," Romney conceded. "I came in and first thing we did was find out that we'd just sent a million dollars to our landlord, and we called and cancelled the check and called the landlord and said, 'We have bad news. The check has been sent but it's not going to clear because we've cancelled payment.' And we did that around the world. We cancelled payment on real estate, we cancelled all sorts of suppliers and did everything we could to preserve cash so that we could meet payroll. It's a crime in this state to employ someone knowing or having reason to know that you won't be able to pay them at the end of the pay period. It's a crime and we were perilously close to not being able to meet payroll. So, we watched this like a hawk."

The partners worked a lot of Saturdays, veterans of this turn-around recall, and they parceled out the sacrifices so that everyone bled at least a little, and some bled a lot but not so much as to make the workout less attractive than its cost. Only one partner jumped ship. After nearly two years of crisis mode, Bain & Company recovered its footing and continues to thrive as one of the preeminent consulting firms in the world.

"There was not even a hint of sharp corners," David Roberts, a Bain & Company partner at the time of the Romney-led turnaround, told me. Romney simply did the hard things that needed to get done: Reduce physical space. Take a hard look at the partners—those who were producing and those who weren't. Arrange bridge financing. Keep a focus on recruiting the very best talent from Harvard Business School, Stanford, and the other leading business schools. Rescind offers that were reaches.

Romney was always "doing the right thing, even though it was the hard thing to do," Baker concluded of those years.

Mitt Romney resurrected the consulting company's finances and then returned to his enormously successful and profitable Bain Capital. Mission accomplished.

The "Bain way" has thus brought success to Romney on many levels and in many situations. Outside of business, it has worked for him at the Olympics (discussed in the next chapter) and with his own mentor, partners, and close friends when the stakes were personal and the climb to success very steep indeed. What does the "Bain way" involve?

"There were two key things that I learned at Bain," he told me: "One was a series of concepts for approaching tough problems and a problem solving methodology; the other was an enormous respect for data, analysis, and debate."

"Think about this," he continued. "You're a company like Bain. You get hired by Chrysler Corporation to figure out how to fix their company, and they are going to pay you $250,000 a month. And you know nothing about the auto industry other than how to start your own car. It takes a lot of chutzpah. How do you possibly justify getting paid millions of dollars by Chrysler Corporation?"

Many executives, discomfited by the invasion of outside consultants, ask this question.

"The answer," Romney offered, "is because you have some conceptual framework for solving problems that is different from what they have inside the company. You're going to get data that they have but have never analyzed in the proper way, and then you're going to tear it apart and debate it amongst yourselves and with them and find new and bold answers. That approach has served me, Bain & Company's clients, and Bain Capital well."

How well has it served?

"Bain Capital is one of the most successful private equity investors in America. The years that I was there, I don't think there was a single fund that did better than ours. I think it was the best performing fund. I can't prove that, but among the major funds that I'm aware of, it was the best performing fund in the nation. Why is that? Because of the approach to analysis and decision making I learned at Bain & Company. No question about it."

An impressive record for equity investing and management consulting, but will the "Bain way" work for the issues confronting the federal government?

I asked the governor if he could solve the Social Security mess.

"Absolutely," he replied without hesitation. This is the confidence that smart people have in the idea of applying intelligence, experience, and good will to thorny problems. This approach works in a bottom line–driven business world with the objective realities of profits and losses, shareholders and CEOs. But that world is not politics. Politics is messy, and seems almost at times to be the triumph of the irrational over the necessary. The deadlock over Social Security reform in 2005 was the perfect expression of the victory of political expediency over if not urgent then at least necessary reforms. Harry Reid and Nancy Pelosi, egged on by a hard Left sheep-dipped in Bush hatred, simply refused to join the debate. They would not engage, and with a forty-vote veto over any plan in the Senate, succeeded in killing off not just reform, but even the conversation about reform. The "Bain way" will not work against such mindless obstructionism. The "Bain way" presumes a common interest in success.

Would the "Bain way" work if applied to the behemoth that is the Pentagon?

"I don't know a better way," Romney replied, and cited all sorts of settings in which he employed the process of assembling diverse viewpoints, massive amounts of data, and serious, sustained argument and counter-argument.

"My experience in working with very different settings—whether it was consulting to hospitals, buying a pizza company, starting an office supply company, or at the Olympics where you had strong factions pulling in different directions—was always the same: the approach of gathering people who represent different viewpoints and then insisting that they argue but with data and analysis allows people to reach consensus and points out where self-interest is driving a particular argument rather than mutual interest."

Romney then cited Doris Kearns Goodwin's bestselling work of political biography about Abraham Lincoln, *Team of Rivals*, as charting a historical parallel to the process he has used over and over again. Lincoln assembled a cabinet of his chief rivals for the leadership of the country in 1860, and harnessed them all to the goal of preserving the union. Lincoln was not afraid of great talent, "an approach which I believe has worked time and time again in government," Romney pointed out.

First, "let people sit at the table and let them bring in different viewpoints and arguments and then support them with reviewable data that can be confirmed. Generally that process will yield a consensus and a decision that the group will stand behind. I think what I've seen in organizations is that when you have a leader that comes in and 'knows' all the answers without the benefit of anyone else's input or data, there is going to be a rejection."

Romney proceeded to part two: "Secondly, if you have a leader that can't make a decision and brings everyone in and just talks but no one can decide, then you can't proceed. You have to have a leader who is strong enough to drive the process, to reach a decision, knowing that not everyone is going to be in agreement when it's finished. But people will feel that they have been heard and that their argument has been made and that they've had a fair chance."

Many Beltway barons will say they have seen this before and seen it fail, and will predict certain doom for the "unsophisticated" or naïve outsider approaches.

Romney partisans will ask: Who, in fact, is unsophisticated? Has genuine, modern management ever been applied to the Pentagon, much less to the domestic agencies? Has data as opposed to agendas ever really driven any Washington "policy process"?

If elected, Romney should be free of the yoke that burdened President Bush from even before he took the oath of office, which was Florida 2000. The poisonous aftermath of Al Gore's decision to contest the vote that included the bitter arguments—from the "butterfly ballot" to the Gore-Lieberman attempt to disenfranchise military voters who had cast ballots overseas, the Florida Supreme Court's naked partisanship, and the "selected, not elected" meme that sprang from the United States Supreme Court's calling a halt to the charade—all have followed Bush from the first day of his presidency, manifesting itself in a furious anti-Bush hatred that has few rivals in American political history outside of hatred for Lincoln and the very earliest battles of the new Republic.

If Romney wins, there is a chance that he will begin his presidency free of that sort of deep hatred from the Left. For one thing, a

Romney victory will almost certainly mean that the hard Left of the Democratic Party, as represented by the bloggers DailyKos and MyDD, will have worked with Howard Dean and George Soros and the rest of the MoveOn.org activist Left to have led the Democrats over not just one cliff, but three of four cliffs—2002, 2004, and 2008. (And 2006 was hardly a great year for the Ned Lamont boosters.) Romney will have slain the Clinton dragon and assumed the office on an explicit "come, let us reason together" appeal that is premised on the idea of objective data and thorough analysis. This is a crucial part of Romney's core appeal: a commitment to finding solutions, but only those solutions that are acceptable in light of America's core values and political traditions.

Here we arrive at a crucial point regarding Romney's commitment to facts, analysis, and the logic of persuasive argument. It's not absolute—it's limited. Romney believes in a higher law, a law "of nature and nature's God" that cannot be abandoned because of efficiencies in the offing, or political convenience.

A pure Bainiac would see no problem, for example, or even an issue in the idea of harvesting stem cells from a production line of embryos. There are efficiencies there, and the promise of great gains for the sick, as well as great profits for the university-research complex that has come to rival the military-industrial complex that Ike warned about.

Romney has seen that complex at work. It came and lobbied him in the form of big brains from the Harvard branch of the university-research complex. Douglas A. Melton, co-director of the Harvard Stem Cell Institute, paid a call to Romney in 2005 hoping to enlist the Massachusetts governor in the plan to jump-start an assembly line of embryos created for the sole purpose of harvesting their stem cells. Romney rejected the appeal: "Some of the practices that Harvard and probably other institutions in Massachusetts are engaged in cross the line of ethical conduct," Romney told reporters. "My wife has MS [multiple sclerosis], and we would love for there to be a cure for her disease and for the diseases of others. But there is an ethical boundary that should not be crossed."

Bainiacs are not generally presumed to worry about "ethical boundaries" that are undefined by law. Clearly Romney brings a set of values to the consultants' table that set him apart from the purest form of MBA mercenary.

The United States has had one MBA president, George W. Bush. Bush's career was not similar to Romney's. President Bush has enjoyed the role of "decider-in-chief," the CEO who listened to options and issued crisp, no-nonsense decisions. This is not the profile of a Bainiac, who disassembles complicated fact patterns and reassembles new and improved organizations.

There are different kinds of MBAs, just as there are different sorts of MDs and lawyers. Bush and Romney could not be more dissimilar.

If he becomes president, will the ingrained habits of the "Bain way" influence Romney for the better? We have two case studies: his tenure as head of the Salt Lake City Olympics, and his four years as governor of the bluest of states.

Chapter Three

A Gold Medal Performance

When Mitt Romney arrived on the scene of the Salt Lake City Olympic Games in February 1999, the situation was a public relations and management disaster. Actually, it was much worse than a business disaster. It was a scandal that had become a crisis. There was no good reason to take the job as chairman of the 2002 Winter Games, and there were plenty of reasons to say no. But Romney took it.

"I had the bug of wanting to be more involved," Romney wrote in his Olympics memoir, *Turnaround*. "I wanted to make more of a difference in people's lives."

Get used to the corny if you pick up *Turnaround*. At the conclusion of our first extended interview, the governor proudly told me as he signed my heavily annotated copy, "You know, I wrote this myself. Tim Robinson helped, of course, but I had to pound it out, night after night."

As a one-time ghostwriter, I believe Romney. There's actually no doubting him. The voice in *Turnaround* is too authentic for a ghost to have been pounding out the text, which is why the reporters, producers, and editors covering Campaign 2008 will need to get a copy. It is quite unlike every other candidate book I have read.

First of all, it is far too earnest even for the genre of campaign books that has sprung up in recent years. Mitt Romney and his Salt Lake Olympic Committee (SLOC) turnaround team used every imaginable motivational tool in the effort to rescue the sinking Salt Lake City games, and all of those gimmicks are recounted in the book, including the almost impossible-to-believe-in-this-cynical-age christening of "gold medal performances" which Romney bestowed on SLOC staffers who had completed crucial tasks.

"Given what we faced," he wrote, "average performance wasn't going to cut it. Great talent, teamwork and a commitment to a shared vision were indispensable. We would need gold medal performances from every member of the senior team and from many of the middle and junior staff members."

"At SLOC, we were flush with crises and thus with opportunities for gold medal performances," he continued. And after a dose of leadership and motivation?

"Gold medal work was everywhere at SLOC." Corny, yes, but deeply sincere and probably resonant for the segment of America that is still moved by *Mr. Smith Goes to Washington.*

The book is also too raw to have been vetted by many people with a political agenda. There are plenty of folks likely offended by his memoir, folks who will be too eager to play payback as a result. I expect the Hillary team is already hunting down the former head of U.S. Olympic Committee's marketing efforts, John Krimsky. It would hard to point to a more unflattering portrait in print than the one Romney delivers—almost always with a backhand—than the one leveled at Krimsky.

"Krimsky and his team in Colorado Springs were my marketing arm and they were just not getting the job done," Romney wrote. "I had asked to join in sales calls and they had been enthusiastic about having my help, but I got no calls from them. Either they thought I couldn't be of help to them or they had no sales calls."

Krimsky up and left the USOC in the middle of the rescue effort. Romney's few lines on the subject leave no doubt that he evaluated Krimsky's reasons for leaving and found them lacking the ethical basis Romney seems to assume is a necessity for an Olympics manager.

By the time Romney arrived on the scene in Salt Lake, though, there should have been few illusions about the Olympics. Past events such as the brazenly corrupt officiating that gave the Soviets a win in the 1972 basketball championship, numerous drug scandals, and a general high-handedness by Olympic grandees had given the world good reason to look sideways at the Olympics "movement," and judge it less than the noblest of all endeavors.

When a "games for bribes" scandal engulfed the Salt Lake City Games in the late '90s, it triggered an "unprecedented attack on the Olympic industry," according to University of Toronto professor Helen Jefferson Lenskyj, whose *Inside the Olympic Industry* is a painstakingly researched account of the many corruptions that had seeped into the modern-era Olympics:

> "[I]t was the guys in the suits," who had messed up, Romney recollected. The original promoters of the Salt Lake games spent lavishly on the IOC members who would select the venue for the games. Allegations of cash bribes and "escorts" rolled out against the backdrop of ongoing Department of Justice and Congressional investigations. The charges and countercharges accumulated so quickly as to make effective responses impossible, and heads began to roll as the Utah establishment struggled to find a way out of the scandal swamp.

Romney was the one-man advance guard for the cleanup crew. He came. He saw. He employed the "Bain way." "When he arrived," the *Salt Lake City Tribune* recalled when the paper declared Romney the "Utahn of the Year" at the end of 2001, "the picture was bleak. SLOC had not signed a new sponsor in 14 months; morale was low. Some wondered aloud if Salt Lake City ought to throw in the towel." But, the paper noted, Romney had moved "through the scandal's stench," and revived the effort from "the moral and financial ashes of the bid fiasco."

"When I went to the Olympics, it was just like going to a Bain consulting client," he told me. "Do the analysis, get the data, find out what the financials really look like, conduct a strategic audit. It was that same approach. It's a learning approach."

"It was a mess," Romney told me about the SLOC when he arrived. Not only was the operation deeply in debt and paralyzed by a still unfolding scandal, the brand was so badly broken that many talked about canceling the Games. In January 1999, Salt Lake City Council member Deeda Seed told PBS that "in light of recent events, it may be difficult for our organizing committee to raise the funds to host these Games. We are still $250 million short of what is needed, and I think any reasonable person would wonder if a corporate sponsor would want to sign on, given what has happened."

"I knew that I had to get sponsors," Romney told me. "I had to get volunteers. I had to get community donors. The only way that I could communicate to them was through the public image of the Games. Media was a big part of it."

How did he do it? Transparency was one tactic.

"My experience has been that openness is a very powerful antiseptic. Sunshine is the best disinfectant, and that openness is the best process. Being direct and honest with people is the best procedure."

Part of the turnaround was tough fiscal management. When Romney arrived, the Games faced a $379 million projected deficit. When they closed, he left behind a $55 million *surplus*.

Pundits will soon start to keep count of the number of times Mitt Romney draws on his Olympic experience on the campaign trail. But even as that number climbs, and the press inevitably comes to that point in the campaign when it begins to mock his recalling his years as head of the Salt Lake City Games, Romney won't stop telling and retelling his stories. Audiences love them, because Americans love the Olympics, even non–sports fans (but especially sports fans who for two weeks every two years binge on round-the-clock broadcasting even of such obscure competitions as curling, ice dancing, the skeleton, and speed skating).

When Romney took on the 2002 Winter Games, the most pressing problem involved rescuing the brand from its near total collapse in the eyes of America's corporate elite, which in large part funds the athletic extravaganza. Salt Lake's successful bid back in 1995 had been swaddled in bribery and shady practices. The scandal had all but killed the expensive corporate sponsorships that make the Games possible. Because the Games were in the city associated with the Church of Jesus Christ of Latter-day Saints, there was an additional layer of complexity over the scandal; the media loved the charge of hypocrisy, easily aimed at the Olympiad often branded "The Mormon Games." There was no small amount of glee among a cynical press when the scandal broke and brought week after week of fresh revelations.

The Olympics have never been as clean or as amateur as the myths from the pre-professional era make them out to be. Their story has been told often and in highly critical books that detail the huge amounts of money that flow through the "Olympic Movement." It's not just money, but an air of arrogance and elitism that has surrounded the Games ever since their resurrection in 1904. The rhetoric of the Games' leaders—often best described as insufferable—had built up a lot of enemies in the working sports press over the decades. When the corruption of the bidding process surrounding the 2002 Winter Games came to light, there was no doubt that the knives that came out would be long and sharp.

The effect was to destroy the financial footing of the Games while their reputation dissolved.

Romney was recruited to lead the Games by senior leaders in the Utah business community and those few still standing at the Salt Lake Committee. Romney enjoyed a deserved reputation for business shrewdness and turnaround talent. It was the Bain & Company and Bain Capital brand that made Romney attractive as a rescuer.

That and his Mormon faith.

Because these games, like all Olympic Games, were so completely intertwined with the city that hosted them, and because the city was so intertwined with the Mormon Church that founded it, an ability for the Games' leader to work with, trust, and be trusted by the LDS General Authorities was essential to the success of the Games. When the search commenced for a Mormon business executive with undisputed ability as well as the telegenic appeal and communication skills necessary for a massive PR repair effort, it didn't take long for the hiring committee to think of Romney, now back at Bain Capital after his rescue of Bain & Company.

Romney tells the story of his recruitment in *Turnaround*, and his account lays most of the decision to accept what looked like a near impossible task on his wife, Ann, and on the family's tradition of service.

Also noteworthy, though, is that when he received the offer, Romney was a strategic planner with a taste for politics who had realized that buying, building, and selling companies wasn't interesting him as much as it once had. He no doubt sensed a rare opportunity with huge upside and only limited downside.

The Games' financial books were a disaster. The marketing had crashed. The scandal revelations kept coming. The costs kept accumulating. If he hadn't been able to pull it off, Romney in all likelihood could have walked away unblemished saying, "I tried, but no one but God can resurrect the dead."

But he did pull it off, and not just by a whisker, but in spectacular fashion. His accomplishment grew even more significant because the Salt Lake City Games were held against the backdrop of 9/11. The deeply moving opening ceremony saw the tattered flag from Ground Zero carried into a totally silent stadium. It was a ceremony watched by hundreds of millions around the globe; it was watched with particular pride and purpose by a still deeply traumatized America. To put together the opening ceremony's coda involving the flag from Ground

Zero, Romney had to fight against the Olympic bureaucracy which, though 9/11 had occurred only months before, cited rules against the display of the host country's flag in anything other than very strictly enforced protocols that Romney's proposals violated. With the help of IOC president Jaques Rogge, a compromise was negotiated that resulted in the memorable and moving entrance of the flag.

The Games also proceeded under the very real fear of another terrorist attack, and with unprecedented security because of the still deeply felt vulnerability that lingered in the country (and in informed regions, still does). They were wonderful, as all Olympics are wonderful. Youth is itself a tonic, as are sports, and especially in an injured and grieving country, the combination was exactly the right salve.

Most Americans are hard pressed to recall many specifics from the Games when it comes to athletes. Derek Parra, the speed skater who has become close to the Romneys and who lived in their Utah home between the 2002 and 2006 Games while training for the latter, is one who stands out, as does Sarah Hughes, the surprise champion in figure skating. Some might recall the judging scandal that marred the pairs figure skating competition, or the rings emblazoned on the mountain or the appearance of President Bush among the athletes, especially the moment when one handed him a cell phone so he could say hi to mom, but most memorable was the spectacular opening ceremony and the solemn arrival of the 9/11 flag.

The significance of Romney's Olympic stewardship for Romney's presidential bid is much more in the stories he tells of the Games than in the awful numbers he and his colleagues confronted and reversed. To be a story teller is a great advantage for a candidate, as President Reagan demonstrated. But the ability to spin a yarn is much devalued unless accompanied by material. Romney's got a box of business stories, but no matter how intriguing the launch of Staples was, it can't compare with the planning for the torch relay, or the tale of tempting the *Today Show* with a promise of a Romney run on the skeleton (head-first on a sled going ninety miles an hour). Expect to hear these stories because the public loves them, and as Kissinger once quipped about one subject or another, they have the additional advantage of being true.

Beyond the easy claim of a significant and difficult accomplishment and the treasure trove of anecdotes, there are some additional aspects of the Olympics experience that will inform Romney's candidacy and if successful, his presidency.

For one thing, as I discuss in more detail in a later chapter, there's media and then there's *media*. There's nothing—nothing—like the media gauntlet a presidential candidate must run both in terms of quantity of coverage and level of scrutiny.

But if there is a close second, it would be as head of a scandal-plagued Olympics.

Mitt Romney basically went to media-management school in his three-plus years as head of the SLOC. It will help him in the campaign.

It was also a graduate course in crisis management of a sort that neither business nor pure government experience can provide. The SLOC had almost no inherent authority to command, only to cajole, beg, and persuade. In order to accomplish anything, Romney had to first divine the correct course of action and then get a variety of players to buy in to his plan. In this respect, Romney has had a glimpse of a president's position vis-à-vis an intransigent Congress. Truman once famously predicted that Eisenhower would be deeply frustrated by the presidency as the erstwhile Supreme Commander would quickly discover that he could order A and B only to find that A and B just didn't happen for a president as they did for a five-star general.

And then there is the experience in constituency management.

All elected officials have to manage various constituencies. All federal office holders have to of course deal with the other branches of government. Legislators must handle their colleagues in their own legislative body. For presidents or governors, there are staffs both personal and in numerous executive agencies. For all politicians, there are political supporters and contributors, family and friends, the media, and of course the people. Each has an agenda, and each his urgent needs and demands, and sometimes—actually often—they all cannot be reconciled.

At the SLOC Romney had many masters.

The International Olympic Committee was the supreme authority, and could hamper his efforts or greatly assist them as its members saw fit.

The United States Olympic Committee is the permanent Olympic power in our country, and it had its hooks into the Salt Lake Games as well, including as a partial beneficiary of the lucrative sponsorships that Team Romney could land.

The sponsors themselves had very definite needs, especially the pressing question of just what they were branding themselves with.

Congress had a huge role—and John McCain was a prominent critic of the Games past and scrutinizer of the SLOC—as was the Clinton and then the Bush White House.

Then Utah governor Mike Leavitt—now Secretary of Health and Human Services—was perhaps Romney's chief boss, but every member of the Utah legislature was in a position to help or hurt the Games, as were the scores of local jurisdictions with a piece of the action because of the widespread location of the various venues.

The SLOC had a staff of course—of about a thousand. And bankers. And contractors.

Each sport has a committee, and each committee an international and national body.

There were the ticket holders. The broadcast networks. The vendors.

And, above everyone else, there were the athletes and the fans. The Olympic Games, when stripped of all the promotion and the money, are still games. The prime numbers of the Games are the athletes, and right behind them, the audience. Romney's understanding of his prime numbers is manifest throughout *Turnaround*, and it will become a necessary text for Campaign 2008.

Most importantly, Romney recognizes that his prime audience in '08 will be the voters, and a relentless focus will follow as a result.

He knows that to reach the general election voters he has to satisfy a dozen different constituencies, from media scribblers and talkers, to precinct chairmen and phone bank callers, maxed-out contributors and fifty-buck grannies, and eventually primary and caucus voters.

All of this cycle's candidates "know" this when they set out. And some have lots of experience with single-state races, and some single-state races can involve a lot of media attention in the pressure cooker of multiple and competing constituencies.

But only six have surfed a sustained, big wave: Hillary, John Kerry, John Edwards, John McCain, Rudy Giuliani, and Mitt Romney.

And only three have done so outside the context of a presidential campaign: Hillary, Rudy, and Mitt. And when Rudy was called to the international stage it was in the aftermath of 9/11, when there wasn't the typical animus among the press to diminish him or the city he led.

It thus won't be surprising if the finals in 2008 match the two best prepared among the dozen would-be presidents to handle the media tsunami.

And only one of those will have taken a skeleton ride down a thousand-foot chute.

So he arrived at the start of his successful campaign for Massachusetts governor with an impressive record of achievement at the Games and in finance. And he did not arrive alone, but backed by a closely knit family that will almost certainly be as closely examined as Romney's management of the Games or his success as an entrepreneur.

Chapter Four

A Christmas Card Family

" I read but few lives of great men," Ulysses S. Grant once proclaimed, "because biographers do not, as a rule, tell enough about the formative period of life."

"What I want to know is what a man did as a boy," concluded Grant.

Mitt Romney was born in postwar Detroit, the fourth child of one of the Motor City's rising young executives. George Romney had been a lobbyist for Alcoa in Washington, D.C., when an opening to run the Detroit office of the Automobile Manufacturers Association appeared in 1939. Romney eagerly accepted the offer of the $12,000-a-year job, and when the war transformed Detroit, it transformed George Romney's career. He became the managing director of the Automobile Council for War Production and traveled extensively in pursuit of its wartime production goals. After race riots shook Detroit—thirty-four were killed in the June 1943 spasm—Romney joined with the United Auto Workers' Walter Reuther to organize the Detroit Victory Council as one step in bringing the city and its vast engines of production back to order.

"Romney was now a man with highly impressive credentials," wrote D. Duane Angel in a short, but well researched and sourced 1967 book, *Romney: A Political Biography*, which was timed to the start of the 1968 campaign, and with which George Romney cooperated. Angel recounts how Romney's rise through various lobbying and governmental relations post combined with his wide contacts throughout Detroit would perfectly position the young executive in postwar Detroit. Romney joined the Nash-Kelvinator Corporation as the executive assistant to its president, George W. Mason.

Nash-Kelvinator was a sprawling manufacturing company that made cars as well as one of the first modern, side-by-side frost-free refrigerators, the "Kelvinator Food-A-Rama Side by Side Refrigerator." Though his duties were widespread throughout the company and included international travel for trade shows, George Romney threw himself into the development of two cars—the Metropolitan and the Rambler. In May 1954, Nash-Kelvinator and Hudson Motors merged to become the American Motors Corporation (AMC). Less than six months later, on October 12, 1954, George Mason died of pneumonia. George Romney became chairman, president, and general manager of American Motors. He was forty-seven.

Romney bet his career on the Rambler and the success of American Motors, and the bet paid off. The compact car became a hit with Americans, and Romney ended up on the cover of *Time* on April 6, 1959.

"Romney himself believed fervently in the compact car," Allen Walrath wrote in an assessment of the Rambler's success in the late 1950s, "and discontinued the Nash and Hudson nameplates at the end of the 1957 model year to concentrate all of AMC's efforts on the Rambler."

"At about the same time, the country was in a deep recession, in which sales of nearly all 1958 cars plummeted," Walrath continued. "But it was a different situation for American Motors, where Rambler sales began to soar."

Sales doubled in 1958, and again in 1959.

"For three of the next four years, the company sold in excess of 400,000 units annually," Walrath concluded, "despite direct competition from the Big Three in 1960 with the Ford Falcon, Chevrolet Corvair and Plymouth Valiant, and a continuing proliferation of compacts in succeeding years."

As the Ramblers began to sell, Romney moved his wife and four children to the Detroit suburb of Bloomfield Hills in 1957. Mitt Romney was ten.

"Harry Truman liked to say in his later years," historian and biographer David McCullough reports, "that he had the happiest childhood imaginable." Mitt Romney will no doubt argue for a tie, at least, with Give-em-Hell Harry.

By many accounts, George and Lenore Romney were among the most remarkable people of their time. They combined outsized drive and talents with a sincere compassion for and interest in people of all walks of life. They also had an enormous love of family.

George Romney "was unlike anyone I've ever met," his grandson Tagg recalls. "He was so driven, so passionate about whatever he was doing and had so many interesting stories about growing up. He was just fascinating. Even though you looked at him and knew that he was an important person, he just made you feel that you were the most important thing to him."

Lenore—"Mahz" to her grandchildren, as George was "Barta"— "loved to sing," Tagg continued. "She was always singing."

"She had had a lot of health problems," Tagg explained. "She had been beautiful younger and then had a lot of health problems, and so she seemed so frail and her legs were toothpicks."

"Probably six times that I can remember," Tagg recalled, "we all thought she was going to die, but she was just a fighter. She would come back. She'd break her hip and be in the hospital with pneumonia, and everyone would gather around; time to say goodbye to Mahz. And then six months later, she'd be up again singing, and she was the most positive human. She never—to the point to it was sometimes silly—she would never say anything negative about anybody. If you started to say anything negative about somebody, she would sing a song and make something up."

Tagg concluded with a smile. "She was a character."

Mitt Romney was the youngest child to these parents, trailing his next closest sibling, brother Scott, by six years. Accounts from the years of George Romney's early career in politics—leading a bipartisan effort to update Michigan's state constitution, and then his first campaign for governor in 1961 and 1962—placed a young Mitt at rallies and in parades with his parents. Mitt grew up in politics, comfortable with the public eye.

"He loved doing pranks and just doing fun things," recalls Lynn Moon Shields, a longtime friend of both Mitt and Ann Romney going back to their days in junior high school and, for a few months in 1964, a steady date of Romney's. "He was just lively. He made you feel good. He was just a very positive guy."

Shields dated Romney in the fall of that year, just before Romney met Ann Davies at Lynn Moon's surprise sixteenth birthday party (which Mitt attended even though Shields and Romney had stopped dating). "The way that we stopped dating is that he just stopped calling to ask me out," Lynn Shields recalled with a laugh. "And he's so nice. He'll always say that I dumped him. He was by far the best date that I had in my high school career. He was such fun and such a gentleman and just—he's obviously very handsome and I was fifteen I think. He would have been seventeen or so. I was a sophomore and he was a senior."

Bloomfield Hills is a small (less than 4,000 residents) and wealthy suburb of Detroit. At the close of 2006 it was rated the fourth-wealthiest city in America, and the richest outside of California and Florida. In the late 1950s and early 1960s, though, it was a suburb for the successful, not the hyper-wealthy. It was also home to the Cranbrook School for Boys, an exclusive boys school paired on a beautiful campus with the Kingswood School for Girls. (The schools became a single entity in the 1970s.)

Romney was no athlete but very much a presence on the campus, and not because his father was the governor. "That didn't seem to me to be a very big deal," Shields recalled. "It wasn't the way it is now, with the way politicians are sort of made out like there royalty or movie stars or whatever," Shields added, "I don't know when it changed, but certainly prior to the '70s, being a politician was certainly no more of a special position than doing something else."

In an enclave like Bloomfield Hills and at a school like Cranbrook, a governor's son in the early '60s would not have been the subject of much curiosity. But Romney was a prankster, and that did earn him a reputation.

"He and a bunch of friends," Shields recalled, "dressed up in very formal clothing and set a formal table in the median strip of Woodward Avenue, the main drag that runs through Detroit. They had somebody, I think, playing the violin as entertainment for the table, and they had a meal right in the middle of this eight-lane road." The police eventually arrived and broke it up, but in the early '60s, such was the stuff of high school fun, a fact that painfully underscores how far the culture has traveled since.

As mentioned, Romney was not an athlete, and Shields, like both of Romney's sons I interviewed, recalled a Romney cross-country race into which Romney put so much effort that, upon crossing the finish line (nowhere near first place, both sons make certain to relate with relish) he passed out cold and had to be carried from the field.

The stories of Cranbrook High School have a very familiar, Dobie Gillis-Patty Duke feel—football games, basketball games, dances, the prom and homecoming and a lot of ice skating. Romney had a car, a Rambler of course. The Beatles had arrived; the girls were smitten with them, and the boys had to pretend to be at least. Vietnam had not yet begun to trouble the plans of young people.

Even then Romney had a reputation for smarts. "I know my mother claimed that she thought all along that he was incredibly bright and that he would be a great president, and she says that she thought that when he was in seventh grade," Shields recalled.

Romney gave a ride home from the Moon house on the night of Lynn Moon Shield's sixteenth birthday to Ann Davies, and as Lynn Shields says, "The rest is history."

When Mitt Romney's father fell for Mitt's mother, Lenore, George Romney pursued the beautiful young actress with the same relentlessness that would later put the Rambler in millions of American garages. George Romney was single-minded about his intended, and where Lenore went—including Hollywood for a career in the business—George followed.

Decades later, having been smitten as a senior at Cranbook School outside of Detroit by the sophomore Ann Davies, Mitt Romney took a page from his dad's playbook and never let up until he got the girl of his dreams.

"Did you ever in your wildest dreams imagine that we'd be here at the Olympics?" Romney likes to tell audiences he once asked of Ann. "Mitt, you weren't in my wildest dreams," is the punch line, and it always gets the laugh. Romney also gets laughs when he recounts the collective astonishment of his five sons at Romney's prominence in the sports pages once he took the job in Salt Lake. (Romney often mocks his own abilities when it comes to sports, but as a self-professed lover of fast things, he once used a jet ski to rescue a group of desperate, capsized boaters in the lake that abuts his summer home in New Hampshire. Tagg Romney recalls that his brother Craig heard some cries for help. His dad then "hops on the jet ski and drives out, recognizes they are in trouble, and he comes back, gets another brother and another jet ski, and they go out and ferry people back and forth.")

It would take a Barrymore to convincingly act more devoted to his family than Mitt Romney: one wife, five sons and five daughters-in-law, eleven grandchildren and the hope of many more. Along with not having served in the military, Romney counts his other great regret as not having had more children. Five boys exceeds the American norm when it comes to kids by more than 100 percent, but Mormons generally—and Romneys specifically—have lived a deeply committed family life that often expresses itself in large broods of children.

When talking about his mother and father, his wife, or his kids and grandkids, Romney quickly gets emotional. He credits Ann with the hard work of raising boys when as a Bainiac he spent long hours at the office and many weekends on the road. I asked if his five boys had all become Eagle Scouts. They hadn't. Only the younger three.

"We didn't quite figure out the Eagle Scout thing," he explained with a laugh. "I wasn't an Eagle Scout. I should have been, but again I manipulated my mother into not forcing me to go to Scouts."

Ann's role?

"After the first two boys, we realized getting to Eagle Scout—it's the mothers that make it happen. So she became a merit badge counselor, and she did what was necessary to drive the next three boys to all become Eagle Scouts."

Ann Romney's role in Mitt Romney's career and success goes far beyond raising the boys and seeing to merit badges.

Ann Davies entered Romney's life when he was a senior in high school, and has never left it. "I was just completely consumed with Ann, and fortunately it was somewhat reciprocated."

"Going to Stanford was very hard because it meant that I would be away from her," he told me in our first interview. Romney immediately set to work getting jobs to raise airfare back to see Ann. "Unbeknownst to [my mom] I took various jobs. I got a job with the Physics Department driving a van between the linear accelerator and the main campus and earned enough money to buy airfare to fly back to Michigan unbeknown to my parents. They had a home in Bloomfield Hills. My father was elected governor and was living in Lansing. The home in Bloomfield Hills was empty, and there was a car there. So I would fly home when I could earn enough money or save enough money and stay at the house, use the car, take Ann on dates. Her parents were on to this little secret."

Not his, though. "Dad came home once while I was there, and I had to escape out [the back] to keep from being found out."

"I was never found out," he announced, but he did tell his unbelieving parents years later.

When Romney received his mission assignment for the LDS, it was to France, which meant a thirty-month mission instead of the standard two years, as he needed the extra six months to learn the language. "I thought my heart would break," Romney said of the extra months. "Two and a half years at that age is forever."

When he returned from France in December 1968, all was not well. "I came home Christmas, and Ann, darn her, was dating some other guy!"

Romney was met by his parents, family—and Ann. He proposed to her in the car ride back to his home:

I was distraught that she was dating. She had dated a lot of people who had proposed to her. On the ride back from the airport, my family was there—my mother, my father, my sister and so forth— and Ann was there. She was there to meet me. They put us in the very back row of this Oldsmobile Vista Cruiser station wagon. We were in the third back row, just she and I, and all the people in the front are all laughing and talking, and Mitt's home, and we've got him, and let's have dinner and so forth. I'm in the back with Ann, and we're talking. I said, "I don't feel like I've every been away. It's the funniest thing. I just feel like I've always been here." And she said that she felt the same way. It's like we've always been together. I said "Do you want to get married?" and she said yes.

The First Lady of Michigan was not pleased:

So we got back home and got out of the car and went into the living room, and I said to my mom and dad, "By the way, Ann and I want to get married." My mother just about died. I mean she wanted a year with her son, adoring her and so forth, and I had no interest in my parents. I was totally in love with Ann.

This was Christmastime of '68. They called over Ann's parents, and the four of them sat down with us and told us that this was foolish and that we couldn't possibly get married that fast and that they had to organize a wedding and so forth. My dad thought this was all very amusing. He loved it. He very much identified with me, and he loved Ann. He saw in Ann what he had seen in his own bride. He saw her as this young, wonderful young woman, and he saw our love as very much their love. We'd fallen in love in high school as they did, and so he thought it was great. But the other adults prevailed on him and on us to wait until March 21st. We waited until March 21st, which turned out to be the fourth anniversary of our first date. March 21st of 1969 we got married, and then one more coincidence was that a year later to the day, our first son was born. A year after that, we asked ourselves what we did on our first anniversary. Then we remembered, we were in the hospital.

Ann's parents hosted a civil service for the young couple in their home before they flew to the nearest LDS Temple for a church wedding—in Salt Lake City. This arrangement, common among Mormons when one of the young couple has parents not of the LDS faith, avoids the unpleasantness of the non-Mormon parents being unable to attend the nuptials. (Only Temple permit-carrying Mormons may enter a Temple.)

From Salt Lake City it was on to Hawaii for a honeymoon that was a gift from Ann's parents, and the couple's sons began arriving a year later.

Taggart ("Tagg") Mitt Romney arrived on the Romneys' first wedding anniversary, March 21, 1970, and family became the center of Ann Romney's life until the youngest boy, Craig, stepped out of the home and headed to BYU in the fall of 2001.

Tagg Romney was followed by Matthew ("Matt") Scott on October 21, 1971, Joshua ("Josh") James on August 13, 1975, Benjamin ("Ben") Pratt on June 5, 1978, and Craig Edward on May 13, 1981.

Tagg graduated from BYU in 1994—interrupted by a mission to Bordeaux—and from Harvard Business School in 1998. Until leaving to take up duties with the Romney campaign in Boston, Tagg Romney was head of marketing for the Los Angeles Dodgers. He married Jennifer Dyan Thomas and they have three children.

Matt and Josh followed Tagg's path, graduating from BYU in 1996 and 1998 respectively, and from HBS in 2003 and 2005. (They didn't share the same undergraduate tastes, as Tagg majored in Economics, Matt in Political Science, and Josh in English. Matt did a mission to Paris; Josh to Leeds, England; Ben to Australia; and Craig to Santiago, Chile.)

Matt married Laurie Liljenquist, and they have three children. He is in real estate development in San Diego.

Josh married Jenifer Marie Chappell, and was kind enough to provide much of the biographical data on his brothers as he and Jenifer awaited the birth of their third child. They live in Utah, and he is, like Matt, working in real estate development.

Ben graduated from BYU in 2003, and Craig in 2005, but Ben broke from the MBA trail and is at Tufts Medical School, where he is scheduled to graduate in 2008. Ben married Jade Ande Paul and they have one child.

Craig married Mary Irene Case, and he is working as a music producer for an ad agency in New York.

The boys are close, as Romney was with his three siblings, his sisters Lynn Romney Keenan and Jane Romney Robinson, and his brother Scott, and as Ann is with her brothers, Dr. James Davies and Rod Davies. Lynn and Scott live in Michigan, Jane and James live in California, and Rod in Colorado. Mitt and Ann Romney have thirty nephews and nieces from their siblings.

Though the care and management of five bright and typical boys was the primary focus of Ann Romney's life, she was always deeply involved in her husband's business and political career and in the public life that almost inevitably accompanies substantial business success, including longtime involvement in leadership positions with the United Way of Massachusetts Bay and a number of other Massachusetts charities and advocacy groups. Since her diagnosis with MS, she has been on the board of the New England chapter of the MS Society, and is very active in raising funds for research on the disease. The disease has not hindered Ann Romney's favorite diversion from work and family, which is horses. She is an avid and very accomplished equestrian, competes often, and in 2006 earned silver and gold medals from the United States Dressage Federation. Though she does not avoid the press, Ann Romney is cautious, and with reason. In the 1994 Senate campaign, the *Boston Globe* did a hatchet job on her that still provokes anger among her friends, though none of the Romneys brought it up.

"The *Globe* just totally smeared her," Lynn Shields recalled. (Shields and Ann Romney have remained friends, seeing each other at least occasionally and staying in touch as much as two busy moms married to two very successful and high-profile Boston businessmen and community leaders can.) "They had a couple-of-page spread on her and they—I don't remember specifically what they said, but they basically said that she's too good to be true, which saddened me because— in other words they didn't find fault in her. She hadn't had an affair, taken drugs, hadn't gotten drunk and gotten in a car accident. It was like that was the only thing that could make her human was if she'd done some of those things, and I thought how sad that somebody who's lived a pretty good life and certainly done a lot of volunteer work and been very generous in life has been slammed for that."

The *Globe's* story is recalled by others as a typical cynical media savaging of a public figure they couldn't figure out. It also occurred before Ann Romney's diagnosis with MS, a chronic illness that makes less likely though not completely out of the question any repeat of the '94 article.

"Probably the biggest challenge that we faced as a family is Ann's diagnosis of MS," Mitt Romney told me. "Ann is the angel in the family. If you ask the boys who is the really unusual member of this family they will point to Ann. She's an angel. She's unbelievable. She's an amazing person. When she was diagnosed with MS it hit us very hard, and it continues to be a concern to all of us."

Tagg and Josh Romney talk of their mother as an esteemed friend now. As both are now parents, they also speak with an unvarnished admiration for how she managed a household of five boys and a dad.

"I remember her always saying, 'Could you please be quiet?'" Tagg Romney recalled, "and I remember thinking, 'Why does she want it to be quiet?' Now that I'm a parent, I understand what she meant."

Of course they weren't quiet—anything but quiet. It was a family devoted to sports and games—played or watched, always at high volume. And the family had the predictable outcomes of such a setting.

"I've broken almost every bone in my body," Tagg told me. "I've had my head stitched up five or six times. I've broken my shoulder, my elbow, my ankle, my femur, most of my toes, most of my fingers."

"My mom joked that they were going to name a wing after me" at the hospital.

The subject of Tagg Romney's title of Emergency Room King of the boys came up in the course of discussing the family's rituals at Christmastime.

"It was a family deal," Tagg began. "On a Monday night shortly after Thanksgiving, we would all get together and play Christmas carols on the stereo, sing Christmas carols together, and then pull out all the decorations and decorate the tree all together."

It was unusual for his dad to be away during the holidays, but Tagg can easily recall when he was.

"In fact," he paused, pointing to his hand, "I've got a scar right there from the year that my dad had to go away on business and we were cutting down the family tree. He wasn't there so it was my responsibility to cut down the family tree—I missed with the hacksaw."

"As brothers we played a lot together," Josh added in a different interview, apart from his brother. "We played a lot of basketball. We wrestled, we fought, we had a pretty normal childhood."

"We lived near a couple of high schools," Josh continued. "There was a private high school right near our house. We used to go play in the field out there and get into mischief and there was a large kind of forest right behind us and we used to go play in there as well. I could say we'd leave in the morning and come back at night. It was never really a big concern."

Ann Romney's MS has followed a course familiar to many MS patients.

"Her disease has almost been worth studying," Mitt Romney commented, "and I think she's actually part of a study group at Brigham and Women's Hospital to understand the course of her disease." Romney described his wife's experience:

In 1998 when she was diagnosed she was quite sick. Her right leg was quite numb. She couldn't get up and down stairs very easily. We were getting ready to put an elevator in the house, and we went out to the Olympics and that turned out to be an extraordinary stroke of good fortune. She had a great doctor here who helped her enormously but then going out there she got into riding again—horseback riding. She hadn't done this since she was a little girl and that really helped, whether it was psychologically or the physical exercise. She got a doctor—a guy that did reflexology who would press her pressure points and so forth and stimulate her nervous system—whether this is all poppycock or makes any difference, who knows?—but it's working. And so she has rebounded and has literally no physical impact as long as she doesn't get overly tired. If she doesn't get in until ten or eleven or midnight, then it's going to take her a day to recover.

As long as she gets her rest and doesn't press her travel too much, she goes riding every day. She follows a very careful diet and exercise, but she's receiving no drugs. There're no injections, and she's had no physical impairment for probably three years now.

Ann Romney's illness will receive a lot of attention through the primary campaign and beyond. But it should not be the primary focus of analysis as to her role in Mitt Romney's life, which has been and continues to be central.

Through the birth and raising of five sons, the hard work and long hours of his early years at Bain & Company and then the founding of Bain Capital, the quixotic and disappointing run against Teddy Kennedy in 1994, and his tenure at SLOC and as governor, Ann and Mitt have been an inseparable couple, and her counsel has counted first and most, as every aide and friend attests. She was, for example, responsible for his taking the Olympics job:

The friend who called with the invitation was Kem Gardner.... SLOC's chairman, Robert Garff, had recently been in my office at Bain Capital to talk about financing for a new car dealership concept he had in mind. Steve Coltrin, the New York public relations executive bidding for work at SLOC, had met me at a New York event. Utah senators Orrin Hatch and Bob Bennett were acquaintances familiar with my background. All have since taken a piece of the credit, or blame, for thinking me up. But it was Kem who made the call.

Would I consider taking the helm of the troubled Olympic committee? Could I restore the public credibility of the organization, overcome the growing political resistance, and work with a hobbled International Olympic Committee, United States Olympic Committee, and other partners to stage successful Games? Would I allow my name to be considered?

If Kem had put these questions to me directly, I would have shot him down on the spot. But Kem knows that. He knows I don't suffer foolishness well. So he deployed a flanking maneuver: he called Ann instead.

Gardner sold Ann, and Ann sold Mitt. "[A]fter hanging up with Kem, she called me at the office. Before I could get beyond 'hello' she put me on notice, 'Now whatever you do, don't just say no out of hand. Hear me out on this before you dismiss it....'"

Romney added, "She continued the lobbying when I got home that evening." And it worked.

"Ann's arguments had resonance, but they had resonance because she knows my core beliefs and my life aspirations," Romney concludes his account of the decision to accept the SLOC job in *Turnaround*. "She knows that somewhere deep inside, I hoped to commit myself to things greater than making a living or building a fortune. It was the spirit of service in one form or another—a family poltergeist that has haunted my ancestors for generations. It was the legacy of my heritage, and of my youth."

It was also the persuasiveness of a talented and energetic spouse who saw an opportunity for her husband to get beyond his very successful business career into a public life he had once unsuccessfully sought.

Jim Davies, Ann's brother, describes his sister as a mover behind the 1994 Senate bid against Kennedy as well.

"She has always been one to encourage others to stretch in trying to be their very best," he wrote me. "A classic example comes to mind of Mitt reading and grumbling about an article in the *Boston Globe* covering the lurid details of Teddy Kennedy's escapades in Florida. He said to Ann, 'Somebody has to get this guy out of office—he's an embarrassment!' to which she replied, 'Mitt, why don't you run against him?' Mitt demurred, but she told him she was serious and thought he should do it. She really believed he could win; and thus was born Mitt's career in politics." Davies confirmed the account of Ann's role in persuading Mitt Romney to say yes to the appeal from the SLOC. "Though neither of them fully realized just how bad things were in Salt Lake," he admitted, "her belief in her husband was such that she knew if anyone could turn a mess into something magnificent, Mitt was the man who could do it."

Dr. Davies—a very successful eye surgeon in northern San Diego county and like Ann a convert to the LDS church—is, no surprise, an unabashed fan of his sister. "Although there are four years between us, and though I was probably the most obnoxious little brother known to man, Ann and I have always been close," he wrote. "My childhood reminiscences bring to mind a tender-hearted girl who found joy in anything life sent her way. Ann loves to laugh, but never at the expense of another." His response to an invitation to opine on his sister bears full quoting:

Ann is an undying optimist and a very hard worker. When she puts her mind to a task, it is already a fait accompli before she has even begun. There is absolutely no quit in her, as long as her cause or pursuit is just and good. Whether it's learning to play tennis (at which she would regularly humiliate me), performing at a championship level (as a relative novice) in the very challenging sport of dressage, helping the inner-city girls of Boston to build a promising future for themselves, or battling multiple sclerosis (MS), Ann will simply not give up or give in.

The optimism she feels in her own life is contagious and allows her to lift and inspire others. She learned well the lessons of our father, the immigrant son of a disabled Welsh coal miner; Dad taught us that we could achieve anything we set our minds to. Ann believed him, and she has spent her life teaching others the same valuable lesson.

Ann is a deeply spiritual person who led all of us in the family as she sought to understand the nature of God and His purpose for her. It was because of Ann that we began attending various churches as a family, and this in spite of our father's agnosticism. He could never say no to his darling daughter. Through her persistence we eventually joined the Episcopal Church as a family, just a short while before she met and began dating Mitt.

Ann's life has always been guided by principles that lie at the core of Judeo-Christian teachings. It's true that we can have a profound effect, for good or ill, on our siblings. I couldn't have asked for a better sister and am deeply grateful that she has played such an important role in my life.

If you know any Mormons, you will recognize in the portrait of the Romney family generally—and in the specific anecdotes relayed by Davies and others—what Denver Seminary's Craig Blomberg refers to as the LDS's "biblical emphasis on numerous fundamental moral values, including putting family relationships as a central priority in life." Keeping a marriage together and strong for thirty-seven years isn't easy. Raising five boys isn't easy. In fact, raising any child or children is hard. I asked Romney about the work of bringing up five boys and its degree of difficulty.

"Very hard," he replied, "and Ann did most of the heavy lifting. I was working at Bain Capital and Bain & Company and worried about whether I was going to lose everybody's money. I agonized over the responsibility of caring for others. When I raised that first fund to $37 million, I was scared to death that I'd go out and lose other people's money. It kept me awake nights and worked hard, but Ann led in the home. When I came home and the door shut behind me, I didn't work. I was with Ann and the kids because that's what life is all about."

Mitt Romney did bring the hammer down when necessary, his boys recall.

Tagg Romney brought up the dad on the sitcom *Everybody Loves Raymond*. "Raymond's dad," Tagg explained, "had this thing, 'The Step.' For Raymond and his brother, if their dad took 'The Step' towards them, they knew right away: whatever they were doing wrong, they had to stop.

"My dad had 'The Step.' If he stepped towards us and he had that look, we knew Dad was serious, and we had to stop whatever it is we were doing. He was the enforcer, but only when he needed to be. The only time that he really needed or felt like he needed to be a disciplinarian was when we didn't treat my mom with respect. I remember that was the number one rule growing up—treat your mother with respect, kindness, and love. If we backtalked her in any way, it was a serious offense."

They were the ordinary conflicts and ordinary joys of a family, though perhaps on a slightly larger scale than most Americans. Mitt Romney laughs a lot looking back on his days as a dad of teenagers. He recalls that Tagg accused him of intentionally wearing his pants too short to embarrass the then teenaged oldest boy.

"Yes, I was convinced that he did," Tagg conceded. "I was convinced that he's wearing his jeans or whatever in public and I was embarrassed. He had floods on, and I was convinced he was doing it to embarrass me."

To keep parents' eyes on the ball, the Mormon Church stresses "Family Night," which is Monday, and which is supposed to be the night all other commitments are put aside and focus is put on the family. It didn't always work out that way for the Romneys.

"We had family night," Romney allowed. "I wasn't very regular. My boys would say, yeah we had family night, about every two months. But for us, it was mostly games and fun, and I felt guilty that I wasn't more regular. But we did a lot as a family. The most enjoyment that my life knows is having all of my family together."

The greatest test of a family: does it continue to hang together? The Romneys' experience:

"We have a deal. Every Christmas which is on the even years, they all come to our home. So it's all the boys and their wives and kids come to our home," Romney told me. "On the odd years they go to their in-laws' home. In the summertime we all agree that we spend a week together at Lake Winnipesaukee. When I'm there with my kids—Ann and I—it almost brings us to tears. It is such a great source of joy."

"It's paradise," is how Tagg describes the summer get-togethers. "It's my favorite place on earth because we are all together, we're water skiing, we're playing tennis, basketball, volleyball. We're playing soccer, whiffle ball, and home run derby and then at night we get the kids to bed and watch a movie. It is a lot of fun. There's a lot of people. It's a lot of commotion, but we all like it."

About his five boys Romney is direct: "Let me tell you, raising them was filled with its own challenges. Each of them had his own problems." Is he proud of them? "Oh, they are extraordinary boys. I'm very proud of them."

His oldest son, Tagg: "Brilliant, focused on his family and his faith and an extraordinarily perceptive and conceptually skilled person. Very, very bright and tender."

Matt? "Matt," Romney smiled, "as a two-year-old announced that he was unusual and I think he was right. Matt sees things that others don't see. He's got a great ability to perceive opportunities and to perceive strengths and weakness in other people. He is a devoted father—well, they are each terrific fathers. Matt can accomplish anything because he has the most determination of almost anyone you've met. He refuses to back down. He is unrelenting."

The third son is Josh.

"Josh is good-natured," Romney began, "liked by everyone, the most stubborn in the family and a person who is bound for success in anything he does. He has a can-do attitude, nothing is too hard for him. He is always optimistic and happy. I've never seen Josh depressed in my life."

"Ben," he continued, "is the most reserved of the five. He is highly intellectual, is able to solve complex problems whether it be mathematical or in philosophical endeavors. He's going into medicine, will be a superb researcher or physician as his path may take him. He is an intellectual powerhouse."

The last Romney son is Craig.

"Craig being the youngest in the family is, of course, our entertainer," Romney concluded. "He is loved by all four of his brothers, which is very hard to do in a family. He has a warmth and an enthusiasm which lights up any room. He is exceptionally creative, musical, innovative, and a natural leader."

About his five daughters-in-law, Romney was expansive.

The boys, he said, "all married up, which is a family tradition. That they succeeded in marrying up was a surprise, but their wives are a good fit. In each case their spouse was someone ideally suited to them. They seem well married."

Two of the sons agreed to lengthy interviews, a not unrisky proposition going in. But after talking with Tagg and Josh, it was easy to see that both had been around the political block a few times, and knew when to answer and when to demur.

I asked Josh if his dad had a volume dial on his voice that he could raise.

"He can," Josh allowed, "but he's pretty level. You definitely know he's got a temper. I think it's a Romney trait. We all have it. He was very even-tempered with the kids and particularly with my mom. You never saw my parents fight at all. They were the perfect couple really. Never saw them fight growing up. I'm sure they did. They've made claims in the past that they didn't. Who knows what went on behind closed doors, but we never saw it."

How did they gig their dad?

Josh gave up the boys' favorite assault on their dad. "We love to scare him," Josh began, and then drew on an apparently unlimited set of anecdotes about the attempt to make their dad's heart stop.

"Once—the garage for our house wasn't an attached garage and it was pretty far from the house. There was a tree and you came up a walkway," he began a story that had obviously been told a few times.

"The tree kind of overhung the walkway, and my brother Matt was hiding in the tree as my dad came home from work. Just as my dad was walking up in front, Matt jumped down from the tree and screamed 'YEAAAAA!' My dad sat there for about three seconds without moving and then just started to chase Matt, and chased him into the house. I remember Matt come running into the house screaming 'HELP!' and going upstairs and locking himself in the bathroom for about three hours. It was pretty funny."

Josh was not an innocent in this long-running "jump dad" contest.

"The best ever was, we had this basement, one of those scary, scary basements. If you didn't have to go into it, you didn't want to. It was an old house basement, and it had one of those lights—it didn't have a switch as you walked in. You actually had to take four or five steps into the room and pull down one of those little rope things."

Josh relished the telling.

"My dad," he continued, laughing at the recollection, "I heard my dad coming down the stairs and I was in the basement and I thought 'oh, boy.' I heard him say that he had to get something that I knew was in a room in the basement, so I went and ran and hid in that room, terrified while I'm in there. So I'm hiding in there, and I see him walk in. It's so dark you can't see anything. He's kind of feeling around for the string, and I just reach out and grab his hand and absolutely killed him. He was just like floored. So scared."

"I was just on the ground laughing," he concluded, even as Mitt Romney laid on a good-natured pummeling.

"In fact it's kind of a family thing," Josh concluded. "We scare each other. My older brother is probably the worst and then Matt. He scared me a couple of times literally out of my wits."

Talk long enough to any of the boys and the picture emerges of a sort of Norman Rockwell-meets-the-'70s family, full of sports and the necessary adventures of any family with five active and achievement-oriented boys, including the epic car drives. In the Romneys' case, there was an out-and-back station wagon excursion to George and

Lenore's Lake Ontario cottage every summer—eleven hours each way.

"Those are family bonding experiences right there," Josh related. "That was an eleven-hour drive and we would take the old Chevy station wagon, the Caprice. I don't know that it was a Caprice but it was a white station wagon with wood panels on the side."

"It was endless," Josh declared. "So we acted up and we were terrible in the car. With five boys you have three in the back seat and two in the very back. The two in the very back are getting sick the whole time and complaining, and the three in front are complaining. My dad was always about making good time, and so he wouldn't pull over for bathroom breaks—he'd just make you hold it. In fact, the only person that he'd pull over for is my mom. If she had an inkling that she had to go, he'd pull right over, but for us boys, it was all business. We were driving straight through."

Like many achievement-oriented dads of that era, work was important, and the Romney boys got that message early.

"He always wanted us to do something," Josh recalled. "He was big on work. He was really big on work and kind of even before sixteen he had us out. He'd make sure every Saturday we'd put in a few hours of manual labor. I remember he borrowed a bobcat once from a friend—a developer friend of his—one of those little bobcats you know. We'd just bought a new house, and there were a lot of giant rocks in the front yard, so he had me out there moving rocks. I think that was a month of my life was moving those rocks. He was funny. He kept pushing me to move bigger and bigger rocks and there was one that was just so big, I'm like, 'Dad, I'm not sure I can move this one. It's kind of big.' He'd always be out supervising and doing the hard work, and I was just in this bobcat. He convinced me to lift it up, and sure enough it flipped me over. It was pretty funny. He always found projects. I think he'd make projects up for us on Saturdays so that we'd always work."

How smart is their dad?

"Off the charts," Josh responded. "It's pretty frustrating. Growing up I always kind of wanted to be an inventor or create products or whatever, and I always had these crazy ideas that I'd come up with. I'd run them by my dad, and he blew me away how much he knew about every industry. I'd study up on the most random industry, health care or whatever it was and say, 'Hey, Dad, I want to do this.' And he'd say, 'Well, have you thought about this, this, this, and that. Because in this industry this happens,' and he just knew a little bit about everything."

Josh Romney, like Tagg, a product of HBS, knows now the level of effort both Bain & Company and Bain Capital required. Given those demands, how much was Mitt Romney at home?

"He was always..." Josh began, and paused. "He never really came home past seven o'clock unless he was traveling, but once he left Bain & Company he didn't travel a whole lot. I think at Bain & Company he traveled a lot more than he did at Bain Capital. He spent a lot of time at home. He was home for dinners. He was home always on Saturdays and spent Saturdays with us."

"The one thing about my dad is he really is a very generous, kind human being," Tagg Romney summed his father up for me. "He taught us growing up, and I think I told you this: the most important thing in life is serving God and serving others."

"And what he would never tell you or anyone else is the extent he goes to help other people," he continued. "I remember being a teenager and getting a call from some random—what we thought was some random crazy lady—who said her daughter lived in Boston. Her husband was poor, they didn't have enough money for Christmas presents and their heat went out and they couldn't fix it. I remember Dad getting us in the car, going to Toys R Us and buying a bunch of presents, buying some wood, taking some of the wood from our own house, taking it to their house, giving it to her and wrapping up the presents. That was one of my most memorable Christmases, but he was constantly doing things like that and never telling anyone about them. He doesn't want to tell people about them, but he wanted us to see him. He would let the kids see it because he wanted it to rub off on us. He'll walk down the street—he can't pass someone on the street who's asking for money without giving them some money. He just can't do it."

When I voiced my skepticism, Tagg was adamant.

"That's who he is," Tagg concluded, "and behind the facade of the tough business guy and the intelligent problem-solver is the root of who he is. He wants to help, and that's really what drives him."

On the reactions among Americans to this objectively wonderful family, much will hang in the 2008 election. For a family tightly bound, loyal, and loving is something Americans admire very much. Not necessarily journalists, but very much so voters.

When I was asking Romney about the impact of his religious beliefs on his candidacy, one part of his response struck me as almost certainly a key to how the issue of his LDS beliefs will be assessed by a public unfamiliar with or even hostile to the Mormon theology. "[T]o understand my faith, people should look at me and my home and how we live," Romney at one point suggested. "Of course, doctrines and theology are different church to church, but what my church teaches is evidenced by what I have become and what my family has become."

This is a powerful response to opponents of Romney who base their opposition on theology as opposed to differences on issues or questions about experience or character—the big three of politics in America. Romney's evoking of his family is a shortcut through the thicket of doctrinal differences and a bridge over the vast chasm that separates orthodox Christianity and the LDS. There is not a single major Christian denomination that does not put love of and care for family at or very near the center of its practice of the faith. When Romney asks people who are ill at ease to look hard at the family he and Ann have raised, he is very bluntly underscoring that despite deep differences, the practical impact of the Mormon faith on moms and dads and kids is quite obviously productive of tight and devoted families.

When Tolstoy wrote in *Anna Karenina* that "Happy families are all alike; every unhappy family is unhappy in its own way," he was sounding a note of admiration mixed with envy that those with unhappy homes may feel for those who have somehow built the bulwark that most people aspire to. In the American electorate, and especially within the Republican primary electorates in Iowa, New Hampshire, South Carolina, and Michigan, there are millions of voters struggling and succeeding or failing to raise a family that produces healthy, happy, and successful kids within marriages that last. It is extraordinarily difficult to do this, especially if illness or bad fortune intervenes.

When Romney hits the campaign trail, with Ann or any of his small army of sons and daughters-in-law, he's going to be telling stories from his own experience as a husband, father, father-in-law, and grandfather which, regardless of religious beliefs, will be admired by those who aspire to someday tell similar stories of struggle and triumph.

What He Believes and What He Has Done

Chapter Five

Mitt Romney Is Pro-Life

B ecause the courts—specifically the United States Supreme
Court—matter so much to conservatives, I spent a lot of time
asking Governor Romney about his views on the Supreme Court
and on the nominees he would put before the Senate if he were
elected president and vacancies occurred.

"I believe that the Constitution embodies the values that the
Founders thought were critical for a successful nation to survive;
therefore, justices have to hold true to the Constitution to maintain
the foundation of values that make it successful," he began. "I want
justices who will follow the Constitution and will not add to it, not
subtract from it but instead look to the Constitution and the values
of the Founders to set the course for the nation. We have a process
for changing the Constitution. It's an amendment process. The
people are very much involved in that process. I find it a breach of
the constitutional path for justices to effectively change the Constitution rather than allow the constitutionally devised processes for
making those adjustments occur."

I asked about President Bush's two successful nominees to the
high court:

"I thought both Justices Roberts and Alito were *ideal* examples for what we should select for justices going forward," he said, with emphasis on "ideal." "I know I depart from my liberal friends on this front."

Romney digressed to discuss the great divide between Right and Left when it comes to the courts.

"I think many liberals believe that a justice should look at America, see what's wrong, and right those wrongs through their decisions. I believe instead that a justice should look at the Constitution and the laws written by the office holders whom the people elected. A justice should follow those things; if there are wrongs, point them out but don't try to address them by changing the law from the bench. I just think there is a huge divide in this country about the role of the judiciary, and I'm firmly in the camp of those who say we should strictly follow the Constitution and the law and not legislate from the bench."

I went back to the question of "ideal" nominees, and brought up President Bush's political stumble with Harriet Miers. Romney was silent at the time of the nomination and had nothing bad to say about Ms. Miers in our interview, but allowed as how "the ultimate choice," Justice Alito, "was a superb one."

I asked Romney if the Miers controversy ruled out legal practitioners or other less well-known nominees than academics or sitting federal judges.

"I think we all know what the ideal is," Romney responded. "The ideal is someone who is willing to follow the Constitution and who has a track record that is solid and impregnable—an individual whose credentials are such that it'll be very difficult for the liberals to bring him or her down. And, of course, you want somebody who has the kind of skills that, when they meet with their fellow justices, they'll be able to hold their own and perhaps even pull the opinions towards their way of thinking. You want a powerhouse. It's hard to find powerhouses every time you're going to make an appointment, but when you're talking about the Supreme Court of the United States, a fair, thoughtful, and strict constructionist powerhouse is exactly what the doctor ordered."

There's a logic to why I began the chapter of Mitt Romney's pro-life credentials with a discussion of his views on federal court nominees. The key issue for pro-lifers is not the candidate's rhetoric, but what will be the candidate's results when it comes to Supreme Court and federal appellate court appointees. There are other issues, of course, but the pro-life movement's primary goal in the next decade, as it has been since 1973, is the reversal of *Roe* v. *Wade*, which constitutionalized the "right" to abortion and in so doing removed the matter from the people and our elected leaders at both the federal and state levels.

"Would you welcome the overruling of *Roe* v. *Wade* by the Court?" I asked Governor Romney.

"Yes," he replied directly and without hesitation. "I would like to see each state be able to make its own decision regarding abortion rather than have a one-size-fits-all blanket pronouncement by the Supreme Court."

Would he have a "litmus test" of any sort when it came to nominees to the Supreme Court?

"I think we'd all like to apply a litmus test," he began before switching immediately to confirmation realism. "Each of us would like to say: 'Here are all the decisions that are going to come up. How will you vote?'" He continued, as though interviewing a prospective nominee for the high court.

"But I don't think that's the process that you're going to see employed for selecting a Supreme Court justice by me or, frankly, by others as well. Doing it that way would make it very difficult for the nominee to be confirmed."

To ask certain questions is to doom a nominee, and Romney knows this, as does every other presidential candidate, both pro-life and pro–abortion rights.

"There will not be a litmus test," Romney continued. "Instead, there will be a *philosophical* test, which is: *Is this a person who follows the law, who abides by the Constitution, who will strictly construe the Constitution as it was intended, or is this a person who looks to expand upon the Constitution to 'write' laws without the benefit of legislation?* I frankly think the latter kind of judge cannot be brought forward."

These are not answers that can be given by Mayor Giuliani, who is not pro-life, nor even by Senator McCain, who has demonstrated he is not serious about getting good judges confirmed. Mayor Giuliani is an avowed fan of *Roe.* Senator McCain, on the other hand, cannot seriously pretend to care about judicial philosophy after he left the nomination and confirmation process a smoldering wreck with his Gang of 14 improvisation in the spring of 2005.

While Senator McCain might agree with Governor Romney that Chief Justice Roberts and Justice Alito were fine choices—Senator McCain voted to confirm both of them)—he cannot pretend to be mightily concerned about judicial qualifications after he and his gang destroyed the Republican Senate majority's very carefully crafted plan to rescue the confirmation process from its politicized and anti-conservative collapse.

An exploration of Senator McCain's Gang of 14 fiasco is perhaps in order. Following the 2004 elections in which many Republican senators had run successfully against Democratic obstructionism in the confirmation of judges—for the second cycle in a row the issue had been huge with the Republican base and fair-minded independents—Senate Majority Leader Bill Frist counted heads and discovered he had the votes to go to the chair for a ruling on the issue of Democratic filibusters of judicial nominees who had cleared the Judiciary Committee. The chair, who would have been Vice President Dick Cheney, was expected to rule that the practice of filibustering the president's nominees was indeed a violation of the Senate rules, and that ruling would have been upheld by a majority vote and gone on to be a precedent of the Senate. Given that the Constitution vests the confirmation power in the Senate as a whole and does not detail that a supermajority is necessary for the confirmation of judges—as it is to ratify treaties or propose amendments to the Constitution—the Republicans were on the side of the Constitution and basic fairness to nominees who enjoyed majority support.

In a stunning move, John McCain announced on Chris Matthews's *Hardball* that he would vote against the "constitutional option," as Frist called it (the "nuclear option" to others). So great was the outrage among Republicans that McCain, sensing a fatal misstep on his long campaign for the presidency, chose neither to reverse his calamitous announcement nor to stand by it. Instead he engineered a "deal" with seven Republicans and seven Democrats to end filibusters for most Republican nominees. A few fine nominees were sacrificed to Senator McCain's ambitions at the time, and still more languished throughout the long months that followed. A once-in-a-generation chance to repair a badly broken confirmation process was lost, and with it many important lifetime appointments, and in the eyes of many, the Senate majority. The pro-life movement knows that John McCain undid their work of a generation in electing a Republican majority of fifty-five, and it will not accept any words he might offer over his deeds.

Still, it remains to be seen whether the pro-life vote will be as important to Romney as it was first to Ronald Reagan and then both President Bush the elder and President Bush the younger. If staffing the courts still matters, then Romney will be the clear beneficiary of a field in which he is the only candidate to be able to claim with credibility that he cares about judicial nominees with a passion, and you simply cannot be pro-life if you don't get the courts right. The only issue on which a president will have a dramatic impact on the life issue is through his or her judicial nominees. We know that Rudy is pro-choice, as are all the Democratic candidates.

We also know that McCain didn't care enough about the issue to sacrifice Senate privilege and Beltway prestige to the service of rescuing all nominees from the politicized and compromised nomination and confirmation process. Senator McCain's "bold" stands in favor of restricting political speech, defending the right of filibusters, against the administration's September 2006 bill on the trial and treatment of terrorists, and in favor of Ted Kennedy's immigration reform package all resonated with the editorial board of the *Washington Post* and *New York Times*, while digging a deep trench between McCain and the GOP's primary voters.

In the prewar Republican Party of the '80s and '90s (until 9/11, in fact), the issue of abortion presented a hurdle that every would-be presidential candidate had to get over. In the decades since *Roe* v. *Wade* in 1973, more than 47 million abortions have been performed, and pro-life Republican primary voters could not be persuaded that the issue took a back seat to any other plank in the party platform. As abortion-rights absolutists pushed forward with an agenda of no compromise—even to the point of demanding that all abortions, even those in the ninth month of a pregnancy, be protected under law, and that minors seeking abortions not be obliged to consult even with the best of parents—the pro-life voter became ever more insistent on certainty that a Republican presidential candidate was solid on the issues constellation surrounding abortion. We wanted to clearly see a candidate's commitment to the reduction in the number of abortions, to the rights of parents to be informed of a minor daughter's desire to have an abortion, and to the recognition that unborn life was exactly that—life.

Part of the demand for certainty grew out of the "Lucy-and-the-football" experience that pro-life activists suffered when three Supreme Court justices put forward by Republican presidents ultimately supported *Roe* v. *Wade* when it came before them for review: Justices Sandra Day O'Connor and Anthony Kennedy were sent to the bench by Ronald Reagan, and Justice David Souter was sent there by the first President Bush. The pro-life community's deep disappointment over its inability to convert political victories into judicial restraint infused it with a cynicism that is profound and enduring.

It remains to be seen whether the shock of 9/11 has disestablished the power of the pro-life GOP primary voter, or at least diminished it. Early indications of broad support for the extremely pro-choice Rudy Giuliani suggest that clarity about the war and believable purposefulness concerning its prosecution may be enough to overcome the previous automatic out that a pro-choice philosophy earned a would-be GOP nominee. Chances are, though, that the candidate's national security steadfastness will have to be coupled with believable statements about the sorts of judges the pro-choice nominee will put forward to satisfy Republican voters.

But it remains a huge advantage in any Republican primary to be pro-life and believably serious about judicial nominees. Dedicated anti-abortion activists remain ready to denounce as insufficiently pro-life any candidate that fails their screening process.

This is the political landscape that Mitt Romney confronts in 2007 and 2008. Romney opponents hope to use the pro-life issue against Romney because his public views on abortion have changed since his first campaign for the Senate against Ted Kennedy in 1994. Purists don't like change. They instinctively and often resolutely believe change conceals opportunism at best and deception at worst. They hear politicians talk about their commitment to the pro-life agenda, and a big sign in their head begins to blink: Souter, Souter, Souter. These ardent and sincere defenders of life have asked questions of Romney, and the governor has answered.

Mitt Romney's views on abortion *have changed* in the past dozen years, and some pro-lifers (as well as forces aligned with other candidates for the presidency) will surely advertise that fact. While the former will seek at least firm assurance on Romney's commitment to their cause, the latter will hope to use Romney's history on the issue to brand him as untrustworthy on abortion and issues beyond it. Romney and his fans will have to respond to this attack almost daily. Unlike anti-Mormon bias, though, this set of arguments will not have to be disguised by Romney's opponents.

Perhaps the first loud shot in this battle was fired on September 27, 2006, with a searing post by Ben Domenech at the conservative blog Red State. Domenech plucked out Romney quotations from his 1994 Senate campaign against Ted Kennedy, and from Romney's gubernatorial campaign of 2002, and went on to accuse Romney of "lying" about his past.

Almost immediately following its publication, pundits favorable to Romney replied to Domenech's broadside, and did so with the best possible approach: candor combined with the right of politicians to adjust their public positions over time in response to both the field on which they are competing as well as the changing nature of the fact set they are addressing.

National Review Online editor Kathryn Jean Lopez is very favorably impressed with Governor Romney. She is also completely and sincerely attached to her vigorous pro-life views, a not surprising fact given that she is a thoroughly orthodox, weekly Mass-attending Roman Catholic. Upon reading the Domenech attack and the hundreds of comments it generated, "K Lo," as she is widely known to the hundreds of thousands of regular readers of the NationalReview.com group blog, "The Corner," posted a response that confirmed that Romney had moved steadily over the years toward the pro-life position, concluding with a quotation from a *Boston Globe* story detailing Romney's reasons for vetoing a Massachusetts state bill that increased the availability of emergency contraception services:

I am pro-life. I believe that abortion is the wrong choice except in cases of incest, rape, and to save the life of the mother. I wish the people of America agreed, and that the laws of our nation could reflect that view. But while the nation remains so divided over abortion, I believe that the states, through the democratic process, should determine their own abortion laws and not have them dictated by judicial mandate.

Because Massachusetts is decidedly pro-choice, I have respected the state's democratically held view. I have not attempted to impose my own views on the pro-choice majority.

For all the conflicting views on this issue, it speaks well of our country that we recognize abortion as a problem. The law may call it a right, but no one ever called it a good, and, in the quiet of conscience people of both political parties know that more than a million abortions a year cannot be squared with the good heart of America.

You can't be a pro-life governor in a pro-choice state without understanding that there are heartfelt and thoughtful arguments on both sides of the question. Many women considering abortions face terrible pressures, hurts, and fears; we should come to their aid with all the resourcefulness and empathy we can offer. At the same time, the starting point should be the innocence and vulnerability of the child waiting to be born.

Will this appeal to voters—to see Romney's past campaign positions in light of pragmatic reality (a vocal pro-life Republican committed to rolling back abortion rights could not be elected senator or governor in Massachusetts) combined with Romney's explicit promise of pro-life policies and his statements on the qualities he will seek in judicial nominees as president—work?

Dick Morris, America's least principled political commentator and an apparent Newt Gingrinch supporter, hopes not. In a late November 2006 column, Morris leveled the simplistic charge that "Romney seems to be a chameleon who adjusts his positions to suit the need of his environment," and added the absurd declaration that: "On abortion the only thing liberals and conservatives agree on is that they can't stand those who flip-flop on this moral issue," which of course overlooks the evolution of Al Gore, Dick Gephardt, and others from pro-life positions to pro-choice absolutism, as well as similar journeys of many other liberals who have followed their parties' activists into abortion rights absolutism.

What Morris, Domenech, and other critics of Romney's pragmatism fail to realize is that the pro-life community is sophisticated and educated, and quite capable of understanding how a pro-life politician in Massachusetts has to advocate for the possible, and mustn't allow the perfect to be the enemy of the good. The *Washington Post* once infamously described evangelical Christians as "largely poor, uneducated and easy to command," and was buried in a storm of faxed resumes; the *Post* retracted its outrageous assertion the next day. But the elite mainstream media concentrated along the Manhattan-Beltway axis ("MSM") clings to the stereotype of the pro-life voter as an unsubtle and indeed unintelligent creature. This view also undergirds the Morris/Domenech conviction that Romney will not be able to persuade GOP primary voters because of statements he made in a debate with Ted Kennedy more than a dozen years ago.

"I am pro-life," Romney told me pointedly. He went on to explain how his campaigns have provided fodder for his 2008 opponents.

"In my 1994 debate with Senator Kennedy he said that I was 'multiple choice' for which he got a good laugh because I wouldn't say I was pro-choice."

"I said what I would do if I were elected senator, the same thing I said when I was running for governor. I said what I would do if I were elected governor," he continued.

Romney emphasized that he had promised to "not change the law."

"As governor, I indicated that I would not change the law as it related to abortion," he explained. "I would keep it the same. I've had roughly four provisions that have reached my desk which would have changed the laws as they related to abortion, all of which would have expanded abortion rights. I vetoed each of those."

"My record as governor has been very clearly a pro-life record," he concluded.

Romney adopted the "pro-life" label after his battle over stem cell research (discussed below). Will his explanation persuade pro-life voters?

There are six reasons to believe it will.

First, the pro-life critics of Romney are attacking him in strident terms which most in the patient and long-serving rank and file of the pro-life movement reject. I have spoken at many pro-life events over the years, from fund raisers for crisis pregnancy centers to gatherings of political activists. The people of the pro-life movement, perhaps more than in any other movement, understand that progress in this area doesn't come from the vocal showboaters, but from the steady accumulation of changed minds and courts. They know an ardent pro-life activist could never get elected in Massachusetts, and they will be impressed with Romney's vetos as well as his position on stem cell research.

Then there is the Flaherty Factor.

Peter Flaherty spent four years on Romney's Massachusetts staff, finishing as deputy chief of staff, before moving over to Romney's Commonwealth PAC. He will most likely be in a role as a senior advisor to the Romney campaign.

Flaherty is a brilliant, enthusiastic, and energetic former prosecutor who is old-school Catholic as only Boston Irish-American Catholics can be, right down to the Holy Cards in his office and his unembarrassed attention to his daily prayers.

Flaherty is also one of the staunchest pro-life public officials in America. If Romney moves to 1600 Pennsylvania, I would be willing to bet that Flaherty moves into the second-floor offices reserved for the counsel and deputy counsel to the president, or a senior post at the Department of Justice charged with superintending judicial selection. Whether Flaherty was at Justice or in the White House, the Romney administration's judicial selection apparatus would likely be superintended at least in part on a day-to-day basis by the sort of committed and smart lawyer the pro-life movement has always hoped would rise to such a post.

Third, Romney benefits from a field of Republican contenders that lacks a strong candidate with better pro-life credentials.

As noted above, Rudy is thoroughly pro-choice, and has refused to even attempt to "evolve" his position, which includes support for the right of a woman to late-term abortions. About John McCain and his Gang of 14 betrayal, enough has been said.

There will be other candidates, and some like Senator Sam Brownback or Arkansas governor Mike Huckabee may well present much stronger pro-life resumes than Romney, but pro-life primary voters are very aware of how the primaries work, and they will understand that McCain—the nightmare nominee for many—has to be stopped in Iowa, New Hampshire, South Carolina, and Michigan. Many and probably most will not waste a vote on a second-tier nominee, and instead will focus on stopping Senator McCain.

Fourth, the pro-life issues set has expanded greatly in recent years, and now includes very complicated public debates on cloning, embryonic stem cell research, and euthanasia. In each of these areas, pro-life voters long for a spokesman who, having gained center stage in American politics, can use that stage persuasively enough to convince people about the dignity of human life and the need to curb science's unlimited curiosity.

The pro-life movement loves George W. Bush, but they also realize he has been singularly ineffective in persuading the country on the perils of unlimited embryonic stem cell research or even in sounding the alarm on the dangerous approach of human cloning.

In Romney there is the promise of an advocate equal to the task, and with a compelling story to illustrate his thinking.

Ann Romney has multiple sclerosis. It is a tough disease, as anyone knows who has lived with it, or helped a family member live with it. (My wife's mother lived with MS for thirty-plus years as it slowly robbed her of the ability to control her body. A cure for MS would be a wonderful, wonderful thing.) Proponents of embryonic stem cell research urge observers of the debate to believe that MS and a host of other diseases, including Parkinson's and juvenile diabetes, are among those that can be cured through their research. Other enthusiasts argue that major injuries such as spinal cord trauma can be repaired via the medical magic of embryonic stem cells.

Romney, who not surprisingly cites the diagnosis of his wife's disease as one of the greatest blows of his life, is nevertheless alarmed by the aggressive program of embryonic stem cell research consortiums. He has taken a very determined stand against the most ambitious of these consortiums, the Harvard Stem Cell Institute.

Romney's collision with the Brave New World of what I will call the "no limits" school of embryonic stem cell research began when the *Boston Globe* ran a story on October 13, 2004, "Harvard teams want OK to clone." The story began:

> Two separate teams of Harvard scientists are preparing to produce cloned embryos for disease research, and one has officially applied for permission from the university's ethical review board.
>
> If granted permission, the Harvard scientists could be the first to clone human cells in the United States. Worldwide, only one team of scientists in South Korea has successfully grown cloned human cells.

"This is exactly the kind of work that we envisioned for the Harvard Stem Cell Institute," Harvard biologist Douglas Melton told the *Globe*. "We want new ways to study and hopefully cure diseases."

Romney's senior staff spotted the story and also the obvious intersection with state law. Although the *Globe* article asserted that "cloning is legal in the United States," in fact the issue is much murkier, and pursuing unfettered cloning would put Harvard at some legal risk.

Romney invited Melton and other Harvard representatives to brief him on their plans and proposals, a meeting which occurred on

November 9, 2004. At that meeting the peril posed by Massachusetts laws was discussed, as were the ambitions of the Institute.

Romney immediately moved into "Bain way" mode and summoned other experts with contrarian points of view, including Fr. Tadeusz Pacholczyk, the director of education for the National Catholic Bioethics Center in December of 2004, and in January of 2005 Dr. William B. Hurlbut, a consulting professor in the Neuroscience Institute at Stanford and a member of the President's Council on Bioethics.

At the conclusion of this process, Romney had determined that Harvard's ambitions, which would have included the creation and subsequent destruction of an untold number of embryos, went far beyond those that most proponents of stem cell research could in good conscience support.

The Harvard Stem Cell Institute was seeking legal protection for an embryo production line for the purpose of creating and harvesting stem cells, and Romney refused his support and indeed entered into a public debate over the ethics of such a path. When Massachusetts Senate president Robert E. Travaglini introduced legislation to protect the Harvard plan, Romney blasted the proposal in a letter to Travaglini. "Lofty goals do not justify the creation of life for experimentation or destruction." In other remarks he labeled the Harvard plan as "Orwellian."

Romney's views on the stem cell debate would permit for research purposes the use of embryos about to be destroyed by their parents; this position puts him at odds with the President Bush's more restrictive position, but it is still significantly more protective of the dignity of the unborn embryonic life than all of the Democrats' and most of the Republicans' positions. Romney has also never supported state-funded research on embryonic stem cells, and is a believer in the efficacy of alternative means of producing the pluripotent stem cells which are believed by most researchers to be the key to the medical breakthroughs desired by all parties. The vigorous nature of his attack on the Harvard plan also won praise for its boldness and, as noted above, pro-life activists have long wanted a champion capable of carrying the debate into the public square.

Romney's veto of the legislation exempting Harvard from any need to seek state approval for the furthest reaches of its scientific community was overridden, but the attempt to persuade the scientific community of alternative and ethical approaches to the stem cell debate continues. In May of 2005, the President's Council on Bioethics reported that it had been investigating "ways of obtaining pluripotent, genetically stable, and long-lived human stem cells (the functional equivalent of human embryonic stem cells) that do *not* involve creating, destroying, or harming human embryos. We have found that there are, broadly speaking, four such possible approaches," and went on to detail those promising areas.

Many in the pro-life movement will look for candidates willing to master this complex terrain and to advocate for the alternatives that protect unborn life, even in its earliest form. Romney's record in Massachusetts will appeal to such activists.

Fifth, Romney benefits from the views of pro-life leaders like Denver's Archbishop Charles Chaput, who is much more interested in what people believe today than what they believed a decade ago.

"People's views can change," the archbishop told me when I brought up the charges leveled against Romney that the governor had moved toward a pro-life agenda over time. "I care if they have respect for fundamental human dignity today." Given that the Catholic Church and evangelicals as well have to hope to persuade people to their views of the importance of curbing abortion, they almost have to agree that it is the current opinion of a candidate that matters, or they will have to forfeit the idea of changing hearts and minds on the issue.

Chaput's reputation as a high-profile, traditionalist bishop also means a lot in American Catholic circles. He won't be endorsing Romney or anyone else, but he and like-minded bishops will be again calling Catholics to study carefully candidates' positions on the rights of the unborn. To the extent the Catholic faithful do, they will certainly be more at home with Mitt Romney than with any Democrat seeking the presidency in 2008.

Another pro-life champion eager to know what candidates think now rather than what they thought two decades ago is South Carolina senator Jim DeMint, a staunch pro-life voice in the Senate, a Presbyterian elder, and as of January 10, 2007, a Romney backer.

"We're not going to win this battle for life in this country unless we convince a lot of people to change their mind," Senator DeMint told me on the day he announced his backing for Romney. "And I think the very deliberate and thoughtful process that Mitt Romney went through, looking at science, considering when life really did begin, it changed his mind. And I think he has the ability to take that argument to the public debate in a way that people can relate to. But again, if someone changes their mind on something, and they've thought it through, that suggests they do have a mind, and they're willing to use it."

Romney's willingness to accept the status quo while governor in Massachusetts while also vetoing attempts to expand abortion rights and holding the line against the most ambitious of the embryonic stem cell research enthusiasts underscores the evolution that DeMint described and which will be so powerful in advancing the culture of life agenda in the country.

Finally, Romney also benefits from his strong stand on the centrality of marriage in the society, a view he has repeatedly expressed in his battle against the Massachusetts Supreme Judicial Court's diktat on the subject and his support for the Federal Marriage Amendment. Romney's undeniable commitment to the defense of traditional marriage has burnished his credentials among the groups and voters most concerned with the millions of abortions that have been performed in the United States since 1973. Since Romney can be trusted on marriage, this reasoning goes, his stated views on abortion and judges in 2007 and 2008 can be trusted as well.

And Romney can be trusted on marriage.

Chapter Six

Mitt Romney Defends Traditional Marriage

If Mitt Romney succeeds in capturing the Republican nomination, his supporters will have to send flowers to the four justices of the Massachusetts Supreme Judicial Court. Two men and the two women who formed this one-vote majority seized legislative authority in Massachusetts and declared that henceforth, on their order the Commonwealth would be obliged to marry two men or two women when they demanded a marriage license. Never in American history had any state legislature passed and a state governor signed a bill extending the right to marry to two persons of the same sex. But still the Massachusetts court declared itself sovereign on the issue.

On twenty-six of the twenty-seven occasions that Americans have been offered the chance to vote directly on the question of whether marriage should be limited to one man and one woman, they have chosen to preserve the traditional definition of marriage. On the one occasion such a popular test failed—in Arizona, in November of 2006—the campaign to defeat the defense of marriage initiative focused not on the justice of extending the opportunity to marry to same-sex couples. The "no" campaign in Arizona deceitfully argued that the initiative posed a threat to the Social Security benefits of older heterosexual couples living together but who weren't married. _mainstream media_

Because the MSM is fundamentally hostile to the defense of marriage movement—they see in it many things, from an anti-gay agenda to the power of fundamentalists—they have largely missed the way the defense of marriage movement is changing grassroots politics in many states, particularly among conservatives.

Each time an initiative concerning marriage has been on a state ballot, a new network of volunteers and activists has sprung up to defend traditional marriage and to staff the effort to educate voters. These networks do not vanish with the victory, but instead transform into potent values coalitions, or at worst slumber until marriage becomes an issue again. The point is that these networks still exist, and their members have not ceased to care deeply about the issue.

What these networks ultimately desire is a federal constitutional amendment defining marriage as between one man and one woman, an amendment sent from the Congress to the states for the ratification debates that would then follow. Most Democrats and some Republicans oppose such an amendment, and point to the traditional authority of the states to define marriage and to the federal Defense of Marriage Act (DOMA), which prohibits the export of same-sex marriage from states opening marriage to same-sex couples. Amendment supporters counter that the DOMA could be struck down as unconstitutional by federal judges as indifferent to popular opinion and constitutional precedent as the four justices of the Massachusetts high court were. Twice the federal constitutional amendment has failed to gather sufficient votes in the House and Senate, and under the new Democratic majority, the amendment will not even be brought to a vote before the next presidential election.

On both occasions the federal marriage amendment came before the Senate, John McCain voted to kill it. The activists who have spent much time on the project will not forget McCain's "nay" votes, and McCain's advocacy for the Arizona marriage amendment to that state's constitution (the only one to have thus far failed) will not assuage their anger.

Mitt Romney stands poised to be the candidate who benefits from the passion, energy, and financial assistance of the pro-marriage network. He has earned their trust because he has battled against his state's highest court and its overwhelmingly Democratic legislature to return marriage to its traditional definition. His tenure as governor ended before he achieved success in Massachusetts, but he never failed to press the issue. When state legislators waited until after the November 7, 2006, elections to recess with the intent of quietly killing a proposed amendment to the Massachusetts Constitution restoring traditional marriage—an amendment that had been backed by 170,000 signatures and years of intense lobbying to meet the strict amendment procedures of the state's constitution—Romney refused to go quietly. He organized a rally of thousands outside the state capitol on November 19, blasting the legislators for refusing to allow a vote on the amendment after years of pretending to be moving toward such a resolution. His remarks to the crowd struck the central theme in the marriage debate: judges ought not decide this issue.

"It's quite an interesting view I get from those windows," Romney began his speech beneath his office overlooking the Boston Commons in front of Massachusetts's historic State House. "All I have to do is glance this way to see the stream of tourists," he continued. "They come in duck boats, trolleys, and as foot pilgrims."

"They're not here for the beauty," he observed. "They're here for the history."

Romney went on to lay out a theme that will no doubt be a key part of his presidential campaign:

For this was the place where an astounding idea was born. It revolutionized America, it revolutionized the world.

The idea was this: our nation would be guided by the voice of the people.

This nation would trust the voice of the people rather than the wisdom of a king, or anyone else.

The idea was embodied in the first constitution, written by John Adams, here in Massachusetts. It established how the voice of the people would be heard—through elections and votes, petitions and initiatives, representatives and senators.

Lincoln said that as elected leaders, we promise to follow the law, to follow the constitution. He called this "America's political religion."

Last week, 109 legislators decided to reject the law, abandon the constitution, and violate their oath of office.

For the constitution plainly states that when a qualified petition is placed before them, the legislature "shall" vote. It does not say may vote, or vote if its procedures permit a vote, or vote if there are enough of the members in attendance. It says "shall" vote.

A decision not to vote is a decision to usurp the constitution, to abandon democracy and substitute a form of what this nation's founders called tyranny, that is, the imposition of the will of those in power, on the people.

As I listened to the debate in the legislative session last week, I was struck by the irony, and the hypocrisy. Legislators so energized to protect the newly discovered gay right to marry had no compunction about trammeling the long-established, constitutional right of the people to vote.

The issue now before us is not whether same-sex couples should marry. The issue before us today is whether 109 legislators will follow the constitution.

Tomorrow, I will send these 109 a copy of the constitution and of their oath of office.

And this week, we will file an action before the courts, calling upon the judiciary to protect the constitutional rights of our
citizens.

Let us not see this state, which first established constitutional
democracy, become the first to abandon it.

The following day Romney sent each legislator a copy of the state's
constitution, their oath of office, and a letter stating that the oath's
"words meant a lot to me when I said them and I know they still mean
something to you."

Romney's ire was directed not at those legislators who would have
voted against allowing the amendment to be on the ballot, but at the
109 lawmakers who refused to allow the vote on the ballot to be held.
The Massachusetts legislature met on November 9, 2006, as required
under the petition section of the state's constitution as a joint session
functioning as a constitutional convention. Only fifty votes were
required to advance the amendment, fifty votes that were clearly
there in the joint session. Rather than take that vote they would lose,
amendment opponents moved to recess the session, a motion that
carried by a vote of 109 to 89.

Romney refused to allow the legislature to dodge the voters' will.

On Friday, November 24, 2006, Romney and several other Massachusetts voters filed suit with the Supreme Judicial Council asking
the court to order the legislature to hold the vote they had been peti-
tioned to conduct. In December, the court announced that while it
lacked the authority to order the measure to be placed on the ballot,
it did agree with Governor Romney that the state's legislators had
been dodging their clear responsibility.

And on January 2, 2007, an embarrassed legislature voted to
place the measure before the voters. It must do so once more in the
next session, and the people will be allowed to vote on the amendment in 2008.

"If the vote stands and the measure advances," the *Boston Globe* declared that day, "it would be a major victory for Governor Mitt Romney, who leaves office in two days but is widely expected to run for president as a social conservative."

The *Globe* was wrong to suggest there was anything tentative about the significance of Romney's victory. Romney had refused to concede and, crucially, stood on the principle that it was the people who ought to decide such major issues, not four justices with cooked-up legal absurdities. While the *Globe* wants to brand Romney as a "social conservative" for his advocacy of traditional marriage, it ought also to note that he's a "rule of law" and not a "rule of courts" conservative as well. Even if the incoming Massachusetts governor, Democrat Deval Patrick, finds some way to again derail the initiative, Romney left office with an unbroken record of vigorous defense of traditional marriage

There are very few defense-of-marriage activists in the country who are unaware that Romney has fought the good fight that many high-profile Republicans—including Senator McCain and Mayor Giuliani—have refused to fight. Nor did Romney confine his efforts to the battle within his own state.

Because of the importance this issue is likely to hold in the debates among Republicans and in the primary voting, in this chapter I quote extensively from primary documents that reflect Romney's record on the issue. Although the elite media dislikes the issue of the definition of marriage intensely and refuses to believe it will have much resonance, it is in fact a powerful driver of voters, especially among religious conservatives who see marriage as ordained by God for the good of His people. Even among secular conservatives, marriage between a man and a woman is appreciated as a crucial institution, and is widely recognized as the best situation for children to grow up within. The attempt by the Left to argue that there is no difference between same-sex couples and heterosexual couples strikes even gay-friendly independents and many liberals as radical.

Thus no Democratic presidential candidate has ever endorsed the idea outright, and it is unlikely that any will do so in 2008.

Traditional marriage defenders fear that slowly but surely courts will continue to chip away at the historic definition of marriage. We've already seen it begin: first in Vermont where civil unions were mandated by that state's highest court, then in Massachusetts with the *Goodridge* decision, and in October of 2006 in New Jersey by that state's Supreme Court. Defenders of traditional marriage believe that the position of the federal marriage amendment's opponents who argue for federalism's supremacy is disingenuous, a thin veil that does not begin to cover their hostility to traditional marriage. The pro-federalism "let-the-states-decide-for-themselves" argument is undermined by the refusal of those employing that argument to candidly confront the fact that no legislature and governor have ever passed a same-sex marriage law except under judicial duress. The states are not in fact deciding for themselves. Judges are dictating the results, results which have trodden on popular will and which threaten to travel from state to state.

If marriage is not protected explicitly in the federal Constitution, many defenders of traditional marriage believe, the certain result will be the almost universal court-imposed institution of same-sex marriage. The years since *Roe* have taught social conservatives that the Supreme Court is prone to imposing radical social change, and certainly has done so in the area of sexual orientation. The marriage lobby both fears and expects such a sudden shift on same-sex marriage, dressed up in the language of the "Full Faith and Credit Clause" of the United States Constitution.

Mitt Romney has spent a lot of time over the past four years battling this court-supervised social engineering in his own state and warning of its likely spread to other jurisdictions. When the issue arises between now and November 2008, Romney will speak from experience and will, with great credibility, argue that his views were not suddenly formed or likely to be abandoned.

+++

On November 18, 2003, the Massachusetts Supreme Judicial Court ruled by a 4–3 vote that the Massachusetts Constitution required the state to permit same-sex marriage. The case was titled *Goodridge* v. *Department of Public Heath*, but it would have been better titled *Imperial Judiciary* v. *Constitutional Majoritarianism*. The court's narrow majority based its decision on the equal-protection and due-process provisions of the Massachusetts Constitution, arguing that they guaranteed the right of same-sex couples to marry. The language of the decision was sweeping, and dismissive of the vast literature and scholarship upholding the right of the state legislatures to determine the specifics of the state's marriage laws.

"Marriage is a vital social institution," began the opinion of Chief Justice Margaret H. Marshall. "The exclusive commitment of two individuals to each other nurtures love and mutual support; it brings stability to our society. For those who choose to marry, and for their children, marriage provides an abundance of legal, financial, and social benefits. In return it imposes weighty legal, financial, and social obligations. The question before us is whether, consistent with the Massachusetts Constitution, the Commonwealth may deny the protections, benefits, and obligations conferred by civil marriage to two individuals of the same sex who wish to marry. We conclude that it may not. The Massachusetts Constitution affirms the dignity and equality of all individuals. It forbids the creation of second-class citizens. In reaching our conclusion we have given full deference to the arguments made by the Commonwealth. But it has failed to identify any constitutionally adequate reason for denying civil marriage to same-sex couples."

Three of the seven justices dissented, as did Governor Romney. Romney immediately released a statement declaring: "I disagree with the Supreme Judicial Court. Marriage is an institution between a man and a woman. I will support an amendment to the Massachusetts Constitution to make that expressly clear. Of course, we must provide basic civil rights and appropriate benefits to nontraditional couples, but marriage is a special institution that should be reserved for a man and a woman."

Romney's opposition was neither perfunctory nor feigned. In the days following the decision, Romney appeared on NBC's *Today Show* and ABC's *Good Morning America* to denounce the Supreme Judicial Court's ruling. He criticized the decision and announced plans to work to amend the Massachusetts Constitution to ban such unions while pledging to work simultaneously to establish rights for same-sex couples. "I agree with 3,000 years of recorded human history," he said on the *Today Show*, "which, frankly, is a contradiction of what the majority of the Supreme Judicial Court said."

"Of course," he continued, "at the same time, we should [be] providing the necessary civil rights and certain appropriate benefits" to same-sex couples.

This careful and oft-repeated aspect of his argument—Romney will not allow himself to be categorized as anti-gay—is not a uniform sentiment among religious conservatives, some of whom oppose the creation of civil union laws. Most conservatives, it seems, would not begrudge same-sex couples the rights of inheritance, to control care and end-of-life decisions of partners, or other basic liberties and free associations. Romney's careful discussion of these issues is an assurance to moderate voters inside the GOP's big tent that he—like them—is not about to endorse any rollback in the dignity and respect extended to gays and lesbians over the past two decades.

But Romney is adamant that it is not anti-gay to be pro–traditional marriage. He is also clear that any adjustments to the laws regarding marriage ought to come from legislatures and governors, not from courts.

In a written statement Romney put forth the central argument against the Massachusetts judicial diktat and those similar to it: "The people of Massachusetts should not be excluded from a decision as fundamental to our society as the definition of marriage," he wrote.

"This issue is too important to leave to a one-vote majority of the [Supreme Judicial Court]."

The crux is how we are governed, not the specifics of gay marriage or any other issue. Romney declared himself on the side of representative democracy as opposed to judicial imperialism. It is this argument that matters most to conservatives. Because out-of-control courts have swept aside traditional morality embedded in law again and again—and threaten to continue to do so. The debate over marriage is also a debate over abortion, cloning, pornography, and freedom of worship. It is a debate over who decides.

The Massachusetts legislature at first responded to Romney's call for action and to the widespread public outrage at the court's high-handedness, and voted in favor of a proposed amendment to the state constitution that would have prevented same-sex marriage by affirming the traditional definition of marriage while establishing civil unions.

The Massachusetts Constitution is not easily amended, however. The process requires the legislature, in joint session, to approve an amendment in two consecutive sessions. Only then will a proposed amendment go to the people for a vote.

The 2004 legislative elections, however, provided a big blow to the pro-marriage forces, emboldening the advocates of homosexual marriage. In the session following that election, the legislature refused to even vote on the amendment, thus killing the process.

Romney responded by resurrecting the amendment effort, through even more democratic means. The governor led the petition drive to force the constitutional convention which, as noted above, was itself nearly subverted by gay marriage supporters two days after the November 2006 elections.

Though Romney could not immediately force the overwhelmingly liberal legislature to allow the people to repair the harm done to marriage by the state's highest court, as governor he managed to limit the damage. With Massachusetts as the only state in the nation marrying same-sex couples, Romney anticipated an influx of such couples to Massachusetts to get married. To prevent this rush to the Bay State of out-of-state gay couples, Romney dusted off a 1913 law prohibiting municipal courts from marrying nonresident couples if the marriage is unlawful in their home state. "Massachusetts should not become the Las Vegas of same-sex marriage," he declared. "We do not intend to export our marriage confusion to the entire nation."

"Our current laws, as they exist, limit same-sex marriage to people from jurisdictions where such marriage would be legal," he continued. "And our understanding is that same-sex marriage is only legal in Massachusetts. And therefore, by definition, only people who reside in Massachusetts or intend to reside in Massachusetts would be able to be married under this provision." Romney's interpretation of the statute has in fact been upheld by the same court that struck down heterosexual exclusivity in marriage.

On February 5, 2004, Romney wrote an op-ed for the *Wall Street Journal*, "One Man, One Woman: A Citizen's Guide to Protecting Marriage."

"No matter how you feel about gay marriage," the piece began, "we should be able to agree that the citizens and their elected representatives must not be excluded from a decision as fundamental to society as the definition of marriage. There are lessons from my state's experience that may help other states preserve the rightful participation of their legislatures and citizens, and avoid the confusion now facing Massachusetts."

Romney went on to blast the Massachusetts high court's reasoning while holding up marriage as a crucial institution:

> Contrary to the court's opinion, marriage is not "an evolving paradigm." It is deeply rooted in the history, culture and tradition of civil society. It predates our Constitution and our nation by millennia. The institution of marriage was not created by government and it should not be redefined by government.

Marriage is a fundamental and universal social institution. It encompasses many obligations and benefits affecting husband and wife, father and mother, son and daughter. It is the foundation of a harmonious family life. It is the basic building block of society: the development, productivity and happiness of new generations are bound inextricably to the family unit. As a result, marriage bears a real relation to the well-being, health and enduring strength of society.

Because of marriage's pivotal role, nations and states have chosen to provide unique benefits and incentives to those who choose to be married. These benefits are not given to single citizens, groups of friends, or couples of the same sex. That benefits are given to married couples and not to singles or gay couples has nothing to do with discrimination; it has everything to do with building a stable new generation and nation.

Romney went on to urge that pro-marriage activism avoid attacks on gays, that defense of marriage statutes be passed by states, that activist judges be rejected, and that consideration be given to amending the federal Constitution.

Four months later, on June 24, 2004, Romney joined the national debate and endorsed a federal marriage amendment in testimony before the U.S. Senate Judiciary Committee. His statement before the committee remains the most complete statement of his beliefs on the issue, and I reprint it here:

This is a subject about which people have tender emotions in part because it touches individual lives. It also has been misused by some as a means to promote intolerance and prejudice. This is a time when we must fight hate and bigotry, when we must root out prejudice, when we must learn to accept people who are different from one another. Like me, the great majority of Americans wish both to preserve the traditional definition of marriage and to oppose bias and intolerance directed towards gays and lesbians.

Given the decision of the Massachusetts Supreme Judicial Court, Congress and America now face important questions regarding the institution of marriage. Should we abandon marriage as we know it and as it was known by the framers of our Constitution?

Has America been wrong about marriage for 200-plus years?

Were generations that spanned thousands of years from all the civilizations of the world wrong about marriage?

Are the philosophies and teachings of all the world's major religions simply wrong?

Or is it more likely that four people among the seven that sat in a court in Massachusetts have erred? I believe that is the case.

And I believe their error was the product of seeing only a part, and not the entirety. They viewed marriage as an institution principally designed for adults. Adults are who they saw. Adults stood before them in the courtroom. And so they thought of adult rights, equal rights for adults. If heterosexual adults can marry, then homosexual adults must also marry to have equal rights.

But marriage is not solely for adults. Marriage is also for children. In fact, marriage is principally for the nurturing and development of children. The children of America have the right to have a father and a mother.

Of course, even today, circumstances can take a parent from the home, but the child still has a mother and a father. If the parents are divorced, the child can visit each of them. If a mother or father is deceased, the child can learn about the qualities of the departed. His or her psychological development can still be influenced by the contrasting features of both genders.

Are we ready to usher in a society indifferent about having fathers and mothers? Will our children be indifferent about having a mother and a father?

My Department of Public Health has asked whether we must re-write our state birth certificates to conform to our Court's same-sex marriage ruling. Must we remove "father" and "mother" and replace them with "parent A" and "parent B"?

What should be the ideal for raising a child?: Not a village, not "parent A" and "parent B," but a mother and a father.

Marriage is about even more than children and adults. The family unit is the structural underpinning of all successful societies. And, it is the single most powerful force that preserves society across generations, through centuries.

Scientific studies of children raised by same-sex couples are almost non-existent. And the societal implications and effects on these children are not likely to be observed for at least a generation, probably several generations. But it may affect the development of children and thereby future society as a whole. Until we understand the implications for human development of a different definition of marriage, I believe we should preserve that which has endured over thousands of years.

Preserving the definition of marriage should not infringe on the right of individuals to live in the manner of their choosing. One person may choose to live as a single, even to have and raise her own child. Others may choose to live in same sex partnerships or civil arrangements. There is an unshakeable majority of opinion in this country that we should cherish and protect individual rights with tolerance and understanding.

But there is a difference between individual rights and marriage. An individual has rights, but a man and a woman together have a marriage. We should not deconstruct marriage simply to make a statement about the rights of individual adults. Forcing marriage to mean all things, will ultimately define marriage to mean nothing at all.

Some have asked why so much importance is attached to the word "marriage." It is because changing the definition of marriage to include same-sex unions will lead to further far-reaching changes that also would influence the development of our children. For example, school textbooks and classroom instruction may be required to assert absolute societal indifference between traditional marriage and same sex practice. It is inconceivable that promoting absolute indifference between heterosexual and homosexual unions would not significantly affect child development, family dynamics, and societal structures.

Among the structures that would be affected would be religious and certain charitable institutions. Those with scriptural or other immutable founding principles will be castigated. Ultimately, some may founder. We need more from these institutions, not less, and particularly so to support and strengthen those in greatest need. Society can ill afford further erosion of charitable and virtuous institutions.

For these reasons, I join with those who support a federal constitutional amendment. Some retreat from the concept of amendment, per se. While they say they agree with the traditional definition of marriage, they hesitate to amend. But amendment is a vital and necessary aspect of our constitutional democracy, not an aberration.

The Constitution's framers recognized that any one of the three branches of government might overstep its separated powers. If Congress oversteps, the Court can intervene. If the Executive overreaches, Congress may impeach. And if the Court launches beyond the Constitution, the legislative branch may amend.

The four Massachusetts justices launched beyond our constitution. That is why the Massachusetts legislature has begun the lengthy amendment process.

There is further cause for amendment. Our framers debated nothing more fully than they debated the reach and boundaries of what we call federalism. States retained certain powers upon which the federal government could not infringe. By the decision of the Massachusetts Supreme Judicial Court, our state has begun to assert power over all the other states. It is a state infringing on the powers of other states.

In Massachusetts, we have a law that attempts to restrain this infringement on other states by restricting marriages of out-of-state couples to those where no impediment to marry exists in their home state. Even with this law, valid same-sex marriages will migrate to other states. For each state to preserve its own power in relation to marriage, within the principle of federalism, a federal amendment to define marriage is necessary.

This is not a mere political issue. It is more than a matter of adult rights. It is a societal issue. It encompasses the preservation of a structure that has formed the basis of all known successful civilizations.

With a matter as vital to society as marriage, I am troubled when I see an intolerant few wrap the marriage debate with their bias and prejudice.

I am also troubled by those on the other side of the issue who equate respect for traditional marriage with intolerance. The majority of Americans believe marriage is between a man and a woman, but they are also firmly committed to respect, and even fight for civil rights, individual freedoms and tolerance. Saying otherwise is wrong, demeaning and offensive. As a society, we must be able to recognize the salutary effect, for children, of having a mother and a father while at the same time respecting the civil rights and equality of all citizens.

Thank you.

Romney critics have argued that his leadership on the marriage issue was a product of his 2006 decision to seek the presidency. *Boston Globe* columnist Joan Vennochi accused Romney of "danc[ing] to the right" in a November 26, 2006, column, and of using the marriage debate as a way to "establish his social-conservative credentials for upcoming Republican primaries." Gay marriage abso-lutist and blogger and radical "conservative" Andrew Sullivan opined that if Romney "were not running as an explicitly religious candidate to a sectarian base, and was less draconian on abortion and marriage, I'd like him a lot." The marriage defense Romney mounted—vigorous and principled—had disqualified him in the eyes of the fanatical Sul-livan. On the same day that Vennochi chided Romney, Sullivan took to the pages of the London *Times* to assert that Romney had sacrificed principle to "appeal to the Republican base," which had obliged him to support "a federal amendment to ban gay unions, and for laws that would criminalize all abortion, except in cases of rape or incest."

Contrary to what leftist critics of Romney like Vennochi and Sul-livan argue, Romney's support of marriage has never changed from the moment the Massachusetts Supreme Judicial Court issued its radical decision, and Romney has never hesitated to use his position to argue for traditional marriage and against its radical opponents and the courts that support and empower those opponents.

One key example: Romney used his platform appearance at the Republican National Convention on September 1, 2004, to under-score his support for traditional marriage.

"Throughout our history," he declared to the convention, "when our country needed us, Americans have stepped forward by express-ing tolerance and respect for all God's children, regardless of their differences and choices. At the same time, because every child deserves a mother and a father we step forward by recognizing that marriage is between a man and a woman."

Three years before the launch of his presidential campaign Romney used his biggest platform to press the case for traditional marriage.

Romney's Commonwealth PAC has also donated to pro-marriage ballot initiatives. At the time the PAC donated $5,000 to the South Carolina ballot effort to defend marriage, Romney released a state-ment which read in part: "We cannot afford to shrink from the time-less, priceless principles of human experience."

Romney almost always addresses the marriage issues in his stump speeches. Here's an excerpt from his June 3, 2005, New Hampshire Federation of Republican Women's Lilac Dinner:

> We're people who believe in a Creator or if not we believe in a purpose greater than ourselves, in purpose-driven lives as Rick Warren has pointed out. We're a people who are self-reliant and independent. We're a people who take care of those who are truly in need. We're a people also who fundamentally respect the value of human life. And at the foundation of our society is of course the family. The family has always been the structure from which we pass along our values and ideals to the next generation.
>
> The Massachusetts Supreme Judicial Court did something, which I think struck at the foundation of the family by saying that our Constitution requires gay marriage. I think John Adams would be surprised. He wrote it; I don't think he had that in mind. And I want you to recognize of course as people we should show respect to people who make different choices in their life, we should show tolerance to other individuals, but we should also recognize that marriage is not about rights of adults, marriage is about raising children. Every child has the right to have a mother and father.

When the Federal Marriage Amendment was brought to the Senate for a second vote in 2006, Romney remained steadfast in his support even though there was much criticism of the effort within the MSM. Aware of Senator McCain's almost certain "no" vote, Romney sent a letter to every senator urging a "yes" vote:

> Dear Senator,
>
> Next week, you will vote on a proposed amendment to the United States Constitution protecting the institution of marriage.

As governor of the state most directly affected by this amendment, I hope my perspectives will encourage you to vote "yes."

Americans are tolerant, generous, and kind people. We all oppose bigotry and disparagement, and we all wish to avoid hurtful disregard of the feelings of others. But the debate over same-sex marriage is not a debate over tolerance. It is a debate about the purpose of the institution of marriage.

Attaching the word marriage to the association of same-sex individuals mistakenly presumes that marriage is principally a matter of adult benefits and adult rights. In fact, marriage is principally about the nurturing and development of children. And the successful development of children is critical to the preservation and success of our nation.

Our society, like all known civilizations in recorded history, has favored the union of a man and a woman with the special designation and benefits of marriage. In this respect, it has elevated the relationship of a legally bound man and woman over other relationships. This recognizes that the ideal setting for nurturing and developing children is a home where there is a mother and a father.

In order to protect the institution of marriage, we must prevent it from being redefined by judges like those here in Massachusetts who think that marriage is an "evolving paradigm," and that the traditional definition is "rooted in persistent prejudices" and amounts to "invidious discrimination."

Although the full impact of same-sex marriage may not be measured for decades or generations, we are beginning to see the effects of the new legal logic in Massachusetts just two years into our state's social experiment. For instance, our birth certificate is being challenged: same-sex couples want the terms "Mother" and "Father" replaced with "Parent A" and "Parent B."

In our schools, children are being instructed that there is no difference between same-sex marriage and traditional marriage.

Recently, parents of a second grader in one public school complained when they were not notified that their son's teacher would
read a fairy tale about same-sex marriage to the class. In the story,
a prince chooses to marry another prince, instead of a princess.
The parents asked for the opportunity to opt their child out of
hearing such stories. In response, the school superintendent
insisted on "teaching children about the world they live in, and in
Massachusetts same-sex marriage is legal." Once a society estab-
lishes that it is legally indifferent between traditional marriage
and same-sex marriage, how can one preserve any practice which
favors the union of a man and a woman?

Some argue that our principles of federalism and local control
require us to leave the issue of same-sex marriage to the states—
which means, as a practical matter, to state courts. Such an argument denies the realities of modern life and would create a
chaotic patchwork of inconsistent laws throughout the country.
Marriage is not just an activity or practice which is confined to the
border of any one state. It is a status that is carried from state to
state. Because of this, and because Americans conduct their
financial and legal lives in a united country bound by interstate
institutions, a national definition of marriage is necessary.

Your vote on this amendment should not be guided by a concern for adult rights. This matter goes to the development and
well-being of children. I hope that you will make your vote heard
on their behalf.

Best regards,

Mitt Romney

The Senate voted 49 to 48 in favor of closing debate on the Federal Marriage Amendment, far short of the sixty votes necessary to
end debate, and nowhere near the sixty-seven votes necessary to send
the measure on to the states for debate.

Arizona's John McCain voted against even holding a vote, the only Republican senator among the four or five then considering a presidential run to do so.

This issue may well divide the Republican electorate throughout the primaries. It has almost certainly deeply injured Senator McCain's effort to repair his standing with religious conservatives for whom this issue, along with the related issues of the protection of unborn life and the increasing imperiousness of federal judges, matter a great deal. At the same time, the small percentage of the Republican electorate who favor same-sex marriage will not throw in with McCain after his late effort to pass the Arizona marriage effort.

An additional point of interest is that Romney's critics on this issue mostly come from the Left.

"He is a fraud," the *Boston Globe* quoted Massachusetts state senator Jarrett T. Barrios of Cambridge of saying after Romney's November 2006 State House rally. "It is a ploy for his run for president."

The paper also quoted Arlene Isaacson, a leader of the Massachusetts Gay and Lesbian Political Caucus, as asserting that Romney needed "to assert his right-wing credentials," and "to show his anti-gay credentials"

These are the sort of critiques very familiar to the marriage activists around the country, and are almost certain to persuade them that Romney has indeed been in the forefront of the effort.

Because the latest assault on Romney has argued not that he was wrong in his defense of marriage, but that he was insincerely using the issue to advance his conservative credentials in advance of a White House run, I asked him about the charge of opportunism.

"The issue was not one I selected," Romney responded. "When I ran for office I said that I oppose same-sex marriage and civil unions."

"There were five debates," he continued, recounting his 2002 campaign. "I probably had that brought up multiple times. I made the same point every time. Actually, my opponent at one point said—in the debate she said that she also opposed same-sex marriage but then she said later that if a bill reached her desk from the legislature in favor of same-sex marriage she would sign it. We seized upon that during the campaign and made quite a deal of the fact that she therefore was supporting same-sex marriage, and I was opposed to it. So my position was well staked out and established before I was elected."

And once elected, he continued, he defended the position on which he had campaigned:

[T]he Supreme Judicial Court here took action. I didn't ask them to take [it]. I didn't know it was going to be taken here. They took action which put me in the spotlight as the person who was virtually alone in this building able to defend traditional marriage. I know that some like Joan Vennochi and others would say, "Well you shouldn't have done that," but had I not stood up for my beliefs and what I campaigned for, I would not have been true to myself. So of course I stood up and said I would do what I can within the law to protect traditional marriage. Those that are critical, they are the ones that have changed their perspective. Not me. I've been in the same place from the very beginning.

Some pro-marriage activists are already arguing that Romney did not do enough, that he ought to have ignored the Massachusetts Supreme Judicial Court. Romney has an answer ready for them.

"First of all," he began, responding to the charge of not having done enough, "we're a nation of laws and I believe in following the law. As Abraham Lincoln said, 'We follow America's political religion and that is the rule of law is abided.' I'm not going to violate the law. Number two, even if I were to violate the law and to say we're not going to implement what the court said, recognize I'm not going to be governor forever, and if I don't change the law then I would have accomplished nothing. So the only way to ultimately protect a marriage is to do so in a legal and binding way."

With the backdrop of the United States Senate's rejection of a federal amendment defending marriage, pro-marriage forces will be looking for someone (1) with the eloquence necessary to argue the case—and to persuade the voters—that marriage matters and (2) who has demonstrated perseverance on the subject even against the media elites who are almost uniformly hostile to the idea that traditional marriage is worth preserving.

Those hunting for that spokesman in the Republican primaries will almost certainly choose Romney. And in a general election, Romney's State House speech from November 19 will be the perfect illustration that this debate is not about gays and lesbians and their right to dignity and the respect they are owed as fellow citizens, but the central issue of the Republic's founding as a representative democracy. The definition of marriage belongs to the people and their representatives, not the courts.

There is a final, crucial reason why Romney will appeal to the pro-marriage activists: Romney is manifestly not anti-gay or homophobic, and this record makes him an even more powerful defender of traditional marriage.

When Romney ran for Senate against Ted Kennedy in 1994, he did so as a staunch backer of civil rights for gays and lesbians. In a letter to the Republican Log Cabin Club of Massachusetts, a membership organization for gay and lesbian Republicans, Romney wrote that "[f]or some voters, it might be enough to simply match my opponent's record in this area. But I believe we can and must do better. If we are to achieve the goals we share, we must make equality for gays and lesbians a mainstream concern. My opponent cannot do this. I can and will." Romney went on to endorse the "don't ask, don't tell" policy governing gays and lesbians in the United States military, calling it "the first in a number of steps that will ultimately lead to gays and lesbians being able to serve openly and honestly in our nation's military."

Romney also went out of his way to include Salt Lake City's gay and lesbian community in the 2002 Winter Games. "On one occasion,"

Romney wrote in his memoir *Turnaround*, "our SLOC board of directors was meeting in a building that I had learned was next door to the headquarters for the Salt Lake City chapter of the Gay and Lesbian Alliance. After the meeting, I walked into the GLA office and asked if they would consider helping recruit volunteers for the Games. They jumped at the opportunity."

Romney appears to be smack at the center of American public opinion concerning gay and lesbian Americans: they are our fellow citizens, entitled to all the rights and respect of any fellow citizen, and children of God equally valued by Him. As a public official he will defend marriage as it has always existed, confident of its central role in the preservation of society, but he will do so without attacks on gays and lesbians and will refuse to allow the debate to degenerate into such an attack. If his views on gays and lesbians serving in the military have not changed in response to testimony from the military on the source of the policy and its necessity, he will be to the left of his party on that issue, but that isn't a driving force in this era of war and terrorism. Romney might even successfully argue that in a time of war, the need for certain skill sets such as proficiency in certain languages fairly demands an exception to the rule.

"I don't ask people's sexual orientation," Romney told me, "and I don't believe in discriminating against people in employment based upon their sexual orientation. I believe in protecting traditional marriage. I don't believe marriage should be extended to marriage of the same gender but I don't believe in discrimination in the work place." When the story of Romney's 1994 letter broke in early December 2006, Romney opponents thought it would be a serious problem for his candidacy. The critics were wrong, and they were wrong despite the willingness of some high-profile conservative activists to declare in stentorian tones the end of his candidacy.

Most Republicans, like most Americans, know and love gays and lesbians in their families, businesses, and communities.

Most Republicans, like most Americans, are repulsed by anti-gay bigotry, just as they are by anti-Mormon bigotry, or any sort of bigotry.

And most Americans value marriage between one man and one woman as the institution best suited to raise children and to perpetuate our society and culture. Most also believe that marriage was ordained by God to be just that institution. And most also believe that if changes are to be made, the agents of change ought not be the courts, but the people and their representatives.

On marriage, Romney advocates for the mainstream position in the country, a position that happens to be conservative and that rejects extremist solutions and denounces extremist rhetoric.

In such balanced and considered approaches, most voters will find a great affinity.

Chapter Seven

Under the Golden Dome: Romney's Governorship

A sk yourself if you have heard of the actions or achievements of any governor in the United States other than your own over the past four years.

Chances are you will recall the collapse of judgment and the inability to act of Louisiana governor Kathleen Blanco in the aftermath of Katrina, and the almost opposite response of Mississippi governor Haley Barbour after the monster storm came ashore.

In Florida, Jeb Bush has had hurricane duty on many occasions and has always acquitted himself well.

There was a scandal in Connecticut, but you can't remember that guy's name, right? And Taft in Ohio and Murkowski in Alaska, if recalled at all at this point, are simple examples of political failure on a colossal scale.

Everyone gets at least a little bit of the Arnold drama, of course.

On the Democratic side, the recently retired Mark Warner had a nice turn as Virginia's chief executive, but he was known nationally mostly for winning a red state and seeing to it that he was followed by another Democrat. His brief dance with a presidential run ended in early October 2006, and that's that for the Dems.

Generally though, Americans don't know much about the governors of other states unless disaster strikes, and even then the credit given is low for successful management of the bad days.

By contrast Mitt Romney's four years have been unusually high profile, and for reasons mostly not of his doing.

Romney did not plan for his state's supreme court to mount a radical assault on traditional marriage, but it did, and that thrust him into the spotlight on an issue of national interest. Likewise, Romney happened to be governor when Harvard's scientists decided to try to push beyond the recognized limits of experimentation on human life in its cellular phase. This is an issue of intense interest in many communities, and Harvard is a high-profile antagonist with considerable resources. As a result of their joust, Romney's views on embryonic stem cell research became far more important than, say, the stem cell research positions of Idaho's governor.

Romney also welcomed the Democratic National Convention to Boston in the summer of 2004, and had a key speaking role at the RNC's gathering in New York City that same presidential season.

The visibility has been partly good luck.

But it has also been partly earned.

Governors who attempt too much accomplish very little. And even the most productive still see their reputations reduced to a few lines or a couple of paragraphs at most. Unlike presidents, the governors who retire after their statehouse tours rarely generate biographies, and if they do, they largely go unread.

California provides a summary of this dynamic. The only of its governors to generate post-Sacramento interest in recent years are the two who stayed employed after their time as the Golden State's chief executive—Earl Warren and Ronald Reagan. The rest have reputations, some have respect, and one still has a career in politics, but those reputations are short courses in long years spent working in the Horseshoe, as the governor's quarters in the California statehouse are known.

Pat Brown was the builder and the UC system protector, as well as the fellow who bested Nixon in '62.

His son Jerry, now the California attorney general, was the moonbeam and the earth child, the darling of the kid vote in the '76 presidential primaries, and sponsor of Rose Bird.

George Deukmejian—the anti-Moonbeam. The solid and serious, crime-fighting steward of a long expansion in the California economy.

Pete Wilson—a very good man to have on the scene when highways collapse after big quakes or huge fires sweep through communities. A Marine. Prop 187. He could have been a contender....

Gray Davis. The. Worst. Governor. Ever.

Arnold. The. Most. Fun. Governor. Ever.

Reagan and Warren get biography after biography, and both deserve them. Their years in the statehouse are dutifully covered and mined for clues as to how they would act as president or chief justice.

For the political class, that's what governorships are—warm-ups for main acts that either come or don't.

Governorships play a special role in presidential campaigns because governors have records as executives, not just as legislators. Senators orate and vote. Governors are obliged to lead, and either sign or veto. Governors hire and fire. Legislators propose. Governors dispose and, if they do not dispose with a veto but sign into law, must execute.

Things happen on the watches of governors, not legislators. There are records there, records to both campaign on and defend against attack.

Mitt Romney took office in January 2003, and his four years were eventful beyond expectation. On the presidential trail those years will be compressed as all records are compressed in that setting. Before long he will have a reputation assigned his efforts as the governor. His rivals will attempt to minimize his record and attack certain aspects of it.

Conservatives might scowl at the very idea of anything good coming out of Massachusetts, the bluest of the blue states, with two Democratic senators and every congressman a Democrat as well as lopsided Democratic majorities in both halves of the state legislature.

Romney's rivals for the GOP nomination will also argue a guilt by association with Massachusetts's reputation as the home of Kennedys, Kerry, Dukakis, and high taxes.

This means, however, that anything Romney has accomplished in such an environment must be graded on the curve: uphill battles are always more difficult, and victories won on such terrain much more worthy of respect.

The marriage and stem cell issues matter a lot, and Romney is already talking about both at every gathering of the party faithful.

But there are six other areas of his governorship relevant when considering a President Romney: executive branch staffing; budgeting and taxes; the universal health insurance mandate; judicial selection; the Big Dig; and Khatami.

Staffing

As soon as he was elected, Romney went into full Bain mode and began reaching out—as he had done at the Olympics—and looking for reliable people from outside government and the usual political and academic circles on which most new administrations rely. Romney wanted a team of individuals with skill sets not ordinarily seen in executive branches.

"I asked Bob White, of course, to head my transition effort," Romney wrote in *Turnaround*. "For two months, Bob worked ceaselessly with the staff he organized to search for top people. We wanted men and women who were not looking for a paycheck but rather a mission to accomplish."

Romney recruited widely, though with an emphasis on the sort of very senior management and finance experience that he has relied

on through the years at Bain Capital and the Olympics. He knew as
well, though, that there are some political skills corporate America
lacks, and so he recruited Beth Myers—a veteran of Massachusetts
and Texas politics and government, and a former big firm litigator
and campaign consultant—to lead his staff, where she stayed until
heading off to become senior advisor to Mitt Romney and the Commonwealth PAC in the fall of '06. She's expected to run the presidential campaign, and could become the first woman chief of staff in
a White House. As noted earlier, Romney has already built a campaign team-in-waiting of formidable depth and experience, and is
adding to it weekly. Every candidate who gets a nomination almost
immediately initiates transition and staffing planning, and does so in
complete secrecy. If nominated, Romney would almost certainly
undertake a similar effort, but one distinguished by the breadth of
his talent search.

Nothing compares to the struggle to staff a presidential administration on the short notice afforded by a win in November, but the
experience of a large state government is as close as it gets.

The Budget and Taxes

When Romney took over the 2002 Winter Games, the SLOC was
$300 million in the red, a considerable sum. He left the SLOC with
a surplus—nice fiscal work given the circumstances.

But $300 million is pocket change in Washington, D.C.

Massachusetts also posed a budgeting task much larger than that
of the Olympics.

Upon winning his election and getting access to all the ledgers,
Romney's team found a $600 million current year shortfall with only
six months left in fiscal year 2002–2003, and a projected deficit of $3
billion for FY 2003–2004.

Romney balanced both the current and following year budgets
without raising taxes.

That's a talking point no legislator can match.

The Universal Health Insurance Mandate

Fighting imperious courts and Harvard make for great headlines, and balancing a budget without raising taxes warms center-right hearts, but what about getting necessary laws passed?

In a state where more than eight out of ten legislators are from the opposite party, that partisan imbalance in the Massachusetts legislature would have perhaps been a sufficient excuse to head out to Iowa with nothing to show but balanced ledgers and a host of veto messages.

Romney appears to have figured out early on, however, that governors seeking the presidency need something to point to, much as George W. Bush touted his education reforms in Texas in 2000, and James Earl Carter his reorganization of Georgia government in 1976.

For Mitt Romney, that signal legislative accomplishment is health insurance reform.

An October 2006 Gallup poll done for *USA Today* and ABC News found that not only did 54 percent of Americans express dissatisfaction with the quality of health care in the country, 80 percent thought it was too expensive. (Only 10 percent were dissatisfied with the quality of the care they personally receive.) The concern about cost reflects the 87 percent increase in health care premiums in the first decade of the twenty-first century, and the overall dissatisfaction rate reflects the almost universal concern that the health insurance system is broken even though the actual medicine currently practiced in the United States is without parallel in human history.

This set of circumstances, opinions, and real problems led Romney to tackle the health insurance policy monster, and to wrestle from the Massachusetts legislature in 2006 an important and sweeping set of innovations on how health insurance will be managed in Massachusetts.

This brilliant bit of legislating was born from a partnering between Romney and his policy team with the conservative Heritage

Foundation. Put simply, the problem of the uninsured is a problem for everyone, as the uninsured still consume health care and the costs of that care must be covered from somewhere, usually general fund tax revenues and in the form of higher premiums assessing the covered population.

Some of the uninsured are the poor or the working poor.

Some are in companies without medical benefit plans.

Some have pre-existing conditions that render them poor risks for companies that insure individuals.

Of the approximately half-million uninsured in the Commonwealth as 2006 opened, however, about 200,000 were healthy "risk takers" who preferred spending dollars on Red Sox tickets or goods and services other than premiums for health care insurance that the figured they probably wouldn't need until pregnancy or their middle years arrived.

What Romney and Heritage discovered is that in fact thousands of these risk-takers end up needing health care, and of the expensive sort. They don't have insurance, so the state and the medical care providers eat the costs, which means the taxpayers and/or premium payers eventually get the bills.

To this group of people who are able to insure themselves but unwilling to do so, the Romney plan gives no choice but lots of encouragement: beginning in January of 2008, they must either insure themselves or be subject to a costly fine. There are provisions to assist in making insurance plans widely known and some common purchasing power deployed as well, but it is primarily a stick that is wielded in their direction.

The poor get subsidies as well as assistance in signing up. Those people who earn an amount less than or equal to the federal poverty level will not have to pay any premiums or deductibles. Those with annual incomes between 100 percent and 300 percent of the federal poverty level will pay part of their premiums based on a sliding scale in respect to their income. Savings from health care expenses previously paid by the state to cover the cost of the uninsured will make up the cost of the subsidies.

The Democrat-controlled legislature tacked on a provision that penalizes companies of eleven or more employees that don't provide health insurance, assessing them a $295 fine for their choice not to provide such benefit plans. Romney vetoed this add-on to his plan as a symbolic and counter-productive departure from the reform's primary emphasis on personal responsibility similar to the car insurance model at work across the country. The legislature overrode his veto.

But the lawmakers still handed Romney an enormous, and to most observers unexpected, victory. They did so because the plan manifestly makes sense to most Americans familiar with the mandate for car insurance (and convinced of that mandate's reasonability).

It made sense. It passed.

Will it work?

There are skeptics who think the costs will rapidly overwhelm the estimates, but even those skeptics don't expect those lines to cross until late 2008.

And even if costs exceed estimates, the idea of trying something other than single-payer or the current maze of law and regulation appeals to a public eager to at least try.

When Romney talks about this program, he is able to remind audiences of his association with the Heritage Foundation, his approach to problem solving, his willingness to assign responsibility to privileged elites, and his willingness to innovate. The wonks will thrash out the details over the years, just as they did with welfare reform and education reform, and the libertarians will never acknowledge that this is an area that can be improved upon by mandates of any sort.

But the law will be Exhibit A in Romney's argument that his background has unique advantages for the problems facing the federal government.

"I attacked here by using the same analytical approach I used at Bain & Company and at Bain Capital," he told me about the health care crisis he confronted in Massachusetts. "In fact, I brought the head of the Boston office of Bain & Company, an investment banker from Morgan Stanley, a professor from MIT, some actuaries, and some politically astute folks to look at health care. We worked on it and worked on it and worked on it, and the first process was gathering all the data, finding out who was uninsured, why they were uninsured. There were some huge surprises as we gathered the data."

"Then we analyzed the data," he continued, "and came up with different hypotheses and came away with a conclusion that has never been reached anywhere in the country before and the answer was this: You know what, we can get everybody else insured without spending any more money. Without raising taxes, without any new government program or takeover we can get everyone in this country insured. Now that was the kind of rigorous analysis that you follow and that I followed back in consulting. It's data. It's analysis."

"And then there were different people with different opinions—strong opposing views. We had long battles," he concluded. "I love argument. If I reach a setting where everybody agrees, I will argue. I don't do it purposefully—it's just in my nature. I'll begin arguing the opposing viewpoint. It's the only way that I've ever found to really reach the right conclusions."

The result was not just the right conclusions and a breakthrough legislative approach to a thorny political/public policy problem, but also a superb exhibit for the campaign trail.

Romney's Robed

Since at least the first President Bush's disastrous appointment of David Souter to the United States Supreme Court, social conservatives have focused on the issue of judicial selection as they have never done before. Republican primary voters used to assume that they'd like a Republican president's nominees to the Supreme Court and the crucial federal appellate courts, but no more. Now they listen closely to what the candidates say.

Prior to 2006, Republicans were obliged to say that they'd look for justices and judges in the mold of "Scalia and Thomas." Now they had better say they'd look for justices and judges in the mold of "Roberts and Alito." And even if they say it, it isn't certain they will be believed.

If Rudy runs, this will be his Achilles' heel. Rudy's views on the social issues make this declaration of intent both necessary, but also hard to believe: if Rudy sees nothing wrong with mid- or late-term abortions, why would voters expect his judicial nominees to be originalists on those controversies? In the hunt for judicial nominees, presidents must look for shared values and cannot impose litmus tests. A tin ear on the rights of the unborn is likely to make Rudy tone deaf to other signals of a Souter-like plasticity in a nominee.

Senator McCain brings the baggage of his Gang of 14 deal to every discussion and debate on this subject. Republican activists marched and contributed and elected senators in 2002 and 2004 on the issue of up-or-down votes for all nominees. It was not John McCain's victory to give away, and certainly not because he valued the traditions of the Senate over the Constitution and endorsed the absurd view that judicial nominees require a supermajority of votes to win confirmation.

Against this backdrop, Romney has a record. He never got to appoint a judge to the Massachusetts Supreme Judicial Court (more's the pity given that body's sorry record), but he made six appointments to the crucial appeals courts of the Commonwealth.

In July 2004, Romney nominated Superior Court Judge R. Malcom Graham and Assistant U.S. Attorney Gary Katzmann to the Massachusetts Court of Appeals. In November of 2005 he nominated Ariane Vuono, and three months later Andrew Grainger. In July of 2006 he nominated sitting appellate judge Phillip Rapoza to be the chief justice of the Massachusetts Appeals Court. On November 1, 2006, he appointed William J. Meade to the Appeals Court.

Graham had twenty years on the bench (as well as a brief stint as a Boston Celtic). Katzmann and Vuono were prosecutors, with resumes telegraphing seriousness on the sort of crime issues with which state appeals courts are often consumed. Grainger had been at a public interest law foundation, the New England Legal Foundation, that seeks to preserve free markets and property rights. Meade had served two years on Romney's staff, was editor-in-chief of the state's law review and was counsel to the Massachusetts District Attorney's Association, a non-partisan organization representing all of the state's district attorneys, at the time of his appointment to the appeals bench. Prior to joining Romney's statehouse team, Meade had been chief of the appellate division within the attorney general's criminal bureau.

The new chief justice of the appeals court, Philip Rapoza, was an associate justice there when elevated by Romney, and his career as a prosecutor and jurist was distinguished and varied. He's widely regarded as very smart but also very affable, and as the grandson of Portuguese immigrants. His is the sort of American story that appeals to the public much as Justice Alito's life story did. Mix in some unusual and extraordinary work—Judge Rapoza spent fifteen months as chief administrative judge for a war crimes tribunal established by the United Nations to prosecute human rights violations committed in East Timor during that country's struggle for independence—and you see the outline of a superb appointment.

Romney is adamant that if given the opportunity as president to appoint a justice to the Supreme Court, he will seek out another Roberts or Alito. As a Harvard JD with a track record of appointing experienced jurists, he has credibility on these statements that other would-be nominees must earn, and that some simply won't be able to.

The Big Dig

On July 10, 2006, the Massachusetts Turnpike Authority killed Milena Del Valle.

The MTA didn't intend her death, of course, but when twelve tons of concrete fell from the roof of the "Central Artery/Tunnel Project," the $14 billion-plus public works boondoggle commonly known as

"The Big Dig," the MTA's recklessness and gross mismanagement had killed.

The MTA had long been a cesspool of cronyism and incompetence. Romney's 2002 gubernatorial campaign was waged in part on the need to bring the independent agency under the control of the governor, but the legislature had repeatedly rebuffed his demands. Even when the roof of the tunnel sprang leaks in 2004, the state's old guard, entrenched in the statehouse and on the top court, refused to listen to Romney's urgent demand for change. Romney demanded the resignation of Matthew Amorello, the chairman and CEO of the MTA, and when he refused to resign and the legislature refused to act, Romney appealed to the Supreme Judicial Court to give him the authority to remove Amorello, whom Romney accused of "mismanagement and financial irresponsibility." The court refused to hear the case, and Amorello stayed put.

Then tragedy struck, and suddenly the Massachusetts legislature realized that the Big Dig was no longer merely a source of lucrative contracts that reeked of cronyism and corruption, but a potential public safety nightmare and political sinkhole.

"It's hard to view Monday's catastrophe as an accident," Romney declared after Milena Del Valle's death. Romney immediately sought and received authority from the legislature to conduct a safety audit of the tunnel and $20 million to conduct it. The legislature passed the law on July 14. "I'm happy to take blame if I have responsibility," Romney declared. "I have a great deal of confidence in the team of state leaders and workers to make me feel that I can sleep at night." Romney successfully forced Amorello out two weeks later.

Shortly thereafter, Romney retained an engineering firm to conduct the "stem to stern" safety review, and formed a five-member panel of experts on engineering, transportation, and construction materials to oversee all Big Dig assessments. "We have many challenges ahead," Romney declared, "but I'm confident we have the right team in place to conduct a thorough review."

The Big Dig wasn't fixed by the time Romney left the Massachu-setts statehouse, and it is doubtful whether the audit will ever be completed.

But Romney's response to a tragedy and a public safety crisis illus-trates how he can be expected to act as president when the inevitable crisis arises: to demand authority and to act, but only with the advice of the best experts available on the issue at hand.

The Big Dig is a monument to the worst features of government, and its consequences have been both tragic and wildly expensive. Expect Romney to discuss it early and often on the campaign trail.

The Khatami Declaration

In August of 2006, the Bush administration inexplicably granted a visa to the former president of Iran, Mohammed Khatami, to visit the United States.

Though not the incendiary extremist that his replacement, Mah-moud Ahmadinejad, has revealed himself to be, Khatami presided over the state that armed Hezbollah to the teeth, refused to bring to justice numerous terrorists associated with the Islamic Republic's long record of murder abroad, and suppressed—often violently—peaceful demonstrations against the regime. He was at best impotent against, and much more likely complicit in, the regime's many crimes against civilization. At worst, he was a clever cat's paw for the mullahs who ruled and continue to rule in the most despotic fashion. At the very least, Khatami certainly participated in his government's head-long rush toward nuclear weapons.

When he was invited by a variety of groups to travel to the U.S. and appear in a variety of settings—including the National Cathedral in Washington, D.C., and the campuses of Harvard and the Univer-sity of Virginia—conservatives and human rights activists reacted with shock and disgust. President Bush defended the decision—weakly—in an interview with Paul Gigot of the *Wall Street Journal*, saying he wanted to hear what Khatami had to say.

But not Romney. He quickly denounced Khatami as a terrorist, and announced that his state would deny Khatami and his entourage the usual courtesies that the Commonwealth extended to heads of state, retired heads of state, and the other various dignitaries who travel to Cambridge or the other great institutions of Massachusetts.

This public declaration was a strategic decision on Romney's part, one key message among many that he is serious about the war against Islamist fascism, and unafraid to declare as much.

"I think it's an outrage that in this season of memory of those that lost their lives," he told me in a radio interview on September 6, five days before the fifth anniversary of the attack on America, "that we would be inviting someone who is a terrorist to this country, and that in particular, this person would be invited to Harvard to come speak on the topic of tolerance. It's outrageous, and for that reason, I have instructed our state agencies, and particularly our executive office of public safety not to provide any support whatsoever for his visit. And that means not to provide the escort and security personnel which would normally be associated with a person of interest of this nature. And it may well lead to them reassessing whether they want him to come to Harvard. I certainly hope so."

The denunciation of Khatami had provoked objection that the former president of Iran was a "reformer," and much to be preferred to Ahmadinejad, and perhaps welcomed in America as a result.

"Well, there's no question that he adopted language that some have called a terrorism of moderation," Romney replied to this objection. "But a terrorist is a terrorist. This is a person who during his years in office, almost eight years in office, presided over their nuclear program. He's a person who has described Hezbollah as a shining sun that illuminates the world. He has endorsed Ahmadinejad's call for the annihilation of Israel. He incarcerated thousands of Iranian students who protested their government. This is by no means the kind of voice of moderation that he pretends to be. He is, in effect, the quintessential wolf in sheep's clothing."

The *Boston Globe* was quick to round up critics of Romney's bright-line stance, reporting on September 9:

"That is not the view of most Iran experts," said Kenneth Katzman, a Middle East specialist at the Congressional Research Service, a research arm of Congress. "I think most experts on Iran would say that Khatami attempted to stop many human rights abuses but did not prevail politically."

Shaul Bakhash, professor of Middle East History at George Mason University and a prominent Iran specialist, said Romney's assertion does not "accord with the facts."

"To say Khatami oversaw the arrest and torture implies that he was directly complicit. I don't think anyone believes that's the case," he said. "You might argue that he was not firm enough or that he did not have enough backbone, but it is hard to argue that he was complicit. . . . I don't think the facts really are in dispute."

Michael Rubin, a scholar at the conservative American Enterprise Institute who is a vocal critic of Khatami, also took issue with Romney's characterization.

"What is factually correct is to say he turned a blind eye" to the crackdown, said Rubin, who was in Iran during the July 1999 crackdown. "He didn't oversee it."

What these academics and experts failed to understand is that the American suspicion of the Islamist theocracy runs very deep, and is very justified. Khatami did not disappoint. In his appearance at Harvard's Kennedy School of Government, Khatami was asked a question about the execution of gays in Iran. While noting that the occasions for such penalties were rare, homosexuality was indeed against the law of Islam and Iran. The Charles River crowd did not boo or even stir, stunned perhaps by the inability of the heady air of Cambridge to soften the "reformer's" matter-of-fact assessment of the Islamic Republic's laws.

It was Romney—now assailed as anti-gay—who spotted the menace that airbrushed Islamist fanatics pose to a gullible West. Romney's candor and firmness earned a great deal approval among the part of the conservative base—both religious and realist—that prefers its foreign policy sober and blunt.

"I'm liking Mitt Romney more and more," noted conservative Wizbang blogger Kim Preistap after the Romney declaration, and this sort of reaction was widespread. Romney had used symbolism against the enemy, a deft bit of public diplomacy that Americans serious about the war cheered and would like to see more of. Much more of.

Romney's run as governor of a deep blue state has been marked by a high profile generated by a series of controversies—none of them manufactured, all of them in fact triggered by others than the governor—each one of which cuts deeply into the consciousness of the Republican Party base.

Romney has balanced budgets, battled imperial judges while appointing traditionalist ones, wrestled with ambitious scientists at the edge of ethics, and worked think-tank wonks to push forward provocative experiments in difficult areas of public policy. When a crisis arose, he asked for the authority to tackle it and did so. And when a moment of crucial symbolism arrived, he did not miss the moment or the right call.

There is much more in his four years that will be picked over by the press and of course by his political opponents. But it is a very solid and in some ways unique platform from which to seek the presidency.

The Campaign Ahead

Chapter Eight

Mitt Romney's Advantages

H ere we switch from reporting to analysis, so be forewarned. What follows is this Republican activist's assessment of the particular strengths that Romney's candidacy has going for it over the next year. They are in no particular order.

1. He's not John McCain

It is hard to overstate the deep dislike that Republican Party activists feel for Senator John McCain, though it is mixed with a great deal of admiration for his undeniable courage. I began describing Senator McCain a couple of years ago as a "Great American, lousy senator, and terrible Republican." When I use that line at public events, it is met with spontaneous laughs and applause. It summarizes the widespread assessment of McCain among GOP voters.

What is the source of this feeling?

First, there was the 2000 campaign, with Senator McCain's barely concealed arrogance as well as the fawning way in which the Beltway media—specifically Chris Matthews—greeted his every pronouncement. Republicans generally despise the MSM, and with good reason. The friend of my enemy is not likely to be my friend, and McCain was wildly cheered and encouraged by Beltway bigfoots long associated with attacks not only on Nixon—though there are still plenty of Nixon people around—but especially Reagan. Republican primary voters know that the MSM had enormous contempt for Reagan, for his gifts, and for his accomplishments. That Senator McCain is their darling is a deeply unsettling fact.

To this suspicion is added the legislative record of the senior senator from Arizona which, while generally acceptable to conservatives (McCain has a lifetime American Conservative Union rating of 83 percent), contains within it some astonishingly erratic votes that call into question his commitment to bedrock conservative principles that Republicans believe in like free speech and transparency in campaign finance. His McCain-Feingold campaign finance reform bill not only overthrew strong and legitimate Republican advantages when it came to fund raising, it actually forbade attack ads on television in the sixty days before an election. Most agreed that this was so blatantly unconstitutional that it could be allowed to pass through the Congress and the president's desk en route to the Supreme Court where it would inevitably be struck down.

But the Supreme Court upheld the awful imposition on election season debate even as McCain's baby supercharged the 527 committees that in short order unleashed George Soros and Harold Ickes on the land.

Sadly, McCain wasn't done. He also wanted immigration law to bear his imprint, and he forced through the Judiciary Committee an awful piece of amnesty legislation, dubbed "McCain-Kennedy." This bill could not survive on the Senate's floor, so distant was it from the basic principles of the GOP. McCain could never admit that he had cooperated to force-feed the country a giant amnesty at exactly the wrong time while ignoring the deep-felt demand for fencing to stop the influx of illegal aliens before those already here could be regularized. McCain's championing of this awful thrust toward amnesty burdened him as well with all the anti-center-right rhetoric that attributed racist motives to those opposed to McCain-Kennedy. When seven hundred miles of fencing ended up being the congressional work-product of 2006, McCain's separation not just from the party but from the center of American public opinion was underscored.

But most devastating to McCain's relations with the GOP base has been his relentless rhetorical assault on those who make up that base. The first blast came in Norfolk, Virginia, on February 28, 2000, when McCain announced that "Pat Robertson, Jerry Falwell, and a few Washington leaders of the pro-life movement call me an unacceptable presidential candidate. They distort my pro-life positions and smear the reputations of my supporters."

McCain explained why: "Because I don't pander to them, because I don't ascribe to their failed philosophy that money is our message. I believe in the cause of conservative reform. I believe that because we are right we will prevail in the battle of ideas, unspoiled by the taint of a corrupt campaign finance scheme that works against the very conservative reform of government that is the object of our labors."

It got worse:

They are corrupting influences on religion and politics, and those who practice them in the name of religion or in the name of the Republican Party or in the name of America shame our faith, our party, and our country.

Neither party should be defined by pandering to the outer reaches of American politics and the agents of intolerance, whether they be Louis Farrakhan or Al Sharpton on the left, or Pat Robertson or Jerry Falwell on the right.

Equating Robertson and Falwell with Farrakkan was a pratfall of the worst sort in American politics, and not one which can be easily forgiven by the supporters of either of these preachers, even as they have mended fences with the senator. When McCain lashed out in Norfolk, he hit not only Robertson and Falwell, but hundreds of thousands of like-minded, patriotic, and hardworking Americans who have felt the steady push from elites urging them toward the exits of American politics. Christians who esteem these men concluded then that John McCain hated not just the preachers, but hundreds of thousands of Christian conservatives as well. That's tough to erase.

Perhaps even tougher to erase is the sense that McCain undercut his party on one of its most important goals—the confirmation of good judges to the bench, judges who had been filibustered.

Others can retrace the fine print of McCain's Gang of 14, as well as the reasons why McCain decided to abandon his party on one of its base's most cherished goals: up or down votes on the Senate floor for all judicial nominees.

Explanations and details don't matter. The primary voters will never forget that on a key issue, McCain threw them overboard. It was the issue on which and for which many had marched and sacrificed in 2002 and 2004. Victory was in sight. The votes were there to support a ruling from the chair that would have established the principle that judges needed fifty-one votes, not sixty as the anti-constitutionalists in the Democratic Party demanded, to secure their appointments. Emotions and principles ran high.

And McCain sold out the party for a "deal" with seven Democrats whose price was the sacrifice of some good judicial nominees as the promise of renewed deadlock in the future. McCain just didn't care what the party felt and what the voters had worked for.

For conservative voters to elect John McCain in November 2008, they would have to do what Senator McCain has routinely refused to do: support the party when it matters most.

But to avoid that possibility, many GOP voters will enter 2008 looking to rally to whoever can beat McCain. And that will likely be Mitt Romney.

2. The Calendar Favors Romney

To win the nomination, a presidential candidate has to win early somewhere and build momentum.

Here's the calendar as it likely stands in January 2007:

1. The Iowa Caucuses: Monday, January 14, 2008
2. The New Hampshire Primary: Tuesday, January 22, 2008
3. The South Carolina Primary: Tuesday, January 29, 2008
4. The Michigan Primary: Saturday, February 2, 2008

As of this writing, the Michigan "limited open" primary's move to February 2 seems almost certain to occur, but is not finalized. (California legislators are also considering such a move.) Romney's allies in his home state of Michigan would like to move up the primary (as do the state's Democrats for their own reasons), and the push forward to February 2, 2008, would be a great coup for the Massachusetts governor certain to benefit from the memory of his still fondly remembered father and mother.

This early run of contests favors Romney for a few reasons.

First, of course, is that Iowa favors the organized and the well-funded.

McCain and Rudy may have the money to go with Romney a few rounds, so that will be a wash in the caucus state, but McCain skipped Iowa entirely in 2000, a memory that still rankles some.

And Iowa is home to a built-in base of Romney enthusiasts.

Start with the Mormons. The basic unit of the LDS church is the "ward," comparable to a Catholic parish. Wards are collected into "stakes," again, comparable to a Catholic diocese. There are eight stakes of the LDS in Iowa, which include more than eighty-five wards. Though of course not all Mormons are going to support Romney, the obvious appeal of a first-ever serious Mormon candidate for the presidency will be large.

And in those eighty-five wards will be an incredible not-so-secret weapon—a core of young people who almost always count among their number a vast array of strong personalities and well-regarded and accomplished youth leaders, not to mention experienced missionaries.

Unlike the out-of-state Deaniacs of 2004 who turned off the homegrown Iowans, these Romney volunteers will be from the neighborhoods in which the caucuses will be held, will learn the sites where the caucuses will be held and will deliver not just themselves but their non-Mormon friends and neighbors to the caucuses en masse and do so with a full grasp of the rules and a deep experience in patience that comes from knocking on thousands and thousands of doors during their time as missionaries.

In the 2002 *The New Mormon Challenge*, Carl Mosser put the number of Mormon missionaries in the field at any given moment at 60,000, which would mean approximately 30,000 missionaries return from their work every year. As about half of the LDS population worldwide is in the U.S., that means about 15,000 experienced missionaries return to their homes, jobs, and studies every year. It is not a reach to conclude that the vast majority of these young men (and women) will be enthusiastic about a Romney candidacy, and equipped with exactly the sort of skill sets that make for very effective political volunteers.

A volunteer effort matters much more in a caucus state than in a primary state, because the commitment to attend and perform effectively at a caucus is much deeper than merely filling out an absentee ballot or driving to a polling place for a five-minute exercise of the franchise. You have to find the caucus, know the rules, and stay as long as it takes.

If you have an organizational edge and a devoted, experienced cadre of volunteers, you want the rules as complex and the commitment as high as possible.

Romney didn't write the rules for the Iowa caucuses, but he almost certainly will benefit from them.

On October 19, 2006, the *Boston Globe* reported on an alleged effort by Romney supporters to tap into the BYU alumni network as a means of organizing campaign support. LDS officials were quick to respond to the *Globe* through its director of media relations, Michael R. Otterson, who labeled some of the paper's more overwrought accusations as "nonsense."

"The Church goes to considerable lengths to emphasize to its members the institutional neutrality of the Church on partisan matters."

While Romney's son Josh and two other Utah supporters had paid a courtesy call on one of the LDS's senior figures, Elder Jeffrey Holland, the *Globe's* breathless effort to generate a controversy over what its headlines called the "Mormon plan" fell flat. Utah political consultant Don Stirling had sent out e-mails that characterized the meeting between Holland and the Romney delegation in ways that embarrassed both the Church and Team Romney, and the Commonwealth PAC was obliged to issue a statement saying that "Don Stirling is an old and dear friend of Governor Romney. He got over enthusiastic and overstepped his bounds. The Commonwealth PAC recognizes the political neutrality of the Mormon Church."

A formal attempt to enlist the LDS Church in Iowa or anywhere else would almost certainly be rejected by the Church and would also be incredibly foolish and counterproductive for the Romney campaign, and unnecessary as well. A campaign organization will attract supporters of all sorts, and will not segregate them by religious background. But the Romney campaign will certainly attract hundreds of thousands of Mormons, just as Jack Kennedy's campaign attracted millions of Catholics new to politics. This is a standard feature of American politics, and much to be celebrated. If, for example, Barack Obama is Hillary Clinton's choice for her running mate, as I predicted in my last book, *Painting the Map Red*, African Americans in great numbers will be energized and will work for a Clinton-Obama ticket in far more energized ways than for a ticket without Obama.

Weeks before the *Globe* story, I had asked Romney if he expected a big surge of support from Mormons excited by the prospect of a president from within their own faith.

"I'll look for help from any good red-blooded Americans that I can find, but if I run for a national office I have to get enthusiastic, committed help from a lot broader group than just the tiny slice of Mormons in this country," he replied. "My message is not about faith, it's about the direction of America."

This is the correct answer, of course, but even as John F. Kennedy's 1960 campaign was lifted by the particular energy that Catholics brought to the prospect of seeing the nation's first Catholic president inaugurated, so too will there be considerable excitement among Mormons as Romney's campaign progresses. And while the Mormon population in America is only around six million, the skills and energy level of this group generally are exactly of the sort valued by political campaigns, especially the skills learned on a mission.

If Romney's candidacy taps into even a small percentage of this talent pool, it will provide an extraordinary boost to his caucus performance. McCain might well want to skip Iowa in 2008 as he did in 2000, but this time can't, because the second stop on the primary trail is New Hampshire.

In 2000, John McCain rolled up 115,490 votes in the Granite State to George W. Bush's 72,262, which makes McCain the prohibitive favorite in the 2008 primary there. The MSM will remind voters nationwide over and over again of McCain's triumph in 2000, and even if Iowa has disappointed the "maverick" Republican senator, he'll be expected to score a second win in the Granite State.

Once again, though, Romney will have the Mormon brigades working for him when it comes to organization. Though there are only three stakes and twenty-eight wards in New Hampshire, that will once again be a formidable head start on the plurality he'll need to rack up a second win.

But there is also the Massachusetts effect: in the New Hampshire primary, it helps to be a neighbor.

In 2004, John Kerry benefited from proximity and the Massachusetts senator rolled up 84,377 votes to Vermont's Howard Dean's 57,761.

In 1988, a different Massachusetts governor, Michael Dukakis, smashed Congressman Richard Gephardt's presidential ambitions by crushing him by almost 20,000 votes: 44,112 to 24,513.

And in 1964, Barry Goldwater lost to Massachusetts's former senator and then ambassador to Vietnam Henry Cabot Lodge, even though Lodge couldn't campaign, with Lodge polling 33,007 and Goldwater 20,692.

Did I mention that the Romney summer home is in New Hampshire, on the shore of Lake Winnipesaukee?

Or that Romney's Commonwealth PAC, New Hampshire edition, has fifty-eight members on its board who are veteran Granite State GOP activists led by 2002 GOP candidate for governor Bruce Keough?

Or that Tom Rath signed on as Romney's PAC's "senior advisor"? Adding Tom Rath—"veteran Republican strategist" in the words of Manchester, New Hampshire's *Union Leader*—was an enormous win for Romney as Rath carries great weight in New Hampshire:

Rath, 61, a former state attorney general who has been in private practice since 1980, has become recognized as an expert in political analysis and strategy.

He is also a New Hampshire representative on the Republican National Committee and serves on its rules committee. In that capacity, Rath has been a watchdog against any GOP efforts to challenge or dilute the impact of the state's first-in-the-nation Presidential primary.

McCain has some organization in the state as well, including possibly Senator John Sununu, but the clout of the heavyweights is with Romney.

Given this organization, money, volunteers, and senior leadership with pull in the state, New Hampshire will be a springboard for Romney even if it puts him in second place, and thus the clear alternative to McCain.

In South Carolina Romney's prospects look dim even after the state's very popular U.S. senator Jim DeMint endorsed Romney in early 2007. If the "Mormon issue" will ever matter, it will be there, and the whispering campaign—and possibly even overt anti-Mormon rhetoric—will take its highest toll in the Palmetto State. A rigorous poll commissioned by an organization founded by a Romney supporter, filmmaker Mitch Davis, found that "33 percent of those polled in South Carolina could not vote for a Mormon."

An early display of this came on September 16, 2006, as retold by reporter Lee Bandy in one of South Carolina's leading newspapers, *The State*:

> The quarterly meeting of the S.C. Republican executive committee Sept. 16 ended on a sour note when one of its more prominent members cornered Massachusetts governor Mitt Romney and grilled him about his Mormon faith.
>
> It was not a pretty sight, according to witnesses.
>
> Romney, a possible Republican candidate for president in 2008, was in town to address the state executive committee.
>
> Cyndi Mosteller, chairwoman of the Charleston County Republican Party, one of the largest GOP organizations in the state, came armed with a bunch of material—and questions— about the Mormon church.
>
> The incident only underlines what could become an uncomfortable debate over Romney's faith if he runs for the White House. The issue will be on the table in South Carolina's early

primary contest, where roughly 35 percent of GOP voters are evangelical Christians, many of whom view Mormonism with skepticism.

Mosteller, an evangelical, said she especially was concerned about the church's attitude toward African-Americans and its stand on polygamy....

Mosteller said the issues of race and marriage concern her. She fears they could become campaign issues and hurt Republican chances.

She had planned to ask the questions in an open committee session, but Romney nixed that idea by ending his short address with a final "thank you."

The governor then proceeded to meet with the media for about 15 minutes.

Enter Mosteller.

Sensing trouble, Romney aides hurriedly ushered reporters out the door.

Afterward, Mosteller said the governor did not answer any of her questions. She described the meeting as "very tense."

Cindi Costa, a conservative Christian from Charleston and member of the Republican National Committee, waited outside the room. She earlier pleaded with Mosteller not to confront Romney.

"This makes me sick," Costa said. "Your personal faith is not game in politics. It's a private matter...."

State GOP chairman Katon Dawson isn't pleased either. "She acted in bad taste."

What this account does not tell you is that Cyndi Mosteller is a longtime John McCain supporter, who has been repeatedly identified as a McCain "adviser." Whether or not she got a prompt from other McCain campaign supporters for this preview of the coming anti-Mormon attractions, this very early display of lowball tactics has to be understood as a foreshadowing of the tough go Romney will have in South Carolina.

But so too does this inevitable assault on Romney's faith carry an advantage of sympathy. Anti-Mormon sentiment is a minority point of view. Any overt displays of this animus will produce sympathy in the North and even in other places in the South. Which leaves Romney with a no-lose situation in South Carolina.

And of course if he wins in South Carolina, it is over.

The rest of the calendar is not yet fixed, though it appears almost certain that Michigan, Mitt Romney's birthplace and a state where the Romney name still carries magic, is almost certain to advance its primary to shortly after South Carolina's. No matter which other states move or don't move, Romney's low expectations for South Carolina will diminish any sting there and Romney will still be in the field when Super Tuesday comes around in early March, and his money and organizational advantages will show best on the broad field with only two likely candidates still standing—McCain and Romney.

3. The Camera Favors Romney

The fates aren't fair when it comes to passing out good looks and full heads of hair. Romney has got both. Do they matter? Anyone who says no is lying or has never been in politics.

The camera also favors the Romney family, from Ann to the rest of nineteen sons, daughters-in-law, and grandchildren.

4. Romney Knows Messaging and Media

"You have the right to remain on message."

Romney quotes this bit of wisdom in his memoir of the 2002 Winter Olympics. He also quotes the same sentiment expressed more bluntly by an LDS president chided by a journalist for non-responsiveness: "You get to ask whatever questions you want," he replied. "I get to give whatever answers I want. That's the deal."

That is indeed the deal. Romney, however, seems ever willing to answer any question, which is both a strength and a weakness, and one once shared by likely rival John McCain. In recent years, though, since the Straight Talk Express went off the road, McCain has been notably unwilling to speak with center-right media though he loves the cozy confines of *Hardball* and *Meet the Press*.

Romney, by contrast, goes everywhere and answers most every question except those few which cross boundaries of good taste. Pages 180 to 193 of *Turnaround* are a baker's dozen of concise and excellent pieces of advice on the management of modern media, the sort of guide that can only be written by someone who has been at the center of an extended and frenzied media circus, which is exactly what the Olympics scandal, recovery, and actual Games were. The runs for Senate and later governor of course had their media challenges, but those are minor league compared to a presidential campaign. But the Olympics, especially a scandal-plagued and then post–9/11 Olympics, are as difficult a media obstacle course to run as a presidential contest.

Only Senator McCain among Romney's primary rivals has run the national media gauntlet before. Of course Rudy Giuliani worked the toughest local beat on the planet for eight years, and after the attack on the country was for months thrust into the nation's spotlight as he had never been before.

After 9/11, though, Rudy had a sympathetic media. The presidential press is geared to seek and destroy. That's what they do. That's what makes their careers and pays their book advances. "This is the business we've chosen," says Hyman Roth in *The Godfather: Part II*. Tearing down aspiring presidential candidates is what the Beltway-Manhattan media elite chose to do (unless that candidate is named Hillary or Barack).

Escaping with your political life is the best that can be done under these circumstances, and that is often only the result of simply being the last target focused on. Someone, after all, has to be president.

Managing the crises—real and those contrived by the MSM—and staying unflappable when everyone else is flapping is an enormous advantage.

As is patience—many media storms pass—and persistence in pushing a particular message. One example from *Turnaround* concerned the "sight lines" at the Salt Lake City Delta Center. The Delta Center was home to the figure skating events, typically among the most sought after and expensive tickets in any Winter Games. Unfortunately, as Romney explained, "[a]t the Delta Center, virtually none of the views were superb for figure skating."

How did he and the SLOC team handle this problem of lousy seats at high prices?

[W]e took every measure conceivable to inform the public of the problem. I acknowledged the matter up front to the media. The managers of the Delta Center were actually quite disturbed that I was so critical of their venue, so I tried to make it clear that there was nothing wrong with the building, just something unusual about Olympic-sized ice. Controversy surrounded who had chosen the Delta Center for figure skating in the first place, the SLOC or the International Federation. It helped draw more attention to the problem: exactly what we wanted.

In our ticketing brochure we described the fact that the Delta Center had sight line problems. On our website, a person buying a seat at the Delta Center would see a pop-up window that said "All seats at the Delta Center have partially obstructed views. Do you want to proceed with your purchase anyway?" The person would have to click "Yes, I accept that my seat will have a partially obstructed view." And the person went to pay at the end of a ticketing order, there was another window that popped up: "You have selected seats at the Delta Center. All our seats have partially obstructed views . . . ." We told the public the bad news ourselves, rather than have the media and others think we had pulled a fast one. It would have been just the kind of story the media loves: we are not the open and honest people we pretend to be. We are trying to get people to pay money for bad seats. We covered up; we hid the truth. What a great story.

I never saw a story saying we had been unfair with our Delta Center seating or ticketing. Sure, there were a few public complaints about sight lines, but nothing that implicated anyone for doing something wrong. Tell the bad news first. It won't go away, but it won't have the sting.

There is in this one story an enormous amount of media savvy and experience, as well as a valuable understanding of the press—"just the kind of story the media loves." Romney's additional anecdotes deal with gotcha journalists, local versus national press people, trustworthy versus duplicitous media people.

In short he's had a graduate school education in handling the MSM, broadcast and print variety. And the management of expectations experience will help dramatically as well when debate time comes around.

And here is the last of his old-media advantages.

Not since the last five minutes before the first Reagan debate against Walter Mondale in 1984 has a Republican audience sat down to watch a presidential debate believing they had the advantage. Some Republicans won some debates, as surely as George H. W. Bush did when Michael Dukakis stumbled on the question about the death penalty for his wife's theoretical attacker, and as George W. Bush did in all three debates with Al Gore.

But they were either clear losses or close-run victories, and the latter were never expected, only gratefully celebrated.

Watching the second President Bush debate was perhaps the greatest trial GOP activists had to endure in the campaigns of 2000 and 2004. The president is best in a conversational setting or in a set piece big speech, but not in the contrived settings of presidential debates.

Though Bush "won" at least five of his six debates against Vice President Gore and Senator Kerry, each was a nerve-wracking experience for Republicans, and they would love nothing more than to have at least a strong competitor to bet on going into these fall of '08 matches.

5. Romney Will Get the Cash, and Cash Is King in the Primaries

Which candidate will raise the most money? Though it is impossible to predict with certainty who will win the "cash primary" in the first half of 2007, or the third quarter '07 dollar sweepstakes, we can look at the performance of the Republican leadership PACs through the first half of 2006. As George Washington University's presidential campaign tracking website P2008 explains, such PACs "can generate goodwill by making contributions to candidate and party committees," while also allowing a candidate "to fund travel, build a network of supporters, and demonstrate fund-raising prowess."

And not just fund-raising prowess, but also organizational skill and innovative tactics

"Since July of 2004," the *Boston Globe* reported on June 11, 2006, "Romney has set up affiliates of his political action committee, the Commonwealth PAC, in five states." The paper continued:

> By having donors spread their contributions across the various affiliates, Romney has been able to effectively evade the $5,000-per-donor annual contribution limit that applies to federal committees, which most presidential aspirants set up to build initial support for their candidacies.
>
> The multistate system is helping Romney raise money quickly from relatively few contributors, and foster valuable political relationships around the country. It is also a strategy several potential opponents for the Republican nomination cannot use: Federal office-holders, under new campaign finance rules, are barred from operating such state affiliates.

Rich Bond, a former chairman of the Republican National Committee, told the *Globe* that the Romney innovation was a "brilliant strategy," one that was "fully compliant with the law, yet allows Romney to deploy political assets in a comprehensive fashion."

The five states where *son-of-Commonwealth PAC* PACs have been established by Romney? Arizona, Iowa, Michigan, South Carolina, and New Hampshire.

The precise amount of contributions are difficult to track, but in the first nine months of 2006, Romney's federal PAC had raised $1.6 million compared to John McCain's Straight Talk America PAC, which collected $6.9 million.

But Romney's federal PAC's reporting does not reflect the amounts reported in his state PACs. In Michigan, for example, in the first seven months of 2006, the Michigan affiliate of Commonwealth PAC pulled in $1,018,270. In the second quarter of 2006, Romney's Commonwealth PAC South Carolina banked $236,000.

George Washington University's P2008 project did the work of collecting all the receipts data for all the Leadership PACs at the mid-year mark in 2006. Romney's organizations had banked $4.3 million, McCain's $3.8 million, Frist's $2.8 million, with Rudy Giuliani in fourth place with a total of $1.6 million.

Romney won the money primary for the first half of 2006, and his momentum was just beginning. *Washington Post* blogger-reporter Chris Cillizza has opined that "Romney's Mormon faith will allow him to tap a massive fund-raising source not fully exploited by politicians in the past," and while that is certainly true, it doesn't explain how, for example, on August 17, 2006, Romney raised more than $1 million for the Commonwealth PAC from just under 1,000 guests at the St. Regis Monarch Beach Resort in Laguna Beach, California. The event was attended by almost the entire top tier of the Digital Coast's entrepreneurial elite. This is the rising MBA class, and Romney has huge numbers of supporters among it because of the widespread belief among such upper-management types and their professional counterparts in law and medicine that the political class is increasingly unsophisticated on matters relating to economic growth and technology. For accomplished and very financially successful people like those who filled that particular room, Romney's religion was a marginal consideration because of his resumé and the very distinct sense of momentum that had begun to surround Romney as the fall of 2006 opened.

The Romney campaign opened its drive for the cash to wage a national campaign with an all-day, high-tech telethon from the Boston Convention Center on January 8, 2007. More than 350 volunteers gathered to call potential donors from around the country, and when the day ended, the campaign had amassed more than $7 million in contributions and pledges, an unprecedented one-day display of fund-raising prowess. Notice was immediately served that Campaign 2008 would be very different indeed from past efforts, and that innovation at every level but especially fund-raising would be a hallmark of the Romney effort.

6. The Team, the Technology, and the Blogosphere

Michael Murphy was the senior strategist to John McCain's 2000 presidential bid and, many believed, the key force behind McCain's early success. Murphy was also senior strategist to Mitt Romney's 2002 gubernatorial campaign. He's a founding partner in the D.C. and Sacramento consulting firm, Navigators. From the Navigators' web site:

> Mr. Murphy has been called a "media master" by *Fortune* magazine, the GOP's "hottest media consultant" by *Newsweek*, and the leader of a "new breed" of campaign consultants by *Congressional Quarterly*.
>
> He has advised Republican candidates from the local to presidential level and has handled strategy and media for over 20 successful senatorial and gubernatorial campaigns, including Governor

Jeb Bush, Governor Mitt Romney, Governor John Engler, former governor and former secretary of Health and Human Services Tommy Thompson, former governor and former Environmental Protection Agency administrator Christie Whitman, Governor Dirk Kempthorne, former senator and former secretary of energy Spence Abraham, Senator Lamar Alexander, Senator Jeff Sessions, and many other GOP leaders.

In 2003, he served as a senior strategist on Arnold Schwarzenegger's victorious gubernatorial campaign in California. In 1999 and 2000, he served as senior strategist for Senator John McCain's presidential campaign.

One of the crucial moves of Campaign 2008 was engineered by Mitt Romney in 2002, when he signed Murphy to run his campaign for governor. When Romney inked Murphy in 2002, he took Murphy off McCain's team in 2008.

Murphy is telling everyone who asks that he is sitting out the primary campaign as it will involve two close and valued former clients. But when either Romney or McCain exits the primaries, expect the return of Murphy to the victorious team in some capacity.

In the interim and perhaps for the full campaign, who will run the Romney campaign?

Romney, of course, and a few of the Bainiacs will likely be (even if only unofficially) on board—especially Bain Capital's Bob White and Kem Gardner.

Bob White is the "first friend" and a sort of fellow adventurer with Romney in his various breakouts from the world of high finance and consulting—the 1994 Senate run, the early days at the SLOC, the campaign and transition to governorship. White's easy charm and complete confidence will almost certainly be useful in preventing the sort of internecine warfare that has plagued many recent campaigns.

A Utah real estate magnate and the friend who persuaded Ann Romney to go to work persuading Romney to take on the 2002 Winter

Games, Kem Gardner was co-founder of the Boyer Company, which has developed more than twenty million square feet of real estate projects in the past thirty years. Like White, he brings to the campaign the confidence of the candidate and the real-world experience of initiating and successfully completing many difficult projects. It's the kind of experience that career political consultants can only pretend to possess.

Spencer Zwick will be doing everything for Romney like he has been since he joined the Olympics staff in Salt Lake. "Spencer Zwick had been daily strategist and advisor during the [gubernatorial] campaign," Romney wrote at the close of his Olympic memoir. "We traveled together virtually every day." Zwick, who attended the University of Utah before graduating from BYU, is the former deputy chief of staff in the governor's office who left to become finance director of the Commonwealth PAC and who continues to travel extensively with Romney. At twenty-seven, Zwick has been with Romney every step of the run-up to the presidential race. While not a Rovian figure, he is more a right arm than a personal aide. Zwick has been called a "young Jack Oliver," after the George W. Bush confidant who stunned the political world in 2000 and 2004 by operating the most sophisticated and successful fund-raising operation in presidential history.

As noted above, Romney's cash machine is expected to break the Bush records, and if it does, the credit will go in large part to Zwick's tireless efforts.

Day-to-day management of the campaign will fall to Beth Myers. A veteran of Massachusetts government and politics, Myers was chief of staff for Romney's statehouse office until she left in August of 2006 to become the director at Commonwealth PAC. The mother of two, Myers is a veteran of political campaigns and consulting in both Massachusetts and Texas, but she also spent five years on the staff of former Massachusetts state treasurer Joe Malone. Myers earned high marks in the statehouse for the efficient operation of Romney's office.

Julie Treer and Eric Fehrnstrom were Mitt Romney's spokespeople as governor, with Treer moving over to the Commonwealth PAC in March of 2006 where she took on the additional title of "political director." Both have worked hard to "feed the beast," as Romney described the process of media management in his memoir, and Treer's outreach to center-right pundits during the 2004 Democratic National Convention in Boston was an early indication of the skill she, Fehrnstrom, and some veteran RNC alums will bring to the care and feeding of the Manhattan-Beltway press elite.

Peter Flaherty's solid conservative credentials were mentioned in Chapter Five. His counterpart on the political team is Sally Canfield, a veteran policy wonk with D.C. ties to the Bush administration, including with the 2000 Bush-Cheney campaign, with Tommy Thompson at HHS, and with Tom Ridge for whom she was deputy chief of staff at the Department of Homeland Security in the department's early days. Canfield also has worked for House Speaker Dennis Hastert. Her Rolodex is deep.

The national political organization added A-Team talent when one of the country's finest election law lawyers, Ben Ginsberg, signed on as counsel to Commonwealth PAC. National Media, Inc. contributes Alex Castellanos, Robin Roberts, and Will Feltus, a trio of media professionals that guarantees Romney's message is carefully crafted and professionally placed. Ron Kaufman, a top advisor to the first President Bush, is a senior executive at Dutko Worldwide, one of the Beltway's biggest names in lobbying, and has been busy introducing Romney around the city for years.

The team is there, and with it the technology to manage the modern presidential race, which is heavily weighted to voter identification and turnout. What Bush-Cheney 2004 proved is that the Rove-Mehlman emphasis on turnout of core voters is perhaps the crucial instrument in electioneering in the periods of political normalcy that dominate between the sort of realigning crises such as the Depression,

Pearl Harbor, the seizure of the Americans in our embassy in Tehran, and 9/11.

Identifying and motivating the "base" is a specialized talent, and Romney has brought on board the best in the business presently available to do just that. Given the results of the 2006 vote, the crucial importance of this nuts-and-bolts voter turnout operation has increased in importance. The RNC's past chair, Ken Mehlman, and Arnold's campaign gurus (also Team Bush veterans) Steven Schmidt and Matthew Dowd remain at this writing the three supernovas of the GOP world as yet unaligned with an '08 campaign. If any or all commit to, or even lean noticeably toward Romney, that will be a sign of inevitability.

What Romney has carefully avoided to date is the acknowledgment of a senior foreign affairs advisor in the mold of a Henry Kissinger, Zbigniew Brzezinski, or Condoleezza Rice. He has huddled with experts in a variety of areas, but seems determined not to tie himself to the views of any particular academic or veteran of the foreign affairs community—a shrewd bit of positioning in a political season that will almost certainly focus more than any recent one on the future of America's national security affairs.

The list of experts on the war with whom Romney has met is large and growing, just as his reading in the area is diverse and deep. Asked whom he has met with on the war, Romney cites Generals Casey, Marks, McCaffery, Ralston, and Zinni. He has sat down with Paul Bremer, Henry Kissinger, Bill Kristol, Colin Powell, and Brent Scowcroft. His staff was setting up briefings from Michael Ledeen, Victor Davis Hanson, and others as 2006 came to a close. "I form my own views and opinions from a number of things," Romney told me. He seeks the "perspectives of a lot of different people with different experiences" to combine with "a lot of reading."

Romney's well-known love of books will also be a key advantage for him. When I pressed him on what, exactly, he was reading on the war, he reeled off a list of titles which, while not complete, telegraphs a comprehensive approach: Walid Phares's *Future Jihad*, Michael Gordon and Bernard Trainor's *Cobra II*, Bernard Lewis's *The Assassins*, Fareed Zakaria's *The Future of Democracy*, Lawrence Wright's *The Looming Tower*, Mark Steyn's *America Alone*, and General Anthony Zinni and Tony Koltz's *The Battle for Peace*.

There is a final area of excellence for which the early signs point to a decided Romney advantage, which is in the new media world of cable, talk radio, and the blogosphere.

Romney has always been ready, willing, and very able to meet the broadcast pundits whenever they called. I have interviewed him on air on numerous occasions and know for a fact that he is very good indeed at maintaining energy and pace while avoiding pratfalls and pushing a particular message. He's also been a regular on the cable circuit, and is relaxed and jovial whether it is CNN or FOX News or anywhere in between.

Rudy has begun to make these rounds as well, but not John McCain, whose distrust of talk radio is nearly complete, but which becomes problematic in the setting of a Republican presidential primary season. Rush, Sean, Laura, Bill, Michael, Dennis, and, yes, me, have large and attentive audiences that lean to the right and participate in politics. Giuliani and Romney are already staples on most of these shows, but Senator McCain has made only one very brief appearance on Laura Ingraham's program, and is a regular only on Bill Bennett's. Voters will notice if the Straight Talk Express is actually a local operating between D.C. and the West Side of Manhattan.

On the blogs Romney has an enormous head start, and a lead he is not likely to relinquish.

Visit RomneyForPresident.com for an easy-to-navigate list of the Romney cyber grassroots, and the impressive group of talents there signal a sophisticated if uncoordinated explosion of volunteer partners in the Romney effort. Two examples bear particular mention.

Article6Blog (www.article6blog.com) sprang to life following an accidental interview I conducted with its two proprietors—Lowell

Brown and John Schroeder—at a live broadcast of my radio show. Both were already bloggers and both are center-right conservatives. Lowell is a partner with the Los Angeles office of Foley and Lardner, specializing in health care law, and a member of the LDS. John Schroeder is an environmental health and safety consultant, and a former staff member for Young Life, an evangelical para-church organization dedicated to outreach to teenagers. As two successful professionals from very different religious backgrounds, they have voluntarily begun a blog that focuses almost exclusively on the anti-Mormon sentiment working against Romney's nomination. Both had already been successful bloggers, but they teamed up to produce a single-issue blog that will be of increasing importance as the Romney campaign unfolds. (We'll be taking a closer look at the Article6Blog in the next chapter.)

Similarly, EvangelicalsForMitt.com is a blog by and about evangelical Christians supporting the Romney candidacy. As with Article6Blog, this is a spontaneous effort by web-savvy evangelicals to directly address and rebut the idea that evangelicals can't or won't support Romney. "Evangelicals for Mitt exists because we want a president who shares our political and moral values and priorities, can win in 2008, and can govern effectively thereafter," the site explains. "We believe that the leader of the free world should not only understand, but also articulate why, a values-based governing strategy will result in a more humane, just, and compassionate society. We believe we have found just a person in Mitt Romney, the governor of Massachusetts. He's not just a candidate evangelicals can support—he is the best choice for people of faith. It's not even close. That's why we launched a grassroots effort earlier this year that helped earn him a terrific victory at the first presidential straw poll, and that's why we're starting this web site."

Three web sites do not a blogosphere landslide make, but the Internet activists of the center-right are very aware of genuine as opposed to paid for ("Astroturf") blog support and Romney has it.

And he has the most impressive official online effort yet mounted. At www.MittRomney.com there is a comprehensive set of multimedia links and resources, as well as an easy to use online contribution button—a feature of most campaigns. Most important, there is a continual effort to update the site and distribute through it not just a daily press release, but news of the campaign from various sources, and an almost instant response to any story touching the campaign.

As soon as Senator Frist declared that he would not seek the nomination, Romney hired Stephen Smith, who had been running Frist's elaborate online operation at Frist's PAC, VOLPAC. Smith immediately strengthened the already strong ties with the new media, and began the steady stream of pointers and tips that leave even hostile bloggers impressed and neutral-to-supportive bloggers pleased. By treating the new media like the old media, using access and information, Smith quickly built the same sort of reputation as a respected press spokesman and liason that campaign press secretaries of the past have sometimes enjoyed with the old media.

"Perhaps the clearest indication of Romney's belief in the influence of online information is his hiring of Stephen Smith, 24, formerly web guru for Senate Majority Leader Bill Frist," the *Boston Globe's* Scott Helman noted not long after Smith arrived. "Steve is going to serve as the conduit both from bloggers and the online community, as well as from the campaign to the bloggers and the online community," Helman quoted an unnamed senior campaign official as confirming. "He's building bandwidth between the two," the advisor continued.

The Smith hiring would not be more than window dressing unless the campaign and the candidate actually believed in the importance of the new media. They do, as has already been demonstrated and which has already paid dividends. One example underscores this.

In early January 2007, someone (not pleased with Romney's very good week that featured the huge opening day fund raising success and the endorsement by South Carolina's Jim DeMint) launched a

YouTube attack on Romney, cutting and pasting clips from his 1994 debate with Ted Kennedy, a video designed to bleed Romney with the pro-life community and to paint him as a Kerryesque flip-flopper.

Almost instantly, an interview for podcast with Professor Glenn Reynolds and Dr. Helen Reynolds had been arranged, and the large online reach of www.Instapundit.com was used to disseminate not just a response to the video, but also to showcase Romney's mastery of many subjects and comfort level with the new media. The podcast of the interview with the Reynoldses was—with the Reynoldses' permission—posted on YouTube even before it appeared on the Instapundit site. The key exchanges as far as the life issue was concerned were transcribed by the Romney campaign:

Dr. Helen Smith: So, what is it about this YouTube video from 1994 showing you as a flip-flopper? What is that about?

Governor Romney: Well, I just got a look at the excerpts from my debate against Ted Kennedy in 1994. It reminded me of why I ran against him in the first place. Someone had to give him a run for his money.

Now, it also shows what thirteen years will do. I'm grayer. I'm a little heavier. And I hope I've grown a bit wiser as well.

"Of course, I was wrong on some issues back then. I'm not embarrassed to admit that. I think most of us learn with experience. I know I certainly have.

"If you want to know where I stand, by the way, you don't just have to listen to my words, you can go to look at my record as governor. Frankly, in the bluest of states, facing the most liberal media in the country, I've led the fight to preserve traditional marriage. I've taken every legal step I could conceive of, to prevent same-sex marriage.

I have also taken action to protect the sanctity of life. I vetoed bills that authorized embryo farming, therapeutic cloning, Plan B emergency contraception, and of course a redefinition of when life was going to begin as well.

I've also fought for family. I've promoted abstinence education in the schools.

I fought for English immersion in our schools and school choice. And of course, as you'd expect from a Republican, I've held the line on taxes, and I've worked to re-instate the death penalty.

And I'm proud that at the same time, I've fought discrimination. I believe every American deserves equal opportunity.

Now, that's my record. And maybe that's why people on the other side are dredging up thirteen-year-old history and attacking me now.

Instant attack, instant response, all within the confines of a single news cycle. That is Campaign 2008, and Mitt Romney is willing to live and prosper within the new rules.

7. Room to Maneuver on the War

There is reason for optimism on Iraq, and reason for pessimism as well.

Iraq is just one front in a global war with Islamist extremism, and Afghanistan is not the only other battleground in this vast conflict.

Whether in Somalia, Pakistan, the West Bank, or the increasingly radicalized Muslim communities of France, Great Britain, and other European countries, the virus that is radical Islam spread with a ferocious intensity throughout the '90s, and the long war has barely, in fact, begun.

Our country's greatest enemy at this time is Iran, and the nuclear ambitions of its mullahs pose an existential threat not just to Israel, but perhaps to the rest of civilization as well. (For a sober primer on this subject, consult the chapter on the devastating potential of electro-magnetic pulse-generating weapons in the Center for Security Policy's 2006 book, *War Footing*, edited by Frank Gaffney. It won't take dozens of nukes on intercontinental ballistic missiles to cripple America, just one, and it doesn't even have to land.)

So the war and its conduct will be the central issue of the primaries and the general election that follows.

Every Republican contender is pledged to a vigorous war policy. While John McCain has often slammed the Bush administration on the particulars of the war from troop levels to interrogation policy, Rudy and Romney have been supporters whose differences, if they exist, have been muted.

Like the other two front-runners, Romney has been in both Iraq and Afghanistan and will return during 2007. All three can be expected to try to stay abreast of the developments there and to be able to demonstrate a complete grasp of the intricacies of the Iraq rebuilding as well as of the deep divisions within the country.

Will Romney be able to convey to a country at war and under threat, and one that may have been hit again before the next election, that he has what it takes to be president in this age?

"Right now, I'm really thinking about my grandkids and the country they'll have," he told me. "I'm thinking about national office because I want for my grandkids the kind of prosperity and security that I had. I think I may be able to help do that."

After that declaration, I asked Romney if he had considered what presidents are sometimes called to do, which is order attacks that kill lots of people.

"I don't think anyone who loves this country and is a person of strength and character would shrink at doing whatever it takes to protect America," Romney replied. "America's first responsibility is to keep America safe. America must remain the world's economic and military superpower, and the best friend peace has is a strong America. You can't be strong if you're never willing to exercise that strength and show that strength. By the way, a 150-pound kid has to get in a lot of fights. A 250-pound kid covered with muscles who knows judo rarely has to fight."

"If you have a strong enough military, no one will test you, and I think one of the reasons we face the challenges we do and we're being tested on so many fronts is that people see we haven't done a great job in the post–major conflict period in Iraq," he continued. "We've been tested and have been found a little wanting. I think we need to be stronger. I don't shrink at all from the need to protect this country and our sovereignty and our pre-eminence in the world."

In that response was the beginning of a critique from the right of the size of the American military, though not necessarily of the Bush administration, which, in Donald Rumsfeld's famous phrase, had to go to war with the Army it had. Would a larger American military be required?

"I'd anticipate additional troops being needed," he said, but when I asked for detail—was a three-hundred-ship navy sufficient?—Romney demurred.

"I'll leave it where I am, which is we're going to have to have a military which is unquestionably capable to deal with the challenges that we're going to face in this coming century. A holiday from history, as George Will called it, is something that we can no longer afford."

As president, Romney almost certainly would order up one of his Bain-style strategic audits of the force posture of the American military, one that would go far beyond the mandated Quadrennial Review and that probed exactly what the nation needs in terms of the size of the military for the decades ahead.

And here he may well be the best positioned of all the candidates to assess and then project the genuine military needs for a long war, a process denied to a country first surprised by the savage assault and then moving rapidly through the early stages of the war to destroy the obvious bases for our enemies and cabin the states that could not be directly assaulted.

Congress has ordered that every four years the secretary of defense conduct a comprehensive examination (the "Quadrennial Defense Review") of the national defense strategy, force structure, force modernization plans, infrastructure, budget plan, and other elements of the defense program and policies of the United States with a view toward determining and expressing the defense strategy of the United States and establishing a defense program for the next twenty years. The most recent was completed and released in February 2006.

Republican primary voters and the general electorate are ready for tough talk on an expanded military and especially for the sea power that recent budgets have shorted. Reagan's six-hundred-ship fleet has been cut in half, and the end of the Cold War saw dramatic force structure reductions that have not been reversed even since the hot war exploded on September 11, 2001. The Republican primary campaign can be expected to review this ground extensively, with Senator McCain using his military experience and his record on Iraq to lead a charge for a military build-up.

Romney can not only match this argument but also persuasively argue that the build-up process will be managed more diligently by an outsider than by the combined military-Beltway insider that John McCain has most certainly become over the past two decades. If the nation is going to again ramp up its military, it will be better served, Romney will argue, if that process takes the best of the last thirty years of management thinking and avoids both the McNamara era bean-counting and the often paralyzing deference to brass that some secretaries of defense have been prone to.

Romney has credentials that go to the heart of managing a war complicated far beyond the old strategies, and the necessary energy as well as the independence from the war-generated Beltway rivalries to stake a campaign claim to the skill set necessary to conducting the war.

Because he has not been a D.C. figure in these years when the shock of the attack, the recriminations, and the endless, exhausting assault on the Bush administration have unfolded, Romney begins the primary season with one great advantage: no matter what a voter thinks about the war, he or she cannot blame Romney for it, nor for attacking the president either.

If the country is ready to put the preceding seven years of bitter domestic strife over the war behind it in order to forge a unified approach to the risks and the responses ahead, an outsider will be necessary, but one fully aware of the threat and willing to meet it rather than wait for it behind walls and borders that really cannot be secured.

Those, in a nutshell, are Romney's advantages. There are vulnerabilities as well. And not just of the Mormon variety.

Chapter Nine

The Attack: The "Too Perfect"
Critique—Envy as an Attack Ad

Too smooth. Too rich. Too successful in private enterprise and public service.

Too perfect.

While Mitt Romney's greatest vulnerability during the presidential campaign ahead is his Mormon faith, it may also be the most easily defended after a few rounds of anti-Mormon rhetoric first shock and then appall American voters. Going after the specifics of the LDS faith, or even arguing directly that a Mormon shouldn't be in the White House runs so directly against a deeply ingrained tenet of the American civic faith that Romney opponents will have to view it as a sort of mutually assured political destruction gambit—even if anti-Mormon bigotry would work, the candidate who fired the weapon would surely take himself down with it.

That doesn't mean it won't be used, but it certainly won't pass from the lips of a mainstream candidate. In fact, each of them will sooner or later denounce anti-Mormon bigotry in public settings, perhaps in an early debate when Governor Romney is asked the inevitable inappropriate question. (The Allen-Webb Senate race of

2006 showed us that local media will ask anything if there is a chance of some national attention attached.)

But John McCain is nothing if not relentless. Of course he heroically survived his captivity from 1967 through 1973, one which included harsh conditions and torture. He fought back from his association with the Keating Five scandal, the name given the investigation into allegations of influence peddling following the collapse of Lincoln Savings & Loan whose chairman, Charles Keating, donated heavily to United States senators, some of whom attempted to intervene in the investigations on Keating on his behalf. After his defeat in the 2000 presidential campaign, McCain forced through a campaign finance bill against the opposition of his party and many free speech proponents, and strongly supported the invasion of Iraq, and delivered a key address at the GOP 2004 convention in New York. Despite disastrous mistakes such as the Gang of 14 and the McCain-Kennedy immigration bill in recent years, McCain is raising money at a pace second only to Romney's and was active on the 2006 campaign trail. He won't give up the nomination to Romney and he'll use every tactic available to him that is neither dishonorable nor self-defeating.

The same will be true of every other would-be president, and of the nation's Beltway press bigs who love to level the field and keep the game going. There will be plenty of parties interested in knocking the surging Romney backward. There will be a number of opportunities to do so, and a number of obvious lines of attack.

1. The Ken Doll/Guy Smiley/Game Show Host Gambit

Mitt Romney is handsome, articulate—even eloquent—well tailored, married to an attractive woman, and father to five all-American boys. He's got a thousand stories and an ease with almost everyone, a ready laugh, and an expressive, open face with a touch of gray hair around the temples.

"A little too smooth," one presidential aspirant told me. And that's what they will all say, and perhaps even on the record as the months pass in 2007.

It isn't a political virtue to be seen as envying the success of another, and especially of a rival. But it is a political necessity to diminish the achievements and bring low the very tall. The best way to do so is with humor, and targeting Romney's "perfect package" will be something of a subcategory of election 2008, running alongside conversations about McCain's temper, Brownback's charisma deficit, and Rudy's rough-and-tumble New York past.

The good news for Romney is that one of his thorns as governor has been the *Boston Phoenix,* the city's "alternative" newspaper, which has delighted in jabbing at the governor, and which has done a lot of work in collecting evidence that Romney is far from a "gaffe-free" political superman. In April of 2006, for example, the *Phoenix*'s Adam Reilly even collected Romney's top ten "greatest gaffes" which, while pretty weak beer, nevertheless remind everyone that no one is "perfect" in politics. The Number One Gaffe? "After the Boston Red Sox win the 2004 World Series, Romney decides to personally dismantle the REVERSE THE CURSE sign hanging from a bridge over Storrow Drive. In the course of his labors, the governor causes a massive traffic jam and gives himself a nasty bump on the head." (The *Phoenix* added that "Romney's stumblebum ways are kind of endearing," which makes these sorts of gaffes potential material to be used by Romney, not avoided.)

Even with a track record of useful errors designed to shrink an outsized reputation to manageable size, the Romney resumé still may be more than a little off-putting to middle-class small businessmen and struggling workers. It will not be a direct attack, because envy, though widespread, is nevertheless not a virtue. But it is a subject fit for a murmur campaign, background noise for more direct lines of attack.

2. Vietnam

Mitt Romney didn't go. I asked him about this.

"I respect enormously the people who do serve our country and did serve our country," he began. "I think there are only two things that Ann and I both agree that we regret. One is not having served in the military, and the other is not having had more kids."

"In my life at that time I didn't get drafted," he continued. "I was eligible for the draft. I would have served in the military if drafted, but I wasn't drafted. My course was a different course, and perhaps because of the fact that I did not serve in the military I have a strong sense of a desire to serve in the public sector today. It led me in some ways to go to the Olympics, led me to run for governor, and it may well lead me to run for another office in the future. Each person's life course is a little different, and mine did not include the military experience. I can only say that for those like Senator McCain and others who serve and have served, I salute and honor their service and recognize that their sacrifice is what has kept me and my family free."

The specifics about his draft status?

"Well during the time that I was a student I received a student deferment and then when my church called me to go on a mission, I received a missionary deferment and then when I returned home at some point, and I don't recall exactly when it was, these deferments were no longer applicable," he responded. "They didn't have further student deferments or my status didn't suggest deferment, and therefore I went into the pool of those who were eligible for the draft. I don't recall which year that was—my memory is a little fuzzy—but there was a nationwide lottery of birthdates. If my memory is correct, my lottery number was 300, and so when they got to that number I would be drafted. I don't think they got quite there. I think they got to somewhere around 250-something but these are now distant memories from early 1970s. At the time that I went into this pool—well I don't recall whether I was married or about to get married. It's been just so long I don't recall when that was done."

"There is no question," Romney concluded. "Those that served we owe a great debt of gratitude to."

Romney had a combination of deferments—a religious deferment covered his two and a half years of missionary work in France, which began after his freshman year at Stanford when he was nineteen, and then the college deferment applied upon his return until most deferments were sacked in favor of a lottery, which when it came along in 1969 awarded Romney's March 12 birthday the number 300.

"I wasn't drafted" is a straightforward answer which will either satisfy or it won't. There will be no Clintonesque contortions about how the draft was evaded or interrogations of National Guard records as with President Bush's Texas Air National Guard. The LDS mission to France happened, as did the 1969 lottery, and most men who were young in the era of the draft can recall their number with perfect ease.

Like McCain and Romney, Rudy Giuliani is part of the Vietnam generation, graduating from Manhattan College at the time of the draft in 1965. He immediately entered NYU Law School, and following a clerkship after graduation from there, became an assistant United States attorney.

McCain's service and heroic survival will throw the backgrounds of each candidate into the spotlight, much as it did George W. Bush's in 2000. But absent dishonorable avoidance, Republican primary voters are not going to vote against a candidate because he did not enlist in the military during Vietnam.

3. Wealth

The chairman of the Massachusetts State Democratic Party, Phil Johnston, pegged Mitt Romney's net worth as between $500 million and $600 million in an interview he gave to MSNBC when the spotlight first began to turn to Romney in the run-up to the GOP national convention, "on the same level as Teresa Heinz Kerry's." Johnston neglected to note that Romney had made his money, not married or inherited it. And Johnston may have missed by a factor of 100 percent the true size of Romney's holdings, which many observers estimate as in excess of a billion dollars.

A half billion or a billion, it doesn't really matter. If elected, Mitt Romney would be the wealthiest president in American history—by a lot.

He would also easily be the president who had made the most money during his business career, though George Washington was an assiduous accumulator of land, and at the time of the first president's death was widely believed to be among the ten wealthiest men in the young country.

It has been Romney's practice to release some financial data, but not his tax returns.

"When I ran for governor," Romney explained to me about his charitable practices, "we summarized and they wanted to know what my charitable contributions had been and we summarized my charitable contributions. I don't think it's a dollar amount but as a percentage of my gross income."

Romney has always tithed—given 10 percent of his and his wife's income to the LDS Church—which would mean some very large checks to the Church from the Romneys. And the tax returns would reveal some very large payments to the feds and the Commonwealth. But they would also allow Democrats to guess at the impact of income tax rate cuts on Romney's own bottom line, as well as his family's interest in related matters like the estate tax.

Would his refusal to release his returns fly in a national campaign, I asked him?

"I don't know."

Could he be moved off that position?

"Probably not."

We will see. John Kerry successfully beat back demands that his complete military service records be released during Campaign 2004, even after assuring Tim Russert on *Meet the Press* that it had been and would be done. Kerry, though, was a darling of the MSM and benefited as well from the obscurity of the records being sought and the complexity of the release process.

Most Americans understand tax returns, and they understand itemization of deductions. What is unclear is whether the idea of privacy as to financial holdings trumps public curiosity fueled by a tabloid media in partnership with agenda journalists looking to knock Romney backwards.

One tactic is the blanket and never-to-be-departed-from declaration along the lines of: "It isn't your business or the public's business to know how much I make or anyone else makes. It is the public's right to know if I have conflicts, and I don't and I won't. My holdings have been in a blind trust since before I became governor. They will remain there until after I have finished my term in office if elected. And I sincerely hope the managers are doing a fine job of investing in America's growth which I intend to steward."

Romney will also be able to note that he took no salary as the head of the Olympics, and that he passed on his annual $135,000 salary as governor, but as with his great success in the marketplace, his willingness to forgo pay may strike some folks as an occasion for envy, not for appreciation.

This is uncharted territory in modern American politics. When the Roosevelt money occupied the White House, and later the Kennedy fortune, there was no culture of disclosure, and a sense of privacy that still surrounded the First Family's finances (as well as many other things such as health and non-marital intimacies). Keeping the public guessing will of course spotlight the enormous success Romney has enjoyed by dint of his own efforts, but it will also invite suspicion and certainly envy. It will not, however, be the greatest of his vulnerabilities.

4. Nearly 200 Captured Castles

I asked a former associate of Romney's from the Bain Capital days how many companies Bain Capital had purchased in the years of

Romney's leadership there. Off the top of his head came the answer of between 160 and 200.

That's a lot of companies, a lot of stories, a lot of potential disgruntled ax-grinders waiting to be asked for their view of the Bain way.

This happened to Romney in the course of the 1994 Senate run against Ted Kennedy. "US Senator Edward M. Kennedy of Massachusetts hired detectives to scrutinize Romney's past during the 1994 Senate race, in which Romney, a former venture capitalist, gave Kennedy his most vigorous challenge in his long career in Washington," the *Boston Globe* reported on December 30, 2005. "The effort unearthed information that badly damaged Romney during the campaign: namely, that his venture capital firm had acquired an Indiana paper goods factory called Ampad Corp., fired more than 250 workers, and then rehired them at lower wages, leading to charges from the Kennedy camp that Romney was anti-labor."

Why was the *Globe* writing about the 1994 Senate campaign more than a decade later, and even after Romney had declared he would not be running for re-election? Because earlier that month, the *Globe* reported, "virtually every agency in state government received public records requests" for "any and all records of communication involving Willard [Mitt] Romney dating to 1947, the year of his birth." "The letters, each dated Dec. 7," the *Globe* added, "are signed by Shauna Daly, who only provided a post office box in Washington, D.C., as her address." Daly was the deputy research director for the Democratic National Committee. The opposition research version of the "Big Dig" had begun.

It will eventually get to every company bought, sold, or invested in by Bain Capital during Romney's tenure there, and perhaps afterwards as well. Americans have a vague idea about corporate turnarounds, and after the famed *Barbarians at the Gate* years as well as financial and corporate scandals from BCCI to Enron to Conrad Black and far beyond, the voting public will be interested in tales told out of school by long-ago pushed aside CEOs and COOs, laid off workers and disappointed investors.

It is a target-rich environment, and one which does not seem to have received much attention from Team Romney. One confidant of the governor seemed to dismiss the idea that anything new would be found if it hadn't turned up, like AmPad, in either the 1994 or 2002 campaigns.

There was nothing—in 1994 or 2002—like the decentralized intelligence collection and distribution network that exists today. If Romney is the nominee, expect the bloggers of the Left, assisted by the DNC and of course Romney's Democratic opponent and some 527s, to dig up the name of every company with which Romney has ever been associated and to throw the names into the political waters like so much chum. Whatever is there to be learned will be, and quite a lot of fiction will be thrown up as well as fact.

Justice Clarence Thomas had undergone at least two full field FBI background investigations and Senate confirmations before his nomination to the United States Supreme Court without a hint of controversy. When the stakes got that high, the Left "discovered" Anita Hill.

Once the big show gets under way, literally tens of thousands of amateur and not-so-amateur sleuths will begin the search and destroy mission aimed at Mitt Romney's reputation.

Each one of the 160 to 200 companies that Bain Capital took over is the modern equivalent of a captured castle. Some in each of the castles might have welcomed the arrival of the new baron and his team. Some might have pretended to. And some no doubt got thrown over the walls.

Everyone is still out there, and there's nothing more certain to draw attention to an old grievance than the new status of a participant in the brawl.

The Swift Boat Veterans for Truth, I pointed out to Romney's friend, had never stirred through all of John Kerry's previous campaigns. But once he got close to the presidency, not only did they find new ambition to tell their story, the resources arrived to allow them to do so.

It seems likely that Romney's Bain-imprinted emphasis on data and analysis will result in some pre-emptive work here. I fully expect that Team Romney will be the first to the hunt for the dossiers of every company touched or even passed by during Romney's tenure at Bain Capital. I also expect that a feature of the Romney web site will chart this list, and provide a case history for each company before or since, as well as a Romney commentary on each transaction so that no member of the media will be able to escape a charge of bias if Romney's view of the company's fortunes is not at least recounted if not credited in the course of reporting generated by opposition research. "Hang a lantern on your problem," is an old saying in politics, and it was practiced by Romney at the 2002 Games as with the seating sight lines at the Delta Center. Expect no less with each and every potential political vulnerability. "We tried to stay ahead of potentially damaging stories by disclosing problems up front," Romney wrote in his Olympics memoir. If he follows his own past practice, the media will know a lot more about the companies Bain Capital invested in before the Democrats (or Romney's primary opponents) do.

These are the major vulnerabilities outside of Romney's LDS faith that are obvious as 2006 closed. None are disqualifying, and none seem particularly more significant than those that Rudy Giuliani brings to the primaries (and certainly nothing remotely approaching the huge chasm that separates John McCain from the deep GOP base).

Each can be dealt with, but only if the "Mormon problem" is solved first.

Chapter Ten

Mitt Romney's Got a Mormon Problem (and So Does a Lot of the Country)

Mitt Romney is a member of the Church of Jesus Christ of Latter-day Saints ("LDS," "Mormons," or "Saints,") and not just a member, but a strong believer in the scriptures, teachings and doctrines of the LDS. "I'm very proud of my faith and love my faith and do my best to follow it and certainly believe it," Romney told me after I recounted to him writer Christopher Hitchens' skepticism that anyone as intelligent as Romney could believe in the doctrines of the Church of Jesus Christ of Latter-day Saints.

Romney was—as are many young LDS men at about the age of eighteen or nineteen—a missionary for the Saints, to France. His "call" lasted two and a half years, ending in late 1968, and took him throughout the country. He spent many months in cramped and uncomfortable living quarters with three other young missionaries, using the primitive communal plumbing and taking one shower a week at the public baths. ("That cost money," he explained, and LDS missionaries at that time were limited to a budget of $100 a month, no matter how much money the missionary or his family would otherwise be willing to spend.) For five months, he recalled, he knocked on every door in Le Harve and doubts if he got invited to enter more than one or two.

The number of converts Romney helped lead into the LDS fold? "No more than a handful," he concedes. Romney has retained his French, and if elected will join Thomas Jefferson among the very small number of American presidents fluent in that language.

Romney almost didn't survive his mission. In 1968, he was driving when, heading into a turn, a car headed the opposite way crossed into his lane and collided at a high speed with Romney's car. The passenger next to him was killed, and Romney thrown from the vehicle unconscious. His parents were notified of his death, which George Romney refused to believe.

Romney did survive, and came back stateside to resume his undergraduate studies at Brigham Young University, transferring from Stanford where he had spent his freshman year. After graduating BYU, Romney earned a joint degree from Harvard's Business and Law Schools, and then stayed in the Boston area to pursue a consulting career at Bain and Company.

Throughout his years on the Charles River, and then after his move to the Boston suburb of Belmont, Romney gladly performed his duties as a faithful member of his church. He first became involved in his local LDS "ward," and eventually rose to serve a term as "bishop" of his ward. Later, he became a leader in the "stake," which is an assemblage of a handful of wards, usually between five and a dozen.

The LDS Church is a layman's church, administered at every level except the very highest by men who do so not as full-time clerics embarked upon careers (as say Catholic priests, Presbyterian pastors, or Jewish rabbis are), but as volunteers who keep their day jobs throughout the duration of their church duties. Mitt Romney has graduated through all the various levels of those duties, just as he was confirmed at the appropriate time to the two levels of "priesthood" all Mormon men attain if they keep the precepts of their faith.

Romney's highest position within his church has been as president of a stake, which is a senior position at the regional level of church hierarchy. The Boston stake he oversaw for a time included ten wards and approximately 3,000 members.

Romney holds a "temple recommend," which means his life and his practice of the LDS faith meet the high standards the Saints require of their members who wish to worship at one of the church's temples.

Mormon temples are not open to "gentiles" (the church's term for all non-Mormons) or even to Mormons who have failed in some aspect of their faith and have not yet been restored to good standing by the bishop of their stake. (Prior to consecration, however, newly constructed temples are open to the public, and I have toured one—the Newport Beach Temple in California, which was consecrated in 2005.)

As president of a stake and bishop of a ward, Mitt Romney has had hundreds if not thousands of conversations with Mormons about the practice of their faith and their suitability for a temple recommend. He has heard many, many confessions of shortcomings and sin, and he has counseled and extended both the Church's forgiveness and discipline for those who have fallen short. The practice of Mormon confession and forgiveness falls somewhere between the non-personal Protestant practice and the detailed and routine visits to the confessional undertaken by orthodox Catholics.

"[Y]ou are responsible for interviewing people and determining whether they are ready to take the next step religiously—whether it's a person who wants to become baptized, whether he or she has confessed and made themselves ready for baptism, whether it's a couple interested in going to the Temple to perhaps be married there, whether they have made sufficient commitments to each other, and whether they have repented their transgressions. And so, in some respects, you wear those responsibilities," Romney explained to me. "In our faith, people would only feel a need to confess major transgressions and to ask for a path for forgiveness and for repentance and the Church gives you guidance as to how to respond to that but that's something that I had responsibility for," he added.

Was it a challenging role to serve?

"It's an extraordinarily humbling role to be in a position helping counsel other individuals about how to strengthen their marriage, how to bring a child back who may have gotten involved in drugs or other problems, how to turn around their own life. Many of the discussions relate to employment: people who have lost jobs and who are trying to get back into the workforce; people who have spent too much money, and they're now bankrupt or in dire straits. In that responsibility I was charged with providing Church funds to people who were in need, and you have to be careful to avoid those who are trying to take advantage of the Church and take its money but also to help people who really need help. And so I was responsible for distributing thousands upon thousands of dollars on a regular basis to people who were in need."

Mitt Romney is manifestly not what Hitchens concluded, "Sort of more like culturally a Mormon than he is religiously one. And he's been, I think, quite clever about it."

Wrong.

"Look," Romney told me when I raised the issue of belief in the founding narrative of the Mormon faith, "I believe my faith. I love my faith, and I would in no way, shape, or form try to distance myself from my faith or the fundamental beliefs of my faith."

"But what I can say is this," he added. "To understand my faith, people should look at me and my home and how we live. Of course, doctrines and theology are different, church to church, but what my church teaches is evidenced by what I have become and what my family has become. I am a better person than what I would have been. I am far from perfect and if you spend some time looking into my present and past, you'll find I'm no saint. I have my own weaknesses as did my dad. We're not about to be taken into Heaven for our righteousness. But we're better people—I'm a better person, my kids are better people—than we would have been without our faith. So judge my faith not by how different the theology may be on one point or another, but whether it made me and my family and perhaps others in my faith better people."

Mitt Romney married Ann Davies in the temple in Salt Lake City on March 22, 1969, a ceremony that in the LDS understanding "seals" them as man and wife for eternity. Ann, a convert, could not have her mother or father attend this ceremony because, as noted, entrance to a consecrated temple is strictly limited to Mormons holding their temple permits. This rule applies even for the wedding day, though some Mormon brides from gentile families will hold a second ceremony, before or after the Temple consecration, which is what the Romneys did in the Davies' home before flying to Salt Lake City for the Temple wedding and then on to Hawaii for their honeymoon.

One condition for receiving and maintaining a "temple recommend" is compliance with the church's teaching concerning the tithe: a faithful member of the church must give one-tenth of all his income to the church. There is no doubt that this is a big number for Romney. There is also no doubt Romney has paid it. "You have to tithe, right, to be the stake president?" I asked. "Oh, of course," was the unequivocal answer. Always? "Yes."

All five of the Romneys' sons—Tagg, Matt, Josh, Ben, and Craig—attended BYU. All five went on a mission for the Church. All are married, and all five have been married to Mormon wives in Mormon Temples.

"I love my faith," Romney told me. "I am proud of my church."

Mitt Romney's sincere devotion to the LDS faith should not surprise any student of Romney's family history. Romney's father, former Michigan governor George Romney, was born in Mexico, the great-grandson of Miles Romney. Miles was an Englishman who had converted to the LDS faith in 1837, then emigrated to Nauvoo, Illinois, to join Joseph Smith, founder of the LDS, only to migrate with Brigham Young to Utah after Smith's assassination.

Miles's son, another Miles, also made the "great trek" from Illinois to Utah on foot, and settled with his family first in St. George, Utah, and then in St. Johns, Arizona.

The younger Miles was a polygamist ("four-wived" is how George Romney biographer D. Duane Angel put it) who left the United States for Mexico in 1885 when the Church came under the heavy hand of the federal government in the ultimately successful campaign to oblige the Saints to forsake polygamy. One of his sons was Gaskell Romney, Mitt's grandfather.

Gaskell might never have left Mexico but for the political upheavals then coursing through Mexico. Various factions clashed violently all through the country, with counter-revolution following revolution. The violence grew closer to the Mormon settlement of about 4,000 along the Casas Grandes River, about 150 miles south of the U.S.-Mexican border.

In late July 1912, the Mormons of Mexico began a near complete evacuation to Texas. The future governor of Michigan was five when his suddenly impoverished family returned to the U.S., and made first for Los Angeles, and then after a few years, returned to Utah and Salt Lake City in 1916. George Romney grew up in Salt Lake City, one of the "first displaced persons of the twentieth century" as he put it.

Faith can be passed from father to son, of course, but when that faith has been upheld against persecution and treasured even through very difficult times, it becomes even more deeply ingrained in a family. There may be descendants of Miles and Gaskell Romney who have abandoned the beliefs that their earlier generations sacrificed so much for, but it is much easier to predict fidelity than apostasy from such a history. And not just fidelity, but a deep sense that it was the faith that brought the family through. Among Mormons generally there is this sense that the persecutions and tribulations of their early years mark their faith as divinely ordained.

So Mitt Romney is a thorough-going Mormon. What exactly does that mean, and why is it a problem for some Americans?

And it is indeed a problem. "I don't believe that conservative Christians in large numbers will vote for a Mormon but that remains to be seen," Dr. James Dobson—perhaps the most influential Christian conservative in the U.S. who doesn't hold elective office—told radio host Laura Ingraham in early October 2006.

Many perils await a non-Mormon writer setting out to describe the particulars of the Mormon faith, just as there are for non-Catholics intent on describing the teachings of Rome, or of a non-Muslim in recounting the essentials of Islam.

The good news for me and for Mormons used to seeing their beliefs poorly if unintentionally mangled in non-Mormon media is that this book does not have to set so high a goal. Rather, an outline of the essentials of Mormon belief, and of the essentials of anti-Mormon assertion as to what Mormons believe, will serve.

The former is not difficult thanks to Rex Lee.

The late Rex Lee was one of the country's finest lawyers, one-time dean of the J. Reuben Clark Law School at BYU and later president of the entire university. For four years, from 1981 to 1985, Lee was the solicitor general of the United States. The so-called "Tenth Justice" as the "SG" is often called, is in charge of all arguments made on behalf of the United States before the United States Supreme Court, and frequently appears in morning coat to make those arguments in person.

I got to know Rex Lee when I was a young special assistant to Attorneys General William French Smith and Edwin Meese. Lee briefed the senior staff of the Department of Justice on the cases pending before the Supreme Court, and on the department's legal strategy concerning those cases.

"You've got to be able to count to five," Lee would almost always begin, to the smiles of the special assistants grouped along the wall of the AG's vast conference room on the fifth floor. Lee's "rule of five" was often invoked as a defense to the charge he was too cautious in bringing challenges to Warren Court–era precedents. (I was once called upon, in my capacity as former ghostwriter for Richard Nixon, to arbitrate between Smith and Lee on whether it was appropriate to split infinitives in briefs. I sided with Lee against my boss; the two of us agreed that whatever read better worked better, and sometimes that meant it was best to boldly fracture an infinitive. The patrician and very old-school Smith demurred, but not without some grumbling.)

In 1992, then BYU president Lee wrote a book called *What Do Mormons Believe?* It is brief, and its 116 pages don't pretend to provide anything like a comprehensive guide to Mormon theology. But its first chapter is an excellent summary of the Church's origins as the Church understands them.

"The central message of Mormonism is that there has been a restoration of the church and gospel of Jesus Christ," Lee begins. "Now what does that mean? Basically, it means that the church—the organization, its authority, and its ordinances—established by Jesus Christ during his earthly ministry has once again been brought back to earth." After a few pages, Lee explains how this came to occur:

> The key figure in the Restoration—the person through whom the Lord worked to bring it about—was the first of the modern prophets, Joseph Smith, Jr.
>
> The first event occurred in the spring of 1820, when Joseph Smith was fourteen. In response to young Joseph's earnest prayer concerning which of the many sects he should join, our Heavenly Father and his Son, Jesus Christ, appeared to him. Part of that visitation included this specific message: He should join none of the churches, because none was true. But Joseph was told that if he remained worthy, God himself would one day restore through him the true teachings, church organization, and priesthood authority of Jesus Christ.
>
> Following that initial vision in 1820, the Prophet Joseph Smith had a series of other visits from heavenly messengers, each

with a specific purpose and message. The three most important of the experiences are these:

(1) Joseph Smith received a series of annual visits from an angel named Moroni. Fourteen hundred years earlier, Moroni had been the last custodian of the records of a people who had inhabited the American continents. The records, which Moroni and his predecessors had kept on metal plates, were religious in nature, like the Bible, consisting mainly of revelations from God to his prophets. They also contained, however, historical data and descriptions of how the people had lived and how they governed themselves.

As a resurrected being, Moroni appeared to Joseph Smith and showed him the site of a set of records on gold plates that Joseph would one day translate. At least once a year from 1823 to 1827, Moroni met Joseph Smith at the site, and in his final visit, the angel delivered the set of plates to him. The records that Moroni delivered were principally a compilation prepared by his father of all their people's records. His father's name was Mormon, and the set of metal plates that Moroni gave to Joseph Smith and that Joseph later translated by the inscription of God bore the title the Book of Mormon, because Mormon was the principle compiler.

(2) During the course of translating the Book of Mormon, Joseph Smith and his scribe, Oliver Cowdery, learned of the importance of baptism. The Book of Mormon (as does the New Testament) frequently mentions baptism as an ordinance involving water, necessary for membership in the Lord's church and for forgiveness of sins. Near the Susquehanna River, on May 15, 1829, the two inquired of the Lord concerning baptism. In response, they were visited by John the Baptist, the New Testament prophet. He laid his hands on their heads and conferred upon them the Aaronic Priesthood, which carries with it the authority to baptize. Following this ordination, and acting pursuant to John the Baptist's instructions, Joseph and

Oliver baptized one another, wading into the river and entirely immersing each other in the water.

The Aaronic Priesthood was the authority by which Aaron and his sons and the tribe of Levi administered the law of Moses, as described in the Old Testament. This priesthood, however, did not have the authority to perform the full range of priesthood ordinances or fully govern the church established by Jesus Christ. In that sense, it was, and is, a "lesser" priesthood.

(3) Shortly after the visit of John the Baptist, a priesthood of greater authority, the Melchizedek Priesthood, was restored to Joseph Smith and Oliver Cowdery by the three presiding New Testament apostles, Peter, James and John. This priesthood contains the authority of the apostleship; thus Joseph Smith and Oliver Cowdery became the first modern-day apostles. The Melchizedek Priesthood bears the power to do what the Lord described to Peter: "Whatsoever ye shall bind on earth shall be bound in heaven: and whatsoever ye shall loose on earth shall be loosed in heaven." (Matthew 18:18.) The restoration of these two priesthoods brought to the earth once again the power to act in the name of, and on behalf of, Savior himself.

With this authority, and after a commandment to do so by the Lord, on April 6, 1830, Joseph Smith and Oliver Cowdery organized The Church of Jesus Christ of Latter-day Saints (nicknamed the Mormon Church).

That is Lee's faithful rendering of the founding account of Joseph Smith, but LDS teaching and scripture is not limited to that account. The scriptures of the LDS include the Old and New Testaments— the latter is a King James version with some editing done by Joseph Smith that makes them unique—as well as the Book of Mormon, "The Pearl of Great Price," and the Doctrine and Covenants, which are compilations of crucial teachings of the LDS prophets, beginning with Joseph Smith.

In their well-researched and respected book, *Mormon America*, Richard and Joan Ostling detail how Mormon theology differs from that of orthodox Christianity. They place particular emphasis on the LDS understanding of God and of mankind's potential, which spring primarily from a famous 1844 address by Joseph Smith known as the "King Follett Discourse." From the Ostlings' account:

> The most radical chasm between Mormon belief and the ortho-dox Judeo-Christian tradition centers on the doctrine of God. This is the great divide.
>
> "I am going to tell you how God came to be God," declared Joseph Smith in his "King Follett Discourse" of 1844, the theo-logical culmination of his career. "God himself was once as we are now, and is an exalted man.... If you were to see him to-day, you would see him like a man in form—like yourselves, in all the per-son, image, and very form as man.... We have imagined and sup-posed God was God from all eternity. I will refute that idea, and will take away and do away that veil, so that you may see.... The mind or the intelligence which man possesses is coequal with God himself.... Intelligence is eternal and exists upon a self-existent principle."
>
> Joseph Smith's theology of God is summed up in an oft-quoted couplet by the fifth president of the LDS Church, Lorenzo Snow: "As man is, God once was. As God is, man might be."

In 1905, B. H. Roberts, a member of the LDS "First Council of the Seventy" (who was once elected as Utah's congressman but denied his seat in the House because he was a polygamist), discussed the specifics of Mormon beliefs with a Jesuit priest. Roberts's words in this exchange form a handy summary of the key differences which separate Mormons from Catholics and Protestants alike. The Ostlings quote him:

First, we believe that God is a being with a body in the form like man's; that he possesses body; parts and passions; that in a word, God is an exalted, perfected man.

Second, we believe in a plurality of Gods.

Third, we believe that somewhere and in some time in the ages to come, through development, through enlargement, through purification until perfection is attained, man at last may become like God—a God.

In summary fashion, this is a list of the crucial theological divides between Mormons and most Christians in America.

Perhaps because Mormons are close at hand, and perhaps because of the historical and deep-seated antipathy to them dating from the second half of the nineteenth century before the Church rejected polygamy, some corners of American Christianity have nurtured a particular focus on anti-Mormon argument. In front of me on my desk are some examples: *The Mormon Conspiracy*, *Reasoning from the Scriptures with the Mormons*, and *The 10 Most Important Things You Can Say to a Mormon* are just three of dozens of titles in this crowded corner of the Christian publishing world.

When I first came upon this literature, I was astounded that of all the religions in the world, Christians have dedicated this much hostility towards Mormonism. In my 1996 interview with Elder Neal Maxwell, an Apostle of the LDS—then one of the "Quorum of the Twelve" which governs the church along with the prophet and his two counselors in the "First Presidency"—I raised the issue:

Hugh Hewitt: I told a number of friends I was coming over to visit you and chat in connection with this show ["Searching for God in America"], and my evangelical friends—a few of them— came forward with book after book.

Neal Maxwell: Anti-Mormon literature.

Hugh Hewitt: You bet! I've got a basketful of it back at the house. Why that level of hostility?

Neal Maxwell: Part of it, to give them the benefit of the doubt, occurs because they don't think we're Christians. They use definition as a way of creating exclusion. So our not being Christians, in their eyes, bothers some of them. This creates a plethora of anti-Mormon literature. Interestingly enough, the names Jesus and Christ appear in the formal names of the Church. The Book of Mormon is "another testament of Jesus Christ." We see him as the Light of the World. But we can't persuade people against their will, and so they create a lot of literature. Some people actually have a business interest in anti-Mormon literature. But, again, for me, all that's not consequential.

Elder Maxwell, however, wasn't running for president of the United States. For Mitt Romney the existence of a vast body of anti-Mormon literature and a dedicated cadre of anti-Mormon expositors *is* consequential. Each and every time I speak about Romney on my radio show, I receive e-mails from some of this number who demand that I condemn the Mormon apostasy and work against Romney's candidacy.

Perhaps the leading anti-Mormon writer of the twentieth century was Walter Martin, a prodigious author and communicator who died in 1989. Martin was the original "Bible Answer Man," becoming a regular voice in millions of American homes and cars via a radio ministry that spanned three decades.

Martin made it his life's work to explore, explain, and usually condemn in no uncertain terms the most popular apostasies he found in American culture. His earliest "counter-cult" books included *Jehovah of the Watchtower*, *The Christian Science Myth*, and *The Christian and the Cults*. He also wrote *The Maze of Mormonism* and a short booklet simply titled *Mormonism*. Martin's 1965 tome *The Kingdom of the Cults*, is his central work, and the book's web site asserts that it has sold 750,000 copies

Martin's success proved that there was a market for anti-Mormon books, and publishers have never hesitated to meet demand, especially when they are fired by a belief—as sincerely advanced as it is contested by Mormons—that the LDS is a heretical creed and its adherents denied the saving grace of Jesus Christ.

Martin's *The Kingdom of the Cults* did not go out of print with his death. In 2003 Bethany House publishers released a revised edition. Most journalists will find their way to this book as they struggle to understand anti-Mormon literature as it relates to Mitt Romney's candidacy.

The first thing to notice is that the title includes the term "cult," which almost spits itself from the cover as it does the lips of most people who use it. "Cult" is a term of opprobrium, usually reserved for Jim Jones's "People's Temple," David Koresh's Branch Davidians, or the Hale-Bopp hitchhiker-suicides of the Heaven's Gate cult. For most Americans "cult" carries with it at least a hint (and usually quite a bit more) of physical coercion and brainwashing, as well as an implication of devious secrecy. A nightmare for many parents is the entry of their children into a "cult," and memories of past "deprogramming" controversies are easily triggered by this term.

Thus Martin's title *The Kingdom of the Cults* carries with it the almost audible deep chords of an enormous organ wheezing out doom and deep distrust. But this vision of "cult" is difficult to square with the sunny Mormons one encounters at Boy Scout jamborees, on city councils across the land, or in the professions and business. But for those who do not know any Mormons, or at least not that well, this background music dominates the attitude they bring to the idea of a Mormon candidate for the presidency.

A closer examination of the table of contents in *The Kingdom of the Cults* underscores that Martin cast his net wide in the round-up of "cults," including Jehovah's Witnesses, Christian Science, Bud-

dhism, Scientology, the Unification Church, "Eastern Religions," and
even all of "Islam." While some "cults" on Martin's list may qualify
under the definition most people are applying in their separation of
religious groups into "mainstream" and "marginal" and "extreme," it
is clear that any definition that sweeps in a world religion like Islam
is not of particular use in a secular setting.

But what Romney confronts is the widespread attachment of the
term "cult" to his religious beliefs. This is a political problem of the
first order.

The new edition of Martin's book provides a summary, one-page
indictment of LDS belief, which is a handy reference guide to anti-
Mormon objections. Note that in this list of particulars there is quite
a lot of overlap with B. H. Roberts's summary of the distinctive
aspects of Mormon theology:

The Bible is the Word of God insofar as it is correctly translated.
There are three sacred books in addition to the Bible: The Book
of Mormon, Doctrine and Covenants, and The Pearl of Great
Price.

The earth is one of several inhabited planets ruled over by gods
and goddesses, who were at one time humans on other planets.
Mormonism is polytheistic in its core.

The Trinity consists of three gods born in different times and
places; the Father begot the Son and Holy Ghost through a god-
dess wife in heaven.

Humankind is of the same species as God. God begot all humans
in heaven as offspring of his wife or wives, who were sent to earth
for their potential exaltation to godhood.

Salvation is resurrection, but exaltation to godhood, for eternal life in the celestial heaven, must be earned through self-meriting works.

Does this unique set of beliefs present obstacles to Mitt Romney's candidacy? Why? Should they? And whether or not they should, if they do, how does Romney go about overcoming them?

To the first question the answer has to be an unqualified yes. They do present an obstacle, and a large, but not insurmountable one. Again, 43 percent of respondents to a November 2006 Rasmussen poll replied that they would not consider voting for a Mormon. In mid-2006, a *Los Angeles Times*-Bloomberg poll reported that 37 percent of those questioned would not vote for a Mormon running for president. In September of 2006, Gallup found that 66 percent of people questioned feel that the U.S. is not "ready" for a Mormon president.

These polls registered much higher levels of prejudice against Mormon presidential candidates than the 17 percent who told Gallup in 1999 that they would not vote for a Mormon. This spike in the past eight years may reflect the media attention in the intervening years to the polygamist sects pocketed in some communities in Utah and Arizona which the LDS routinely denounce and which they assert are not really Mormon at all. The bestselling *Under the Banner of Heaven*—which recounts Mormon history while retelling the lurid story of murders committed by a breakaway pair of brothers raised as Mormons who had rejected the church's repudiation of polygamy— is almost designed to confuse the killers' beliefs with modern LDS practitioners. Then there is the television series *Big Love* as well as the 2006 FBI manhunt for Warren Jeffs, both of which helped create a media environment of suspicion for anything labeled Mormon.

My own personal polling—primarily of radio audiences or Republican activists—reveals a still surprising 20 percent who wouldn't vote for a Mormon. And these are not uneducated captives of myth or sensationalism. These folks *do* distinguish between the

LDS Church and the much smaller communities of self-described "fundamentalist Mormons" who practice polygamy in isolated and highly regimented communities that are shunned and condemned by the LDS. Many know and respect Mormons, and count them among their friends and colleagues. They understand that the fringe is not in the LDS Church or even associated with it except in the minds of the fringes' followers.

But still they object, and James Dobson's estimate is as a result a reasonable one as to the reality of the situation as the 2008 presidential campaign opens. Although other evangelical leaders like Jerry Falwell have publicly disagreed with Dobson's assessment of the realities of the political landscape—"If he's pro-life, pro-family, I don't think he'll have any problem getting the support of evangelical Christians," the president of Liberty Baptist University and the Moral Majority told the *Clarion-Ledger* of Jackson, Mississippi, last year—Dobson's assessment remains the reality.

After extensive questioning of hundreds of such objectors to a Mormon candidate for president, I have reduced the list of objections to three—presented in reverse order of importance.

Objection 1: "If there is a Mormon in the White House, Salt Lake City will call the shots, at least on the biggest issues."

Though I have heard this worry, I haven't heard it often, and I have never heard evidence for its being a realistic problem.

In the past, this issue was more salient. In the nineteenth century, Brigham Young was both head of the church and governor of Utah—clearly a tricky intersection of church and state.

During George Romney's 1968 run, David Broder and Stephen Hess, in their book, *The Republican Establishment*, noted that "[a]s recently as 1965, Church president David O. McKay wrote letters to the eleven Mormons in Congress urging them to vote against the move to repeal section 14(b) of the Taft-Hartley Act, which authorizes state right-to-work laws."

The issue of potential influence of the LDS prophet on a president was an issue in the campaign of Mitt Romney's father for the presidency, which George Romney dealt with in typically blunt fashion, telling a group of non-Mormon pastors and ministers in Salt Lake City in 1967 that while the Church should encourage its members to be active in politics, the "Church itself should not become active or identified with a political party or candidate...."

The idea of the General Authorities of the LDS attempting to guide American policy through an adherent in the Oval Office seems these days to be so beyond plausibility that to raise the question is to invite scorn. But raise it I did with Governor Romney because of the need to get an on-the-record response to even the remotest hypothetical:

"Would you ever expect a call from President Hinckley or his successor?" I asked.

"No," he emphatically replied. "Absolutely not. And I'd also note that when you take the oath of office, that is your highest oath and first responsibility. That's true when you become governor, it's certainly true for anyone who becomes president. When I placed my hand on the—I actually think I have it right there, the Bible that my dad was sworn into as governor and as a cabinet secretary and that I used when I was sworn in as governor—my highest and first responsibility was to honor my oath of office and follow the Constitution and protect the Commonwealth of Massachusetts. For those sworn into national office, their obligation is to the nation. It would be inappropriate for Church officials to contact me and it would be less than appropriate for me to take guidance from any institution other than caring first for the oath of office."

It would also be political suicide for the Mormon president and the LDS to take or make such a hypothetical call. As with the overwrought charges about the pope and first Al Smith and then JFK, this will be a non-issue in 2008.

Objection 2: "A Mormon president will supercharge Mormons' missionary work."

The second objection comes from those circles of Christians concerned with the salvation of souls and convinced that Mormons are not "saved," and thus bound for eternal damnation. Among this group of objectors there is the fear that the election of a Mormon president would legitimize a sect that is not merely heretical, but successfully heretical in a way not seen since the rise of Islam in the seventh century.

Very few Americans have not seen the short-sleeved, white-shirted, and black necktie–wearing Mormon missionaries on their bikes in all sorts of neighborhoods. I have encountered a pair of fresh-faced ambassadors for the Book of Mormon on the streets of Tijuana, Mexico, next to the orphanage supported by my Presbyterian congregation. A young friend from Orange County is now in year two of his mission to Zimbabwe. My Constitutional Law class for this year includes a half-dozen returned Mormon missionaries who served in places as far-flung as Brazil and Japan.

At this moment—according to *The New Mormon Challenge*, a 2002 book of essays by evangelical Christian scholars on the growth of the LDS Church—there are approximately 60,000 young Mormon missionaries in the field. The concern among some evangelical voters is that come January 2009 these missionaries will be bolstered in their efforts by being able to point to a Mormon president, and the LDS will win more converts.

For a Christian who believes that hell beckons believers in the Book of Mormon, this is not a casual objection, but a deeply sincere concern that the legitimization of Romney's religion will in fact condemn hundreds of thousands and perhaps millions of souls to eternal torment. This will strike the nonreligious as absurd, and the Christians who believe in universal salvation as an antique and archaic—and embarrassing—claim to exclusivity.

Among Christians, this opens up a broad debate, but we need not enter that here. This concern is a political fact, and Romney needs to worry about it.

Does Romney think he will be held up as a role model of Mormonism, part and parcel of the missionaries' pitch in the remote regions of the world?

"That would kill us," he said with a laugh. "It's hard for me to know what the impact of that would be. I think certainly that's not the reason I'm considering a run and I think it overstates dramatically the impact of the faith of a particular president."

He laughed again. "I haven't actually looked. My guess is if you looked at the conversions in Massachusetts, you wouldn't see any change between before and after I became governor, and I don't think Democrats are flocking to the Mormon church because Harry Reid is the majority leader. I just don't see any evidence of that."

"To suggest that people would say, 'You know, because it's sort of fashionable, I'm going to join this group where you have to give up 10 percent of your income, you can only have sex with your wife.' The dues in my Church are pretty high."

"It certainly hasn't worked that way in Massachusetts," he said, with a final laugh at the idea that a co-religionist president would make the Mormon appeal more plausible.

Objection 3: "It is just too weird."

Dozens of people have struggled to articulate to me their objections to the idea of a Mormon president. These conversations boil down to a combination of unease at the perceived secrecy/exclusivity of the Church and its unusual historical narrative. "How could anyone believe that stuff?" is a common way of putting it, or, as the heading suggests, I have often heard objectors say that while every Mormon they know is an upstanding member of the community, the stuff they believe is just, well, "weird." The bluntest of them, the avowed and relentless atheist Christopher Hitchens, declared that "If Romney's interviewed, and he says he believes that Joseph Smith found a golden book written by an angel, or whatever.... If he says he believes that, then I have to say, well, he convicts himself of being an idiot."

Why?

"[N]o serious person can possibly believe," he harrumphed, "that Joseph Smith experienced a revelation."

It is rare these days for Hitchens to be this wrong, but manifestly millions and millions of very, very serious and very, very smart people do in fact believe just that.

Mormonism is certainly radically different from orthodox Christianity though not, Rex Lee points out in his book, all that different from the widespread conventional Christian acceptance of the idea of miracles and visitations of Mary, various saints, and of course angels.

Mixed up with this "otherness" is also the Mormon discipline—it is a very hierarchical church—which when combined with the exclusivity of some practices (without a temple permit, you cannot enter a consecrated temple, remember) simply scares or offends many, many people.

There is still some resentment of the lateness of the Church's repudiation of the segregation of its priesthood—blacks were forbidden until 1978—and its continued exclusion of women from the priesthood and thus formal leadership at any level.

How will Mitt Romney deal with these objections?

He has been developing a strategy from the moment it became clear that this issue was very much on the table. This recognition may have begun with an astonishing interview conducted by *Atlantic Monthly* writer Sridhar Pappu for a September 2005 profile of Romney, titled "The Holy Cow! Candidate," perhaps the first high–profile injection in the new millennium of the idea of religious background as a disqualifier into the public debate about presidential politics, and the first such discussion in elite circles since the 1960 campaign.

Pappu's first question in what should be at very least a delicate area was jarringingly audacious:

"How Mormon are you?"

One can almost hear the astonishment in Romney's voice as he responded to Pappu:

> "How Mormon am I?" he said. "You know, the principles and values taught to me by faith are values I aspire to live by and are as American as motherhood and apple pie. My faith believes in family, believes in Jesus Christ. It believes in serving one's neighbor and one's community. It believes in military service. It believes in patriotism; it actually believes this nation had an inspired founding. It is in some respects a quintessentially American faith, and those values are values I aspire to live by. And I'm not perfect, but I'm one aspiring to be a good person as defined by biblical Judeo-Christian standards that our society would recognize."

Pappu follows the surprising question—can you imagine an *Atlantic Monthly* writer asking John Kerry, "How Catholic are you?"—with an even more astonishing inquiry:

> "Do you wear temple garments?" I asked uncomfortably, refer-ring to the special undergarments worn by members of the Church of Jesus Christ of Latter-day Saints. (The underwear has markings denoting the covenants of the Mormon faith, and is meant to serve as a reminder of the high standards Mormons are expected to uphold. The rules governing its wear and disposal seem as complex as those pertaining to, say, the American flag.)
>
> He answered, "I'll just say those sorts of things I'll keep private."

Note that Pappu admitted to being uncomfortable in posing that particular question, and it seems to me obvious that the discomfort is rooted in shame at having attempted to pierce the private sphere of personal devotional practice. It would have been similar to having asked John Kerry if and when he last made a good confession—a Catholic duty on the faithful at least once a year. That question was never to my knowledge posed to Kerry and it would have been shameful to have done so. The debate about Kerry's dissent from his church's teaching on abortion was, on the other hand, a familiar extension of the debate that began with *Roe* and which has gone on unbroken for more than three decades, a debate which did not demand of Kerry any personal revelation about private religious practice, and which in any event did not attempt to probe a religious devotional exercise wholly unconnected to any public issue.

Following the Pappu article, the game was on. *Washington Monthly* editor Amy Sullivan seized on these exchanges and concluded: "At that point, Pappu dropped the issue. But the next reporter won't, nor the next, nor the next," indicating that pressing an inquisition about a candidate's religious belief is fair game from her Beltway Bigfoot viewpoint. "That kind of vague answer works for Bush," Sullivan sniffed about Romney's first exchange with Pappu, "but Bush is a Methodist." Thus does Sullivan openly announce a double standard for American journalism, one which Thomas Jefferson and many other American presidents must have been thankful has never before existed.

Sullivan notes that reporters "eat up any chance to explore a new religious angle. They peppered Lieberman with questions in 2000 about whether he could campaign on the Sabbath and followed John Kerry to mass every week during the 2004 campaign to probe his views on the Eucharist." In fact they did not do the latter, but only covered the tension between Kerry's public position on abortion rights and the Roman Catholic Church's public position on who should receive Communion. Reporters pursuing these stories were not out to discredit a candidate by discrediting his faith, though faithfulness to an avowed set of beliefs is a legitimate story, and a potential president's Sabbath practices a necessary discussion in an age when terrible events don't follow a regular pattern.

There were also well-defined limits to the questions posed by MSM outlets. As representatives of the public they can and do ask almost all candidates for an account of their worldview, for an idea of their views on morality and justice and how their faith might account for those views. They also properly inquire about a candidate's personal history and how that might inform his conduct of office.

But sincerity of belief has been off-limits in previous years. Fidelity to the finer points of doctrine—"Do you believe in the Immaculate Conception or the Assumption of Mary, Senator Kerry?"—would delegitimize and stigmatize any reporter who posed them in public. And rightly so, which is why such questions have not been asked before of any candidate.

"It seems to me that [Romney] should be able to set those rules," *Newsweek's* managing editor Jon Meacham told me in response to my question about the appropriateness of such questions. Meacham is a student of religion in America, and his book on the faith of the Framers, *American Gospel: God, the Founding Fathers, and the Making of a Nation* is widely regarded as thorough and fair in its descriptions of the religious beliefs of the men who made the American Revolution.

"I don't think [Romney's faith] is a problem," Meacham said. "I think it's an issue in the way that any candidate's faith is an issue, because character matters, and faith is an essential element within character."

"I think the country is about to get a crash course in the history of the Church of Latter-day Saints," he added, and "[I]f he's going to make his values part of his pitch to the people, which most politicians do, then he's opening the door, I think, to details, partly because they are interesting."

When I pressed the idea that a standard about such questions had been established in all past campaigns, and that the idea of asking Kerry about his confession-going habits, Meacham agreed that indeed there were boundaries. "I think he should be able to set the ground rules in the way Bush set the ground rules on drug use," he mused aloud (not adding, as I would, in the same way that Clinton sealed off the questions about his past extramarital activity prior to his 1992 run).

"I think a lot of people have no idea what Mormonism is, and, you know, he's an interesting figure," Meacham began, making one last stab at coming up with a rule that would honor past practice and yet deal with this new center-stage attraction. "I'm trying to think: Would it be legitimate to ask John McCain, who's an Episcopalian, I think, or certainly a Protestant, whether the world was created in six days?"

He didn't answer his own question, but my answer is emphatically "no," no more than it would have been to have asked Senator Joe Lieberman if he believed Abraham sent Ishmael away, or to ask now Senator Joe Biden if he believed in the finer points of the doctrine of transubstantiation or whether the Virgin Mary appeared at Guadalupe. The point is that interesting questions aren't always legitimate, and certainly aren't when they break the civic religion's commitment to equal rights for all citizens regardless of their religious beliefs.

Perhaps the first major article on the subject of Romney's Mormon beliefs was written by *Weekly Standard* publisher (and my old and close friend) Terry Eastland for that magazine's June 6, 2005, issue. In an article titled "In 2008, Will It Be Mormon in America?" Eastland addressed the same ground as Pappu and Sullivan, but with a respect for the LDS faith and the appropriate boundaries of journalism lacking in their essays. Eastland's article delivered a compact history of the LDS faith and church and provided an overview of the potential issues that Romney's church affiliation will raise in some circles. Eastland also interviewed experts and finally Romney himself on the subject of how Romney's faith will potentially play in the 2008 presidential election.

But unlike his journalistic colleagues who irresponsibly handled a serious matter, Eastland respected the informal prohibition on religious inquisition that differentiates tabloid hacks from responsible journalists: there is a sphere of private beliefs about God that is not right to raise or probe, and though the border is hard to find when there are legitimate issues that need to be discussed, heading for the undergarments angle is disgusting and will appear so to most Americans.

Against the backdrop of these three primary objections to Romney's Mormon beliefs, and his responses to them, the issue becomes how Romney, the media, and the electorate should deal with these sensitive matters over the next several months. The Romney campaign in particular will need to address the reality behind the Gallup poll numbers.

He needs a set of responses or talking points which will be sufficient—if repeated often enough—to turn voters who had nursed suspicions away from those worries, while at the same time protecting him from mischief-seeking headline hunters. These answers should also serve the very important cause of preserving the American consensus that the specifics of personal religious practice and belief are not legitimate subjects of inquiry when those inquiries are designed to embarrass or disqualify candidates from seeking public office.

First, Romney or his surrogates should enlist or at least not discourage high-profile Christians of the most thoroughly orthodox sort to repeat again and again that the refusal to vote for a Mormon on the basis of his beliefs is not merely un-American, but un-Christian. To the extent that the friends of Romney ingrain the idea that it is bigotry to refuse office based on religious beliefs, they will have met their biggest obstacle head on and not through their candidate's exertions, but via proxies.

This process has already begun. Chuck Colson is the founder of Prison Fellowship and among the most widely respected authors and teachers of evangelical Protestant theology as well as a proponent of a robust Christian presence in the public square. He is also deeply experienced in Washington ways, having risen to the near height of Beltway power as a senior aide to Richard Nixon before Watergate took him down and to prison, a journey that also included his conversion.

Colson does not mince words about the theological divide that separates Catholics and Protestants from Mormons. He does not believe, for example, that Mormons are "saved," and thus believes that they are bound for hell unless they abandon their faith and embrace Jesus as evangelicals understand that process.

Even so, he is forceful in his condemnation of the idea that Mormon belief is a strike against Romney. Here is one portion of my interview with him on the subject:

> Mormons and Evangelicals have some very profound differences. They go to the very heart of what the Gospel is and so they are not easily dealt with in theological terms, and most evangelicals would not recognize Mormons as part of the Christian belief system. They would recognize it as something separate from mainstream orthodox Christianity. So everybody tries to gloss over that. I realize that Mormons go out of their way to gloss over it and call themselves Christians and even change the way they identify themselves in public for that purpose. But it's simply [obvious] to any discerning evangelical or discerning Roman Catholic that Mormonism is not orthodox Christianity—"orthodox" with a small "o."
>
> Now having said that, I don't think we should ever put the candidate for president to a theological test. It so happens that I've had long discussions with George Bush about his belief system. He happens to be a solidly orthodox evangelical, which makes me very happy. He's president and as president has made excellent judgments, particularly for the Supreme Court and his passion for human rights. I don't make his faith a test to whether he should be president. I don't think it should ever be a test. I wrote a book in 1986–87 rather on this very point about not putting a

person in office because he is a Christian, and I think back it would be very devastating to you if he put his Christian faith literally to work and tried to impose biblical law. In a pluralistic society it would be a disaster if, as I wrote in *Kingdoms in Conflict*, he tried to bring on the end times by himself. So, I don't think the theological question is on the table with Romney.

I think that what's on the table is competence, remembering Luther's admonitions that he'd rather be governed by a competent Turk than an incompetent Christian. So competence is obviously key. The president of the United States has a huge job and his decisions affect every human being in America and indeed around the world. So you have to look for somebody who is competent and able to do the job.

The second thing that you look at is where does he stand on moral questions? And there we have a great camaraderie with Mormons. So the evangelicals would look at Mormons as soul brothers and certainly co-belligerents in the battles of the cultural war and also how we see Islam, I suspect—although I've never discussed that with Mormons. So, from my perspective, I would not apply an evangelical litmus test to Romney. I would look to his competence and where he stands on the moral issues, and I would find personally where he stands on the moral issues to be a great comfort.

The Romney campaign must seek the ready willingness of such men and women to always be on call when reporters come across the recurring story of a voter or a celebrity who lets fly with an anti-Mormon remark, or any attack on Romney rooted in his faith.

One such voice will be the Catholic archbishop of Denver, Charles Chaput, widely regarded as a champion of traditionalist Catholic doctrine and an inspiring leader of the renewal of the Catholic Church in America.

I spent a couple of hours with Chaput at his Denver home discussing the idea of a Mormon in the White House and followed up that conversation with an e-mail exchange that focused on the three objections outlined above.

The first question I asked Archbishop Chaput was whether he would vote for a Mormon.

"If I believed him to be the right man for the country, a man of intelligence, fairness, good judgment and moral character, yes of course I would," the archbishop replied.

Then I raised the three central objections to a Mormon in the White House which I have repeatedly encountered.

Did Chaput fear that the Mormon "General Authorities" would attempt to influence the Mormon president?

"I think that's very unlikely, and anyway it wouldn't work," he replied. And then he added, tellingly for Catholics: "Exactly the same thing was said about the Vatican and Catholics fifty years ago."

Archbishop Chaput is correct, of course, and this shared religious discrimination of the past may well help Romney with the Catholic vote.

Objection two: will a Mormon president "legitimize the message of the 60,000 Mormon missionaries at work in the world on any given day"?

"If Mormon missionaries are successful, it's because other religious communities are too often doing a bad job," Chaput answered. "A Mormon president of the United States won't materially change the facts of any local person's religious life. People don't sign up for a religion because the current U.S. president is Baptist or Catholic or Mormon. They commit to a religious faith because it speaks deeply to their heart. If mainline Christian churches can't do that for people, somebody else will."

Though Chaput did not say it, there is a challenge to evangelicals and Christians in his response: this would be a silly question were it not for the feeble missionary zeal of much of the post-modern Christian community.

Finally I came to the question of the intellectual reliability of anyone who believed such astounding propositions as are embedded in LDS doctrine. Is Mormon belief so iconoclastic that sincere belief in it calls into question a believer's intellectual strengths?

"Most religions have strange-looking elements when seen from the outside," Archbishop Chaput responded. "From the inside, they may be experienced quite differently. If I believed the content of LDS faith, I'd be a Mormon. I don't, and I'm not. But in my experience, most of the LDS leaders I've met have been intelligent, sophisticated, effective persons. If they're hobbled in any way by their beliefs, they're extraordinarily good at hiding it."

And here is the complete response of the Romney faith: no religious faiths are completely naturalistic. If they were, they would not be "faiths." The demand that Mormons defend their faith as "rational" is unique and troubling in American history, for we have never demanded any such accounting of a would-be president in the past, and to do so in 2008 would be to play into the hands of the secularist extreme.

There is still the practical problem of secular reporters who feel that Mormonism is sufficiently different that their contempt for all faith will be disguised by their interest in this particular sect.

Romney should not dwell on the questions of his faith or allow reporters to do so. He should refer reporters interested in the story to this book and the extensive interviews he provided me or others on the subject as a shorthand way of signaling that the questions have been "asked and answered." He should articulate a line of appropriate inquiry that reporters are not allowed to violate, and should politely but firmly turn them back when necessary. He should be careful to explain that this line is not just in his interest or in defense of his own personal privacy and religious liberty, but reflects a basic American principle deeply rooted in our founding documents and our historical practice.

Romney should also ask his fellow candidates for clear statements regarding the dishonorability of voting against a candidate on the basis of religious belief. This is the "Article VI" argument, and it is a powerful one.

The third clause of Article VI of the United States Constitution bars a "religious test" for public office. This is an obscure portion of the Constitution, but one which will receive a lot of attention over the next year and a half as Romney's Mormon faith receives repeated scrutiny. *The Heritage Guide to the Constitution* gives a brief history of the clause, authored by scholar Gerard V. Bradley:

"Religious Test

...no religious Test shall ever be required as a Qualification to any Office or public Trust under the United States."

(Article VI, Clause 3)

The original, unamended Constitution contains one explicit reference to religion: the Article VI ban on religious tests for "any office or public trust under the United States." Despite much litigation over the constitutional border between church and state, there have been no judicial decisions involving the religious test ban. The clause has been entirely self-executing. We do not know whether the Framers intended the clause to apply to every federal officeholder, howsoever minor; but no federal official has ever been subjected to a formal religious test for holding office.

By its plain terms, the ban extended only to the federal office-holders. States were free at the time of the Founding to impose religious tests as they saw fit. All of them did. State tests limited public offices to Christians in some states, only to Protestants in others. The national government, on the other hand, could not impose any religious test whatsoever. National offices were open to everyone.

The surviving accounts of the Constitutional Convention indi-
cate that the Article VI ban "was adopted by a great majority of
the convention, and without much debate." We know that North
Carolina opposed the prohibition; the Connecticut and Maryland
delegations were divided. All the other delegates were in favor.
But even some "nay" votes were not necessarily in favor of religious tests. Connecticut's Roger Sherman, for example, thought
the ban unnecessary, "the prevailing liberality" being sufficient
security against restrictive tests.

Of course the "prevailing liberality" was not very liberal. The
clause was hotly disputed in some states during the 1788–1789
struggle over ratification of the Constitution. The objection was
simple: "Jews," "Turks," "infidels," "heathens," and even "Roman
Catholics" might hold national office under the proposed Constitution. As more soberly expressed by Pennsylvanian Benjamin
Rush: "Many pious people wish the name of the Supreme Being
had been introduced somewhere in the new Constitution." The
Religious Test Clause was thus a focal point for reservations
about the Constitution's entirely secular language.

Some defenders of the Constitution argued, in response, that
a belief in God and a future state of reward and punishment
could, notwithstanding the test ban, be required of public officers. On this interpretation, Article VI banned only sectarian
tests, such as would exclude some Christians from office. Others
asserted that the requirement that officers take an oath to support and defend the Constitution necessarily implied a religious
commitment. (See Oaths Clause, Article VI, Clause 3.)

In the ratification debates, the defenders of the Constitution
put forward two reasons for the religious test ban. First, various
Christian sects feared that, if any test were permitted, one might
be designed to their disadvantage. No single sect could hope to
dominate national councils. But any sect could imagine itself the
victim of a combination of the others. Oliver Ellsworth noted that

if a religious oath "were in favour of either congregationalists, presbyterians, episcopalians, baptists, or quakers, it would incapacitate more than three-fourths of the American citizens for any public office; and thus degrade them from the rank of freemen." More importantly, the Framers sought a structure that would not exclude some of the best minds and the least parochial personalities to serve the national government. In his 1787 pamphlet, *An Examination of the Constitution*, Tench Coxe wrote of the salubriousness of the religious test ban: "The people may employ any wise or good citizen in the execution of the various duties of the government."

The limitation to federal officeholders was mooted by the Supreme Court in the 1961 case *Torcaso* v. *Watkins*. Relying upon the First Amendment religion clause, the Court struck down religious tests for any public office in the United States. Not even a simple profession of belief in God—as was required of Roy Torcaso, an aspiring notary public—may now be required. Torcaso thus totally eclipses the Religious Test Clause of Article VI. The scope of an individual's immunity from disqualification from office on religious bases now depends upon the meaning of the Establishment and Free Exercise of Religion Clauses, not upon Article VI. Because the First Amendment's breadth is as wide as all government activity, questions about the precise meaning of "office of public trust" are also moot. Whether the Religious Test Clause by itself extends to members of Congress or all the way down to postal workers no longer matters—save perhaps to historians.

The most powerful argument Romney can muster among a Republican primary electorate pledged in word and sentiment to "originalism" is the appeal to the spirit of the civic religion embodied in Article VI. Although of course this article does not outlaw religious bigotry on the part of private citizens any more than the Fourteenth Amendment outlawed racial bigotry on the part of private citizens, it did very much embody the ideal of the Framers. A great majority of the Founding Fathers would collectively shudder at the prospect of voters rejecting a candidate because of what he believed about the Almighty, and not because they feared for their own exclusion or the exclusion of one sect or another from office.

Most Americans from the revolutionary era were Christians, and many of the devout sort, including some of the Framers. James Madison, according to Jon Meacham, was very devout. "He was," Meacham told me, "a complete, straightforward Episcopal vestryman," whose faith was "intensely private." "Adams bounced around," he continued, but "John Jay was a clear Anglican," and Andrew Jackson, "a straightforward Presbyterian."

Many, however, were not, including some of the most famous, including the first three presidents, and many of the revolutionaries who had launched the revolt against George III.

George Washington was outwardly a most regular churchgoer and a vestryman, but as historian Paul Johnson points out, he was hardly a fervent or even conventional Christian.

"His record of church attendance, about 50 percent or less, suggests decorum rather than enthusiasm," Johnson wrote in his biographical essay on the father of our country. "In his twenty volumes of correspondence there is not a single mention of Christ. In no surviving letter of his youth does the name Jesus appear, and only twice thereafter. 'Providence' occurs more frequently than God. He was never indifferent to Christianity. Quite the contrary: he saw it as an essential element of social control and good government—but his intellect and emotions inclined him more to that substitute for formal dogma, freemasonry, whose spread among males of the Anglo-Saxon world was such a feature of the eighteenth century."

Washington "swore the oath of office as president on the Masonic Bible," Johnson noted, "and when he laid the cornerstone of the capitol in 1793 he invoked the lodges of Maryland and Virginia. Indeed at his funeral all six pallbearers were Masons and the services followed the Masonic rite."

Ben Franklin? In his own words, "a thorough deist." Franklin did advise Thomas Paine, unsuccessfully, to keep Paine's atheism to himself, but not out of fear of damage to the faith but rather for Paine's life and limb. Franklin, concluded Aspen Institute president Walter Isaacson in his biography of Franklin, embraced "a virtuous, morally fortified, and pragmatic version of deism. Unlike most pure deists, he concluded that it was useful (and thus probably correct) to believe that a faith in God should inform our daily actions; but like other deists, his faith was devoid of sectarian dogma, burning spirituality, or a personal relationship with Christ."

Then there is Jefferson, scissoring out of the New Testament all references to the miraculous, barely concealing his contempt for orthodox Christianity. Perhaps he was a deist, but more likely he was an agnostic of the most thorough-going sort. Jefferson "did not believe that God intervened in human history at all," records Christopher Hitchens, who also declared that Jefferson's life "in the most unmistakable terms" revealed "that he was not a Christian." As "to whether he was an atheist, we must reserve judgment if only because of the prudence he was compelled to observe during his political life."

And Lincoln? That is the subject of a great deal of argument, and some of the best arguments put him closer to Jefferson's camp than many Christians like to admit. The very widely admired historian Mark Noll, one of evangelicalism's leading historians and previously a professor at Wheaton College and now the Francis A. McAnaney Professor of History at the University of Notre Dame, wrote of Lincoln's faith that "[c]onsiderable uncertainty arises...when Lincoln's own religion is examined."

"On the one hand," Noll explained in 1992's *A History of Christianity in the United States and Canada*, "it is obvious that Christianity exerted a profound influence on his life. His father was a member of Regular Baptist churches in Kentucky and Indiana. Lincoln himself read the Bible throughout his life, quoted from it extensively, and frequently made use of biblical images (as in the "House Divided" speech of 1858). It was said of him, perhaps with some exaggeration, that he knew by heart much of the Psalms, the book of Isaiah, and the entire New Testament. His life also exhibited many Christian virtues."

"On the other hand," Noll continued, "Lincoln never joined a church nor ever made a clear profession of standard Christian beliefs." It is a very ambiguous record:

> While he read the Bible in the White House, he was not in the habit of saying grace before meals. Lincoln's friend Jesse Felli noted that the president "seldom communicated to anyone his views" on religion, and he went on to suggest that those views were not orthodox: "On the innate depravity of man, the character and office of the great head of the Church, the Atonement, the infallibility of the written revelation, the performance of miracles, the nature and design of... future rewards and punishments... and many other subjects, he held opinions utterly at variance with what are usually taught in the church." It is probable that Lincoln was turned against organized Christianity by his experiences as a young man in New Salem, Illinois, where excessive emotion and bitter sectarian quarrels marked yearly camp meetings and the ministry of traveling preachers. Yet although Lincoln was not a church member, he did ponder the eternal significance of his own circumstances, a personal life marked by tragedy (the early death of two sons) and difficulty (the occasional mental instability of his wife). And he took to heart the carnage of the war over which he presided.
>
> Whether it was from these experiences or from other sources, Lincoln's speeches and conversation revealed a spiritual perception far above the ordinary. It is one of the great ironies of the his-

tory of Christianity in America that the most profoundly religious analysis of the nation's deepest trauma came not from a clergyman or a theologian but from a politician who was self-taught in the ways of both God and humanity. The source of Lincoln's Christian perception will probably always remain a mystery, but the unusual depth of that perception none can doubt. Nowhere was that depth more visible than in his Second Inaugural Address of March 1865: "Both [North and South] read the same Bible, and pray to the same God; and each invokes His aid against the other. It may seem strange that any men should dare to ask a just God's assistance in wringing their bread from the sweat of other men's faces; but let us judge not that we be not judged. The prayers of both could not be answered; that of neither has been answered fully. The Almighty has His own purposes." Even more to the point was his reply when a minister from the North told the president he "hoped the Lord is on our side." Responded Lincoln, "I am not at all concerned about that....But it is my constant anxiety and prayer that I and this nation should be on the Lord's side."

Thus it can fairly be said that of the country's three most renowned presidents—Washington, Jefferson, and Lincoln—none would be a model for an orthodox Christian of either the Protestant or Catholic camp.

It also has to be noted that the most orthodox of the Christian presidents of modern times, the Sunday school–teaching and Habitat for Humanity home–building Jimmy Carter, conducted a disastrously impotent presidency which witnessed the Soviet invasion of Afghanistan, the establishment of radical Islamist Iran, and an economic climate that combined rampant inflation with crippling unemployment.

To be sure, there have been devout believers in orthodox Christian doctrine who have served in the nation's highest office—from John Quincy Adams in the nineteenth century to Woodrow Wilson in the twentieth and George W. Bush in the twenty-first. There is a powerful argument to be made that deep faith is a sustaining and nurturing advantage—or even a necessary aid—for a present-day office holder who must necessarily shoulder almost daily briefings on and imaginings of horrors surpassing those of 9/11.

But there is simply no persuasive argument to be made that a great president must be a great and orthodox Christian, or, even, an outwardly observant one. And the Framers knew well the danger of exclusion as well as the folly of denying the Republic the services of any man because of his religious belief—or total lack thereof.

Romney will likely not be the one to make such arguments about past presidents and their religious beliefs, but pundits and supporters alike will quickly discover that essays on the faith tradition of American presidents are going to reveal either a mosaic of beliefs that underscore just how non-judgmental Americans have been on this issue over the centuries, or the ignorance of the writer and speaker.

Finally, and ultimately perhaps the most persuasive of arguments directed at Christians hesitant to openly support or even vote for Romney, there is self-interest.

There is a steep and very slippery slope in front of the passionate anti-Mormon who takes that passion and funnels it into anti-Romney activism because of theological concerns. Such activists are building a weapon of political war that will be used against them and those whom they might approve for office based on theological soundness in this and future cycles.

There is a growing anti-religious bigotry in the United States, and it is firmly nested in the elite opinion machines of the MSM and on the Left, which means within the highest circles of the Democratic Party, as well as in scattered precincts on the libertarian Right.

For three decades people of faith have watched a systematic and very effective effort waged in the courts and the media to drive them from the public square and to delegitimize their participation in politics as somehow threatening. Whether it is the absurd screeds of a Rosie O'Donnell arguing that "extreme Christians are just as dangerous as extreme Islamists," or radical writer Andrew Sullivan's gross and self-caricaturing effort to brand everyone with whom he disagrees a "Christianist," there is concerted effort afoot to discredit tens of millions of Americans who vote in part because of their worldview on such subjects as the protection of the unborn, the central role of marriage between a man and a woman in the preservation of the family, and the evil of human cloning. The cultural Left wants very much to parody and then purge traditional values voters from the mainstream. (To be fair, Sullivan's hysteria, which led to his branding of Romney as a "Christianist," perhaps did more to diminish evangelicals' doubts about the Massachusetts governor's core values than all of Romney's partisans combined.)

If the various and disparate camps within what the Left lazily and condescendingly calls the "religious right" join with the secular agenda journalists of the Left and their allies in the ACLU and other hyper-activists of the "no religion in the public square" extreme in mocking Romney's sincere religious belief, they can expect the same arguments to be turned against them in even greater force than they have already encountered.

If, on the other hand, evangelicals and orthodox Catholics are ready to defend Romney against the attacks on his faith, the laughable idea advanced by Sullivan and his ideological clones in the MSM and on the Left that Christians want to take over the government in order to impose a sort of Christian version of sharia will be discredited (though of course not silenced as access to an audience, even to bitter and bigoted nutters, is one of the crowning glories of our constitutional guarantees).

When all of these arguments have been made—again and again and again—there will still be objectors, and there will still be the risk that the amoral political operatives will mine anti-Mormon bigotry in a primary or a general election's closing days. This happened to Matt

Salmon in the closing days of his 2002 campaign for Arizona's governorship when Salmon opponents attacking Mormonism surfaced.

Something similar happened in Mitt Romney's first political campaign, a 1994 run against Teddy Kennedy. As the campaign intensified in that perilous year for Democrats and the polls showed Romney a very real threat to the senator, Kennedy partisans got nervous—and desperate.

The senator's nephew Joe Kennedy—at that time a congressman—denounced Romney as "a member of the white boy's club," an obvious slam at the Mormon Church which the uncle was forced to disavow, explaining that: "I believe religion should not be an issue," an almost obligatory concession to the obvious irony of any Kennedy appealing to religious bigotry. Nevertheless, the damage was done. While Romney's campaign encountered other serious problems— primarily the idea of defeating a Kennedy in Massachusetts—Terry Eastland noted that "the attacks had their desired effect." Mitt Romney was seriously wounded.

There will be ways to anticipate and counter explicitly anti-Mormon campaign tactics. I asked Bill Clinton's press secretary Mike McCurry, esteemed as media savvy on both sides of the Beltway divide, whether he anticipates these sorts of attacks to occur. "I think they will," he said, but offered the most effective defense:

> I live in the shadow of the Mormon temple here in Kensington, Maryland," McCurry argued, "and there are quite a number of people who live in our community who are here for temporary assignments there. And I'll tell you, you'd be hard pressed to find friendlier, more family-focused folks. And if they attack the denomination, or attack the theology of the church, I think that sets off a whole bunch of things that will have unintended consequences for them.

What sort of consequences?

McCurry acknowledged that Mormonism was vulnerable to mischaracterizations and distortions. Ignorance can cause others to view Mormons as "snake-eating, serpent-dwelling people," he acknowledged. "But, you know," he added, "that gets overridden by so many role models that exist. People who know Mormons, people who live in Mormon families. They know what their ethic is."

"I would find any attack on the religion," he concluded, "if it came from fundamentalist Christian or evangelical Christian groups, it would open up such a can of worms about who's got God on their side that I think Romney would really do well on that."

McCurry's intuition that attacks on Romney's faith might backfire is not widely shared—yet. But there is within the electorate an enormous distaste for any sort of attack on a candidate's religious background.

The "Mormon question" is the near exclusive focus of Lowell Brown and John Schroeder, two bloggers who write the Article VI Blog (www.article6blog.com). The former is an accomplished Los Angeles lawyer and a Mormon, the latter an Orange County, California, environmental consultant and evangelical Christian. They credit me with suggesting they set up a collaborative blog shop on this subject, but both were successful bloggers before they launched Article VI Blog, and their common interest in politics made it a natural pairing.

In addition to posts and commentary on the media's treatment of Romney's religious background, the two have been conducting fascinating interviews with individuals who have unique takes on the subject.

One of the most interesting was a long conversation with filmmaker Mitch Davis, whose credits include 2001's *The Other Side of Heaven*. Davis is a Mormon, and he started a 527 committee named RunMittRun.org, which is focused on the "Mormon problem."

Why, the Article VI bloggers asked Davis, did a successful and busy movie guy divert his time and money into such a cause?

"Several months ago I began to take note of his potential candidacy, started to read articles about him in the *Wall Street Journal* and elsewhere that were encouraging and exciting," Davis told the bloggers. "But I began to notice there was a trend to end all of these effusive articles with the sort of postscript, 'It's just too bad this guy's a Mormon or he'd be our next president.' And as that trend continued, and the volume increased rather than decreased on that particular issue, I just decided it was time to do whatever I could to counteract that. It just felt so unfortunate to me, and, frankly, kind of embarrassing that in the year 2006 in America, this is still the big issue that it seems to be in a lot of people's minds."

Davis understands that Romney's faith may be the biggest obstacle to his nomination by the Republican Party.

"I think that it is clear that the way the field of candidates for president is shaping up at this time, Mitt Romney is unquestionably going to be the candidate whose lifestyle and values most closely approximate and honor those of the evangelical Christians," he told the bloggers. "There's just no question about it."

Davis sees bigotry in the anti-Mormon assault on Romney.

"It's a harsh word to use," he conceded, but added that "I do believe that this is at the core of a lot of what is going on. But the good news is that the bigotry is not based on mean-spiritedness or cruelty. It is based, apparently, on ignorance, or lack of information, misinformation, or disinformation. As we have tried to really assess why people would have a difficulty voting for a Mormon in such high numbers, it is clear that the reasons they would have that difficulty is that they really understand so little about Mormons."

Romney faces a very difficult challenge if his candidacy depends upon him educating people about the Church of Jesus Christ of Latter-day Saints. It is a trap, in fact, and one which he must work overtime to avoid. JFK wasn't responsible for educating non-Catholics on the ways of the Vatican or the specifics of the Baltimore Catechism, and neither Jefferson nor Lincoln was pressed to explain their idiosyncratic views on the Almighty.

Romney's best strategy for overcoming the obstacle of anti-Mormon voters? Bypass them completely. Argue the case for his candidacy based upon his qualifications, and make it so compelling that even a bigoted, deeply anti-Mormon primary voter is obliged to say either, "Wow, he's capable of doing this job," or "Wow, he's going to win no matter what I think," or, preferably, both.

In short, Romney's best strategy is to overwhelm any objections to him based on his faith by demonstrating that he is simply the best-prepared, best-qualified candidate to run for, win, and then serve as president. In so doing, he isolates the prejudice from the process, and forces voters to recognize that they would be indulging a uniquely un-American impulse in voting against him because of his faith.

Because the Mormon hurdle exists and the press loves it, Romney's campaign will have to counter with a lot of biography and a lot of conversation about his record. The campaign and the candidate will have to couple this tactic with a disciplined but sunny refusal to debate theology, a refusal that will be grounded in the American political tradition. "I think he should be able to set the ground rules," Jon Meacham said, and Meacham was correct. I hope the governor sets those rules where they have always been for the benefit not just of his campaign but for the benefit of all politicians and public servants who nurture a sincere religious conviction.

Romney would thus present himself as uniquely prepared for the presidency while at the same time occupying the mainstream with his insistence that American politics have built large levees against faith-based exclusions from office, levees that do not have a Mormon exception built into them. If he succeeds on both scores, the Mormon problem will fade. If he stumbles in either argument, the Mormon problem becomes a handy excuse for unsettled voters to turn another way.

"I know that there will be people that say can Condi Rice be president?" he asked rhetorically in our conversation, hitting a theme I expect will be a feature of many interviews. "A woman? Can a woman be president—a black woman? Can John Kennedy be president—a Catholic? Can Joe Lieberman be president—a Jew? Can Mitt Romney be president—a Mormon? The answer is to all of the above: of course!"

"Ever since I was a little boy," Romney explained to me, "I was told everyone in America can become president of the United States regardless of race, creed, or ethnicity. I believe that. I believe the American people believe that.

"I'm as deeply and fundamentally American as any other person in this country," he concluded, "and I love this land enormously and my consideration of the national race flows from the love of this country."

Conclusion

For Mitt Romney to become the president of the United States, he will have to confront and overcome the opposition of four specific camps.

He will also have to speak clearly and emphatically about the nature of the times in which we live and the threats we all confront. Clarity on this existential threat will be the necessary, though not sufficient key to his success.

First among the four opponents: those fundamentalist Christians who are anti-Mormon.

Second, the MSM which does and will continue to loathe Romney's traditional values and anti-elite politics, even though Romney embodies the success that elite institutions hope to prepare their best graduates to achieve and which Romney has enjoyed in great measure. The jealousy of the elite media is not to be underestimated. Romney is a target that many among the scribbling classes would love to hit.

Third, Senator John McCain wants badly to be president. He is very smart and determined, if not wise or measured. McCain will try whatever works, and may in fact act desperate as it becomes obvious that he has very little in terms of mainstream GOP activist support and quite a lot of suspicion and dislike in that group. The Beltway-Manhattan media machine still counts McCain as its favorite Republican and will ally with him in the rapidly unfolding presidential campaign. All McCain's team will have to do is cue the MSM brigades and they will spring into action on any theme hinted at.

And finally Hillary and Bill, whatever their faults, are brilliant political operators backed by extraordinarily talented professionals such as James Carville, Paul Begala, Mandy Greenwald, Howard Wolfson, and Harold Ickes. Congressional Democrats, suddenly powerful after a dozen years in the wilderness, will be working over-time to support the Clinton restoration even as the appearance of the contest on their side unfolds. I wrote in my last book about the inevitability of a Clinton-Obama ticket and still think it is very likely, though the suddenly bright star of James Webb would bring power-ful themes to a Hillary run. Webb is old school, and took hundreds of thousand of Republican votes away from George Allen. He may well be the only alternative to the Obama bonanza, and his presence on a ticket would magnify Romney's lack of military experience.

It is improbable to think that Romney can clear all four sets of hurdles. Anyone who seeks the presidency who is not an incumbent is by definition a "long shot," and needs a lot of things to work in favor of his or her campaign to be victorious. But Romney does have the significant advantages outlined earlier and the luxury of confronting each of the opposing groups in sequence—not all at once.

It may be that the first hurdle has already been crossed. Romney cooperated with this book project even though he knew its focus would be squarely upon his faith and the problems it presented. It is very early in the campaign, but here in your hands is an in-depth treatment of the central question Romney's candidacy faces. He can point to it and other interviews and articles and say "asked and answered." Will it be enough? "Hang a lantern on your problem" is old but very wise advice for politicians seeking office. Romney has been allowing the spotlights to gather on his Mormon faith, and the issue may soon fade as a result.

It will quickly become obvious, I think, that evangelicals, Mass-attending Roman Catholics, orthodox Jews, and all other people of faith have a stake in getting past the Mormon question.

It is difficult to imagine two more dissimilar American worldviews than those held by Mark Halperin and Dr. Albert Mohler.

Halperin is the political director of ABC News, author along with John Harris (formerly of the *Washington Post*) of 2006's *The Way to Win: Taking the White House in 2008*. Halperin is also the editor of ABC News's "The Note," a daily supply train of political info and editorial snarkiness that reinforces Beltway and Manhattan groupthink about what matters in American politics and models for would-be insiders the appropriately cynical disposition toward it.

Mohler is the president of Southern Baptist Theological Seminary, a prolific author, broadcaster, and blogger, and among the most influential Protestant theologians at work in the United States today. (Mohler is also my colleague and friend at the Salem Radio Network, and I find it hard to overstate his great learning and energy.)

Halperin's voice is the voice of the MSM, perfect pitch, if you will, of elite media's many deep-seated and occasionally acknowledged but not revealed biases.

Mohler is a leader with few parallels among conservative Protestants.

Both are uneasy with the Romney candidacy, for similar but also very different reasons.

When I put to Halperin the question of whether Romney had a "Mormon problem," he began as any student of the American Constitution ought: "I'm on the end that says 'less than most people think,'" Halperin replied.

But then Halperin went on to outline all the ways that Romney had exactly the sort of problem he had just scoffed at.

"I think the ability of Governor Romney to make this not a problem in the nomination fight will depend on his ability to explain his faith," he told me. "He's yet to do that. I've tried to talk to him about it. He's incredibly reluctant to do it. If he's able to explain it, I don't think it would be decisive in keeping him from being the nominee any more than people who think McCain-Feingold is an abomination would keep John McCain from being the nominee. But the precondition is that he has to explain it, which he's not done up until now."

"Look," Halperin continued. "I've spent a fair amount of time since he's become a serious candidate trying to understand the Mormon faith. I'm not a dumb person. I don't quite get it and there are parts of it that are harder to explain to someone who doesn't share the faith than others. I think he's got to talk through what his faith means to him. I think most politicians don't have to do that, *but I think the burden is going to be on him as a political reality to do it.*" (My emphasis.)

This is an astonishing reversal of the American agreement regarding the religious convictions of American political candidates, and it is issued from a very important voice in the American dialogue. Halperin's "The Note" is an important (and unusual) bit of media terrain, and it plays a key role in setting the agenda for Beltway-Manhattan media elites. It is jarring to hear Halperin declare open season on Mormon beliefs.

I asked Halperin if it wasn't untoward for American political reporters to ask Romney to explain his faith when in a way we haven't asked other candidates to do so.

"Like with so much that's in our book," he replied, referring to *The Way to Win*, "it's a difference about what is and what ought to be and I think whether its untoward of reporters to do it, now my strong sense in talking to Republicans is that Governor Romney needs to do it for himself whether he wants to do it by having reporters ask him whether he wants to give a speech, write an article, whatever it is. If faith is important enough for people in the present, this is a religion that is remote enough for enough Americans that I think unfortunately he's going to have to play by different rules and explain it."

This is I think an elaborately constructed apology for the coming inquisition that the MSM is eager to begin and for reasons wholly unrelated to the specifics of Mormon belief.

"Look," Halperin declared in response to my assertion that the *Atlantic Monthly's* inquiry into whether Romney wore Mormon undergarments, "I've asked him if he thinks the Garden of Eden was in Missouri. It's not fair—politics is not fair and other prominent presidential candidates from Massachusetts understood. Politics is not fair. Life is not fair. I think he would serve himself and the process better to not do it in the form of questions on the run from voters and reporters, but just explain it and then he wouldn't have to worry about being misunderstood or being caught up in the freak show. But I do think that it could keep him from winning the nomination simply because I think a lot of voters will be turned off by it."

In the space of a couple of minutes, Halperin went from declaring that he thought the Mormon issue was "less than most people think," to declaring "that it could keep him from winning the nomination simply because I think a lot of voters will be turned off by it."

When I told Romney of Halperin's insistence that Romney answer such detailed questions, Romney laughed. "He's going to have to go ask the Church what their view is." Was he offended by such questions? "I'm rarely offended. Often surprised. Sometimes made to laugh, but I'm happy when people ask me things on their mind." ("The more embarrassing the better," he added, after a pause, surely recognizing that those doing the asking diminished their own reputations, not his, and perhaps confident that the American public will quickly grow queasy about such intrusive drilling into the area of personal faith.)

Why will the MSM be eager to cut up Mormon belief and badger Romney about obscure points of Mormon doctrine?

Romney's LDS faith represents the soft underbelly of all faith-based voters and the candidates they prefer, and if Romney can be bled via an assault on the rationality of his faith, the next candidate of firm religious views can expect more of the same. Halperin is the voice of the anti-religious hyper-secularist MSM, and if this powerful group of religious cynics gets the cooperation of any sizeable number of people of faith in their anti-Mormon project, the press will finally be liberated from the American consensus that faith is not a fit subject on which to evaluate would-be political leaders. In carving up Romney, the MSM will be sharpening the blades for use on every other candidate from every other faith background.

And not just candidates, but judicial nominees as well.

The remade Senate Judiciary Committee under the chairmanship of Vermont's often loopy and always hard-left Patrick Leahy will waste no time in recreating its blockade of originalist nominees to the federal bench which debuted in the first few months of the Bush presidency. Had Leahy retained his chairmanship of the committee that he gained when Vermont's Jim Jeffords jumped parties in the late spring of 2001, there would have been no confirmation for Justice Alito, and quite possibly none for Chief Justice Roberts either.

Leahy and his hard-left colleagues are not committed to up-or-down votes for all nominees, and the GOP majority of 2005–2006 punted away the opportunity to secure such votes when the Gang of 14 undercut the Republican caucus's intent to obtain a ruling from the chair (Vice President Cheney) on just that subject.

The slim but real Democratic majority in the Senate will never allow that vote to occur, and the refusal to advance originalist nominees has to be expected.

And the return to faith-based discrimination against nominees will also be a reality, though the Democrats may work to obscure this feature of their first blockade, as when Senator Schumer objected to Judge William Pryor's "deeply held beliefs," a not so subtle attack on the devout Pryor's Catholic convictions.

The legitimization of inquiries into religious beliefs would have lasting and deeply damaging effects on American politics and government.

I think Dr. Mohler understands the risks that Protestants face in this hyper-secularization of the public square and of the potential for the Left to use attacks on Romney's faith as a precedent-setting example of how to carve up the prospects of candidates and nominees who bring religious convictions to their public careers. Even though Mohler is aware of the risks of allowing Romney to be assaulted on the basis of his faith, Mohler still has not overcome his reservations about the prospect of a Mormon president.

Mohler is of course no fan of Mormon theology. While he could indeed vote for a Mormon president, it is with a troubled note of uncertainty.

"That's entirely a contextual question," he told me when I asked if he could vote for a Mormon president. "I can't commit myself to that until I see how the election shakes, but I can't say categorically that I would never vote for a Mormon candidate for president."

When I asked about the source of his hesitation, he replied candidly that "I have to respond to that first as a Christian theologian."

"With my concerns about the character of Mormonism, I would be hesitant to do anything that would draw attention to Mormonism as a mainstream part of American culture and, therefore, more likely to appear as a legitimate Christian denomination when I do not believe that it is," he continued.

Was he concerned about the LDS church officials attempting to influence a Mormon president?

"That is not my concern," Dr. Mohler responded emphatically, "any more than my concern would be that a Catholic president would be run by Catholic authorities."

Was it the impact a Mormon president would have on the worldwide missional efforts of the LDS?

"Yes," Mohler allowed, "that is one of my central concerns and it especially would be directed at nations where Christian efforts and evangelism now continue and where there are also Mormon efforts."

"The election of a Mormon president would be an enormous boost in terms of publicity for those efforts among the Mormons," he concluded.

When I relayed Governor Romney's noting that his tenure in the Massachusetts statehouse had not seen a flowering of Mormonism in the Bay State, Mohler conceded that "I think that's probably the case," but added "That's why my concern would be in terms of the international scene where especially in many countries which are or might be described as the Third World, the aspiration to be like America would be tied in all likelihood to the aspiration to be like an American president."

Dr. Mohler is also a very studied observer of American politics, and he also seemed to anticipate the Halperin line of attack.

"[M]any of these Mormon claims fly right directly in the face of well-established history and the knowledge of even the formation of the Native American peoples and all the rest," he noted. "There is just so much there that will appear bizarre and strange to mainstream Americans."

Is it wrong—even exclusionary or bigoted—to articulate such concerns?

"I don't think the question is whether or not a candidate is an orthodox Christian in any traditional theological sense," Mohler replied. "I think the issue is what is the worldview held by this candidate and what difference would that make materially in his leadership of the nation. If a person holds a basically secular worldview with some mild religious attachment, then nobody really feels threatened by that. But if this is a heartfelt commitment whether it be Hindu or Mormon or Islamic or Christian, I think the citizen will take that into full consideration."

Is it bigoted for the citizen to do that?

"That's even the wrong use of the word bigotry," Mohler replied. "Bigotry means prejudice based without substance, and I just don't accept for a moment the fact that a Christian response to Mormonism being unbiblical and not a form of Christianity and all the rest [is] bigotry. It's just a natural response to intellectual honesty."

In the combination of the Halperin-Mohler critiques is Romney's major dilemma. The intensity of the attacks by the MSM may work to erode the reservations of the Christian anti-Mormon block. Dr. Mohler will be an excellent early indicator of whether such a dynamic is taking place. The lack of a serious Republican contender to Romney's right will accelerate the process. Romney's unwavering support for traditional marriage generally and the Federal Marriage Amendment specifically will also assist in reconciling Christian fundamentalists to a Romney candidacy.

New media and new Christian scholarship from among the Protestants, combined with a heavy dose of the civic religion and a deep drink of political realism, will thus all help carve this path.

The blogs are already debating Romney's faith, thus helping along the process by which the issue will lose its salience.

Powerline's John Hinderaker, who along with his colleagues Scott Johnson and Paul Mirengoff operate the blog which *Time* christened the "blog of the year" in 2004, is a successful trial lawyer who gets right to the bottom line. Romney's faith is "a drawback," Hinderaker told me, and he worries that the "millions of anti-religious voters" will see Mormonism as a "worse" version of "standard evangelical Christianity," will reject Romney even as Romney forfeits the anti-LDS vote among conservative Christians.

Ed Morrissey of Captain's Quarter's blog was as clear-eyed as Hinderaker.

"The fact that the question has to be asked speaks to some handicap," Morrissey replied. "[T]he question will be how big a part it will play. Part of me wants to say that we have grown in America to the point where religion holds no opportunity for bigotry... and then I stop singing Kumbaya and put out the campfire.

"Some Christians will be put off by a Mormon running for the presidency, no matter who he is," Morrissey continued. "For that matter, some people will be put off by a black candidate, or a female candidate, and so on. Giuliani will get some Mafia references despite his track record of fighting the mob in New York. Romney would be a formidable enough candidate to overcome that, I think. He has proven himself successful in the Olympics—no small feat—and successful in governing Massachusetts as a Republican—no small feat again. For a Northeastern Republican, he carries very little Rockefellerism, and his engaging personality will win people to his side. He and Giuliani both have shown demonstrable leadership in executive positions, which puts them ahead of the presumed candidates thus far."

"If Mitt can avoid too many public connections with the Mormon Church and show some strength in the early primaries," Morrissey concluded, "he can win the nomination. I don't think the Mormonism will be a problem after that."

Hinderaker's and Morrissey's similar replies underscore that everybody who follows politics closely already knows that Romney has a "Mormon problem." They have already been discussing it and evaluating it, and that conversation will continue right through Iowa and New Hampshire. The blogs will push it along much faster than old media would have, and in so doing will make the issue old news much earlier than in previous presidential cycles. As with everything else in American politics, the old stories wither, and the hunt for the new angle propels the news cycle. This early awareness and discussion is immunizing Romney against the Mormon question, a reason he no doubt has agreed to the interviews for this book and in other settings.

Even as Romney campaigns and builds his organization, the immunization will proceed, and the evangelical world will engage in the conversation about the Mormon question that Romney needs to resolve prior to the primaries. It is already under way, but it will flower as 2007 progresses. In this book's appendix is an interview I conducted with two respected scholars from southern California's Biola University, a conservative, traditionalist Christian university which is widely known within evangelical circles as a center for Christian apologetics. These two professors, Dr. Craig Hazen and Dr. John Mark Reynolds, are prolific writers and speakers with a vast network of contacts throughout the Christian academic world.

As you read through their responses to my questions about the standard objections I discovered, you will find a very interesting approach to the "Mormon problem," one that relished the prospect of engagement with the LDS Church and its membership, an engagement sure to advance as a result of the Romney candidacy. Both men are convinced that the opportunities flowing from a Romney candidacy are enormous and to be welcomed. Far from legitimizing LDS theology, both scholars wonder whether Mormonism will itself change as the public focuses on its unique theology.

With new media speeding the conversation along and new scholarship cheering it, Romney will hope that the boundaries for the debate will be set by the consensus the American civic religion reached in 1960 concerning John Kennedy's Catholicism: the American public shudders at the prospect of religious debates framing their secular political choices, and will punish other candidates who appeal to religious prejudice as well as press institutions that play to it.

That was the old consensus, and it will quickly become apparent whether it has survived in the era of new media. Some political leaders—from both parties—will get great credit if they act early and visibly to rebuke anti-Mormon rhetoric and dirty tricks. John McCain and Rudy Giuliani are both going to bear special burdens here, and silence on the subject will not serve them well as the campaign advances.

McCain's candidacy holds one central appeal for conservatives: he knows war and will fight to win the one we are in. On this point McCain is believable and his appeal considerable.

To this central appeal he marries his supposed electability: presumed political strength among "independents" and his famous support within the mainstream. He can beat Hillary, goes the argument, and he will insist on victory in the war.

The GOP may well buy this argument unless it can have the same assurances from some other candidate who is better than McCain on other issues of central concern, chief among them judges, taxes, and spending.

Rudy Giuliani cannot run to McCain's right on judges because of his well-known liberal beliefs on abortion and other social issues. Rudy will say that he will appoint judges in the mold of Roberts and Alito, but it will be difficult to believe.

Rudy can run head to head with McCain on the war, however, and has been doing so for the past two years. Giuliani is many things, but he walked toward the Towers on 9/11, and he knows the enemy and his toughness transcends many political liabilities.

But Rudy lacks credibility on judges and doesn't even pretend to care about the marriage issue. So while he will drain votes from GOPers upset with McCain on party loyalty issues, if those voters are social conservatives, they will want more from a candidate than just being "not McCain."

Romney is believable on judges because he is believable on marriage and has begun the process of explaining his abortion views. His few judicial appointments are solid and his handling of the stem cell research issue also reassuring. Can he match McCain and Giuliani on resolve regarding the war? If so, he wins the nomination, provided his approach to the Mormon issue has succeeded.

Romney will succeed in addressing the Mormon problem if he persuades the Republican base that he can do the one thing absolutely necessary to their hopes and dreams of safety within a country where the laws respect religious liberty and where people of faith are not excluded from the public square by a zealous secular elite disdainful of an understanding of history and life that has God at its center: beating Hillary.

Romney will be talking about Hillary from the first day of his campaign to November 2008. Senator Clinton has some preliminary warm-ups to address, but Joe Biden and John Kerry are not exactly the sort of stuff of which comebacks are made. Only Al Gore would present the sort of real threat that could give a Clintonista pause, and there she would prevail as well, though only after a fierce fight. (Senator Obama is an interesting man, but a presidential campaign on his part is really a vice-presidential campaign, and one that if waged seriously could lose him that second slot.)

As Campaign 2008 unfolds, the GOP's loyalists will be worrying about the return of Hill (and Bill) on a daily basis. They know the pair's amazing political skills and the ferocious loyalty they arouse. They know the money is there, and they fear the MSM's uncritical and unambiguous allegiance to the prospect of a Clinton restoration.

Romney's central appeal is that he is smart enough, and wealthy enough, to beat Hillary and her deep-pocketed friends on the far Left, beginning with George Soros. Romney will ask the GOP to look very clearly at the prospect of the Clintons' return to 1600 Pennsylvania Avenue and to assess the vulnerabilities of McCain—some in the GOP will never forgive him and won't turn out; his mercurial temper will explode at just the wrong time; the whispering campaign about his melanoma that the MSM would suddenly recall if he secured the nomination; his age—and thus to realize McCain won't be able to last the long march from lockup of the nomination until November. Romney, on the other hand, is a fresh face with a talented team, one located far from Washington and the aftermath of the overthrow of Saddam. He's smart and eloquent, trained in the Bain way and owner of a billion bucks, fast on his feet, easy to laugh, a favorite son of one blue state (Massachusetts) and the grandson of another (Michigan) and certain to pick another solid conservative for the number two slot, whether Jeb Bush, Secretary of State Rice, Haley Barbour, or some other experienced figure acceptable to the party's base. He'll get the judges right, and, crucially, he has the fortitude for the war that comes from a genuine and deep commitment to the idea that America is particularly blessed by God and uniquely destined to be a bright city on a hill.

Romney is blessed with a wonderful and winsome family, an impressive grasp of media old and new, the personal wealth to keep going if all he needs is a few million to get over the finish line, and crucially, a field against which he matches up very well indeed. He can indeed win it all, and he will be able to persuade the base of that fact, itself a key advantage in maintaining and growing his early momentum in the race.

Many expect Newt Gingrich to fill the void left by George Allen's collapse, but while the former Speaker will again prove the Keyes-Kucinich rule to be true—the MSM will refuse to disqualify any would-be candidate no matter how implausible their claim to competitiveness—he is not a conservative in the mold of W. or Allen.

Kansas senator Sam Brownback and former Arkansas governor Mike Huckabee are not serious contenders. Senator Brownback simply won't be able to raise the money, and Governor Huckabee will not be able to escape the idea that one governor of Arkansas in the presidency was more than enough, thank you. Former Wisconsin governor and HHS Secretary Tommy Thompson is a thoughtful and experienced conservative as is Congressman Duncan Hunter, but neither will register above 5 percent in Iowa, and less in New Hampshire, and Congressman Tancredo, should he follow through on his threats to run on an anti–illegal immigration platform, will get the career-ending rebuke such a move would deserve.

By March 2008 the GOP nomination will be close to decided, if not already over. If Mitt Romney does not commit a blunder of the sort that has sunk many campaigns in the past, the United States will indeed be on the cusp of nominating a member of a non-Catholic religious minority for the first time in its history. So deep is the distaste for McCain among the GOP regulars that it may well be a simple choice between Romney and Giuliani, and Romney's values will trump Giuliani's social liberalism among the values voters. Why settle for strength on the war when you can have strength on the war and excellent Supreme Court nominations as well?

To achieve this clarity on the choice, Romney will have to use the campaign to establish his bona fides on the war—which he took a step toward doing with his condemnation of Khatami's visit to the United States. But as a civilian and as only a small player in the drama of 9/11, Romney starts out far behind McCain and Giuliani on the war and his commitment to its successful prosecution.

Which means he will have to earn the credibility and believability on the war that McCain and Giuliani already enjoy. If the next year is a serious year in American politics, the Republican candidates will be devoting almost all of their debate to the global confrontation we find ourselves in with both Sunni and Shia Islamist extremism. Of course other issues will be in play, but the first and most important one will be how to advance America toward victory in the war in the post-Bush era. Clarity on the threat and purposefulness in meeting it will be the themes that ought to dominate the nomination months.

Giuliani, Romney, and McCain have all begun the campaign with clear statements of resolve on the war. But as the war drags on in Iraq—and as the war against the war continues with Democrats in control of Congress and the Vietnam-era impacted media elite still in power in the MSM—the temptation will grow to temporize on the threat even as the threat continues to grow—not just in the caves of Afghanistan and Pakistan, but in the nuclear ambitions of Iran and the religious fervor of the Hezbollah and Hamas militants, and their terrorist allies around the globe.

President Bush has never been other than clear-eyed about this threat. He has refused to be deterred from his focus on it, and almost every one of his missteps politically have been as a result of this focus, whether the nomination of Harriet Miers (whom he believed could be trusted on the legal disputes relating to the war) the ports deal (which he thought necessary to cement ties with a close ally) or the retention and then abandonment of Rumsfeld (again, understandable only in the light of Bush's focus on winning the war).

Because of the nature of intelligence in this war, it is very unlikely that any of the candidates fully grasps the nature and extent of the threats which abound, though again and again the president and vice president have referred to them, as have Tony Blair and his senior appointees.

Pakistani scientist A. Q. Khan exported nuclear designs to various murderous regimes around the world, and North Korea is also in the business of selling the technologies of death to any willing buyer. The stockpiles of horrific weapons are growing, and the difficulty of cabining their spread and deterring their use grows more and more incredible with each year. The race against time is actually almost certainly doomed, though presidents and the candidates who wish to become president prefer to avoid discussing this horrible math.

Eventually, a WMD will indeed strike somewhere on the globe, and Jack Bauer won't have been there to prevent it. At that moment a tremendous fear will sweep even this most stable of countries. If the attack has been upon our country, that fear will combine with a rage only dimly foreshadowed in the aftermath of 9/11.

We will be electing a president with the hope that his, or her, policies and people will work with the military, intelligence agencies, and State Department to prevent the awful day from occurring between now and the end of their term.

But if that cannot be the case—and someday in the future it seems almost certain to not be the case—then the next president or a future president will have to be the one to restrain American power and the desire for revenge and to restore confidence in democratic forms and the Constitution that protects them, even as he leads another counterattack. He or she will also have to be able to persuade an enraged public about the distinctions in the Muslim world that many will want to sweep away in their anger, and to resist the almost instant absolute power that will be available to the president in office at that time.

History will record that Bush, like Lincoln, acted with great restraint in the years after 9/11 when he could have taken any power he demanded from a willing and deeply traumatized Congress. Likewise, President Bush could have used the years of the crisis to act as FDR and his generals did in the aftermath of Pearl Harbor, with terrible consequences for suspect populations and faiths.

President Bush did not go that way—though, like Lincoln, he has often been accused of doing so—and that was at least partly because of his religious belief and the character that faith infused in him.

When the next awful-day dawns for America, again it will require a president of great character and courage moderated by a necessary measure of reflexive restraint.

We have entered a long period in which every day's news can bring word of an immense, history-changing event, when a city could disappear, an economy crash, or a pandemic be unleashed that rivals the Black Death in its toll.

Whether any president will be able to lead the country through such times and retain the essential structure that has governed us since 1789 is an open question. Such a challenge would require an awesome array of skills. The only parallel times in history when a democratic republic was set upon with a series of regime-threatening battles or disasters are the era of the late Roman Republic and the dawn of the twentieth century.

In the late Roman Republic, a succession of nation-threatening crises combined with ever-escalating political intrigue and eventually political violence to result in the replacement of the Republic with the Empire. Freedom was abandoned in favor of security and a military prowess that simply destroyed enemies rather than treat with them.

In the aftermath of World War I a shaken and traumatized Great Britain refused to take up its obligations as a superpower, and through the policy of appeasement triggered a second war that saw Britain's eclipse and resulted in the disestablishment of its empire even as the century watched the rise and fall of the most brutal dictatorships it has ever recorded.

There are already alarming signs that the United States is choosing the course of British appeasement of the 1930s with its almost certain outcome of disaster, which would likely be followed by the temptation to "go Roman," as my friend, fellow blogger, and author James Lileks puts it. When anti–illegal immigration absolutist Tom Tancredo refused to rule out "bombing Mecca" as a response to a future attack, he was voicing the repugnant idea that the United States would chose to attack a religion, as opposed to an enemy, as one way of striking back. Tancredo's outburst earned him widespread scorn, but the desire to engulf the world in retribution would not be easy to contain if the United States suffered an attack from a WMD.

This deeply troubling scenario is the backdrop for election 2008— not the interesting and significant (but not urgent) debates over global warming, or the lively and timely arguments over Social Security, Medicare, and Medicaid spending. The campaign of 2008 will be two campaigns: one, the ordinary sort of campaign in which these and other important issues are discussed; and the other, the debate over how the country is going to survive this era of existential threat and proliferation of WMDs.

Winning the presidency will require persuading the public not just of the right approach to this existential threat, but also of the necessity to prepare for it and to contemplate and commit to the restraint that it will be necessary to deploy upon the arrival of the horrible event.

In my closeout interview for this book with the governor, I brought to his attention a November 2000 column by Peggy Noonan, which was eerily prescient about what awaited either Al Gore or George Bush: "The next president may well be forced to shepherd us through the first nuclear event since World War II, the first terrorist attack or missile attack," Noonan wrote. "'Man has never had a weapon he didn't use,' Ronald Reagan said in conversation, and we have been most fortunate man has not used these weapons to kill in the past fifty years. But half the foreign and defense policy establishment fears, legitimately, that the Big Terrible Thing is coming, whether in India-Pakistan, or in Asia or in lower Manhattan."

"When it comes," Noonan continued, "if it comes, the credibility—the trustworthiness—of the American president will be key to our national survival. We may not be able to sustain a president who is known for his tendency to tell untruths."

Would Romney be up to such an event as 9/11—or even worse?

"I think it's a place that no human mind wants to go," Romney replied. "No one wants to think about the unthinkable. No one wants to think about mass destruction through nuclear devices in the modern age. It doesn't have to be. With American leadership in the world bringing together the civilized nations to overwhelm and combat jihadism successfully will keep us from ever having to have a nuclear weapon go off anywhere in the world. That's the job."

Romney was certain that he could lead after such a catastrophe, but he was more intent on conveying a broader point, one which is crucial to judging anyone's qualifications to lead a democratic republic.

"[T]here are many people who could lead this nation through a great time of stress and woe," Romney emphasized. "There's not just one person, there's not just ten people, but at the heart of the American people—at the heart of the leaders of America are people who love this country, who tell the truth, and who could lead it through challenging times."

This is a disavowal of Caesarism, and a crucial one to hear pass from every leader in a post–9/11 era. In this era, especially, we do not want to elect a leader too confident of his or her *unique* ability to lead nation in war.

Romney has clearly been thinking about the war, and not just the Iraq front in the war, but the entire war.

We need, Romney said, to be "waging an all-out campaign against jihadism—against violent jihadism. One part is rebuilding strong military: Navy, Marines, Air Force, Army. That's one part."

"The other part," he continued "is going to have to be moving moderate Islam away from the jihadists."

How to do that? Romney rattled off a half-dozen initiatives, including funding non-Wahhabist schools in Islamic countries, helping to establish banking systems that offer mortgages and micro loans, encouraging export-oriented industries, planting crucial health care innovations, and, crucially, establishing institutions "essential for liberal democracy in the moderate modern corners of Islam so that Islam can reject the extreme."

Romney is part of what has been called the neo-Wilsonian side of the GOP that understands there can be no retreat in this war, and that even temporary withdrawals from various fronts will only be postponing the inevitable. The task of the next president will be to persuade the American public—and indeed the West as a whole—that the war is real and ongoing, and that victory is not only far from certain but is indeed doubtful.

This vital task must be accomplished in an era of media cynicism so deeply etched into every news broadcast as to seemingly make impossible any appeal to the public's better angels. *The Colbert Report* is a brilliant bit of programming, as is Jon Stewart's gig, but together they have come to represent the end result of American media: the refusal to believe anything.

Which brings us back around to the beginning of the book.

Mitt Romney believes extraordinary things—about what Joseph Smith saw and translated, the role of the LDS Church, and the nature of God—but most Americans believe extraordinary things about God as well, though very different extraordinary things from Mormons.

It seems very unlikely that in a time of war, when the country is indeed threatened in very real, very immediate ways, that the electorate will punish a candidate for having a belief in a God who is not indifferent to the conduct of men and women, who hears the prayers of His people, and who believes in compassion toward the poor and justice for the evildoer.

It seems, by contrast, very likely that in a time of war against an enemy both large and yet so very difficult to identify or deter, the electorate will look for a candidate of genuine intelligence and capacity, an ability to communicate with the American people and the world, and with a toughness that does not shrink from hard fights or difficult decisions.

Before 9/11, before Afghanistan and Iraq, and before the long list of terrible attacks—whether in Beslan or Madrid, London or Bali, or dozens of other places—Republican primary voters might very well have parsed the nuances of candidates' pro-life stances, or dived deep into every statement ever made on every issue of some consequence.

But in the first open nomination process since 9/11, the GOP will be looking for a candidate who not only understands the threat, but also the country that faces it, who values that country's deep traditions and love of family, and who will fight for all of those traditions and all of those families with an eye on the Constitution and an appreciation for the vast talent available to call upon and mobilize.

Mitt Romney's campaign may hit a reef, or sink on a blunder. So might any other candidate's campaign.

But if the country gets the debate and the campaign it deserves in the middle of this deadly conflict, the votes will be cast on the basis of the candidate's ability to lead—as a Lincoln, a Truman, an FDR, or a Reagan led—with optimism and purpose, and a conviction of the goodness of the country and the courage and resolve of its people.

Interview with John Mark Reynolds and Craig Hazen, October 2006

Hugh Hewitt: John Mark Reynolds and Craig Hazen, welcome. Can you begin by telling us who you are and what you do, John Mark Reynolds?

John Mark Reynolds: I'm John Mark Reynolds. I'm a philosopher of religion. I have a PhD from the University of Rochester where I specialized in Plato and Plato's view of the human soul. I've been at Biola [University] for over a decade now, where I am the founder and director of the Torrey Honors Institute, which is the flagship honors program for the university where we look at the world of classical ideas from a biblical and Christian perspective.

HH: And Professor Hazen?

Craig Hazen: I've been at Biola for almost ten years, and I did my doctorate work at UC Santa Barbara in religious studies. My specialty was new religious movements and comparative religion. I run the MA program in Christian Apologetics, which has about two hundred grad students and is probably the biggest program of its kind in the world.

HH: Now, let's go in reverse order. What's your experience with the Church of Jesus Christ of Latter-day Saints, Craig Hazen?

CH: Wow, you know, I seem to bump into them no matter where I go. I used to live right next door to a ward. Every time I moved to a new home, I'd live next door to a Mormon bishop, there were missionaries flowing in and out. I've always had a fascination with the Mormon people. I have a deep love for Mormon people. When I became a Christian as a senior in high school, I was fascinated with what the differences were between an evangelical Christian and a Mormon and that carried through. I studied Mormonism fairly in depth for a period of time, and then with my graduate work actually made Mormonism part of my doctorial research.

HH: And you published in the area?

CH: Yes, that's right.

HH: The book is *The New Mormon Challenge*, of which you are a co-editor?

CH: Yes, that's right.

HH: Have you written other books about or articles about Mormons?

CH: Yes. There's a whole chapter on Mormonism in my book called *The Village Enlightenment in America.* It's on an early apostle named Orson Pratt.

HH: John Mark Reynolds, your experience with the Church of Jesus Christ of Latter-day Saints?

JMR: Well, at the University of Rochester, you are in what's known as "the burned-over district." And, of course, I was near Hill Cumorah where Joseph Smith allegedly had his visions and where the Church holds a festival every year. I attended that at least two or three times, because I like to think of the burned-over district as involved in some school projects, thinking about why revivalism was so mighty. Things like Charles Finney, Mormonism, spiritualism, all having their foundation within, let's say, fifteen miles of my PhD program at the University of Rochester I spent a lot of time with Mormons, thinking about them and interacting with them and also found Mormons [to be] friendly interlocutors when I would give a paper at a place like Cornell University. At one point I challenged Mormons to be more Mormon—not to retreat from some of their claims and to try to defend those apologetically, and got a lot of good reaction from scholars at BYU at that time. I've had a lot of friendly academic interactions.

HH: Would you explain for the benefit of the audience or people reading this what the"burned-over district" is?

JMR: Yes. Upstate New York was a center for revivalism in the nineteenth century. It was a strange mix of New England Puritans moving to the far west [of New York State] and loosening up their constraints a little bit. It became a democratic place for religion. Craig's an expert on this area, but if you lived in upstate New York or studied there, you had to have thought about the fact that groups like the Death of God movement near Colgate Rochester Seminary, was a sister seminary to the University of Rochester where I was a grad student. Spiritualism, the Fox Sisters with their "spirit rapping," were in, I believe, Hyde, New York, also close to Hill Cumorah, Joseph Smith, and Mormonism. All these revivalisms, including Adventism with William Miller, saw upstate New York as their center.

HH: I want to locate you two again for our readers at Biola. Biola is a unique institution. It's a lighthouse institution for Christian studies on the West Coast. Craig Hazen, how would you describe Biola University to someone who is reading this for the first time?

CH: Biola is about to celebrate its one hundreth anniversary and it's been an interesting place. It started in the midst of the fundamentalist-modernists controversy. Biola would have taken the conservative side, the fundamentalist side and that was in a day when that term actually meant something good—people who didn't necessarily strap dynamite to their bodies and that type of thing. But Biola really stood for the faith once delivered to the Saints in all of its intellectual prowess. It wasn't an anti-intellectual movement whatsoever, and Biola remains steady on that course. One of the few colleges founded in that era that has remained solidly in the biblical Christian camp.

HH: Before we actually [talk] about how a Christian ought to approach the issue—if it is an issue—of voting for a Mormon for president, can we get you both to tell a little of your own personal faith and what tradition you're in so that a reader can get a plumb line? John Mark Reynolds?

JMR: Well, I am a member of the Antioch Orthodox Church, which is claimed to be the oldest church movement in the world. Our headquarters is in Antioch in Turkey. The patriarch is now in Damascus for political reasons, so I'm part of what most people would call Eastern Orthodoxy.

HH: And Craig?

CH: I'm kind of an evangelical ecumenical. I grew up in this southern California mix where you go to Calvary Chapel on Saturday night and then maybe to an evangelical Methodist church, if you can find one, on Sunday morning, and right now I attend an evangelical Friends Church and that's just been my tradition. Southern California evangelicalism.

HH: Are you both familiar with anti-Mormon literature?

JMR: Yes. I went to Bible college. I view myself as an evangelical and very excited to be an evangelical and so went to an evangelical Bible college where I spent a lot of time thinking about apologetics, cults, and world religions and read a lot of anti-Mormon literature, some of which was absolutely dreadful, and spent some of my life apologizing for that early exposure. So, yeah. I've read a good bit, but not as much as Craig.

HH: Craig, obviously you're part of the colloquy under way between evangelicals and Mormons. Can you describe what that is?

CH: This is a huge breakthrough. It's never been done before, where a group of thoughtful evangelicals, most of whom have advanced degrees in theology or religious studies or history, get together with the senior faculty of religion at Brigham Young University and hash out theological issues. We do this a couple of times a year, and it's just been marvelous. We've formed some tremendous friendships, and I believe there's a lot of progress being made. Perhaps the most important piece of progress is we've learned that modern Mormons do not necessarily embrace all that Joseph Smith and Brigham Young taught. In other words, the Mormon Church of the mid-nineteenth century is a different kind of thing than the Mormon Church today.

HH: Alright. Now I want to get to the issue of politics and the intersection with faith. John Mark Reynolds, would you vote for a Mormon for president?

JMR: Yes, absolutely, and I think that having Mormonism be a disqualifier for office is inappropriate. I've blogged pretty extensively on this issue, and this isn't because I don't think theology is important. I think Mormon theology is severely defective. It's not clear to me that one can be a good Mormon and a good Christian and I've talked to my Mormon friends about this pretty extensively. People can disagree theologically, very seriously disagree, but make common cause in politics. Obviously, my home church, the Eastern Orthodox Church, has had some serious historical differences with Roman Catholics, yet clearly in pro-life issues we've been able to work closely with Roman Catholics and make common cause.

We're not electing a pope, I'm not electing the patriarch of Antioch—they don't ask me for that anyway. But would I vote for a Mormon for patriarch of Antioch? No. Would I vote for a Mormon for a president of the United States? Yes. In a blog post recently I've tried to outline three reasons why I think the Mormon theology is severely defective. [But] It's not a disqualifier for a serious person to consider their theology as appropriate for the White House.

HH: Can you give the URL of the blog?

JMR: Yes, my blog is at JohnMarkReynolds.info. If you do a search for "Mormon" or "Romney," I've written about this on at least three different occasions—multiple pages of why I think it's appropriate to consider Romney as a candidate on his political merits and more [or] less dismiss the theological issues from consideration.

HH: Craig Hazen, would you vote for a Mormon for president?

CH: I would. In the case of Romney, there's something special going on here. If Romney were the governor of Utah or Idaho, I'm not sure that I'd leap forward and say, "Yes, no doubt about it. Here's a guy that could be president." I'd have to dig a lot more deeply, but Romney right up front is a faithful Mormon who's governed Massachusetts for goodness' sake. You don't get elected in Massachusetts because you're "Temple worthy." That's not the issue. A guy who can impress the voters of Massachusetts to vote for him has something going for him. The fact that he's a Mormon actually can intrigue me at that point because his value system in terms of life and family and certain aspects of national security and political conservatism maybe those all come into play in a positive way. I might vote for a guy like that.

HH: I did not know your answers before we sat down. I'm going to ask you more generally, at Biola, among your colleagues on the faculty, and it's a vast university with hundreds of colleagues, do you expect that there is a significant number who will say, "No. I could never vote for a Mormon for president"? John Mark Reynolds?

JMR: I think there are two answers to that question. The first is the initial answer and I can tell you from my own personal family, and my family is very well educated, very thoughtful. The first answer is "Oh! I'm not sure about that," or "Maybe not." But then, if they consider it for more than a minute and they have any kind of dialogue about it and they think about it for a few seconds, the answer is "Yeah, I guess I would be open to that. In fact, I'm tired of being taken for granted by Republican candidates, maybe somebody who is a Mormon and has been put down for his religious beliefs won't be the kind of the person who mocks us from the White House or does things that some people in my family or some of my colleagues might be concerned about."

So, there are two answers to that question. Initially, it's probably 50/50. After a little bit of thought I've found that in my family and amongst my colleagues, it's probably more like 90/10 that we would think about that.

HH: Craig Hazen, you do agree?

CH: Yes, I agree with that. I can only think of a very small handful of people who might step forward and just say, "You know, I just couldn't in good conscience vote for a Mormon for president."

HH: There are three objections which I've run into over and over again in the course of preparing this book. The first is "Salt Lake City will control the White House." Does that concern you, Craig Hazen?

CH: I doubt they are controlling Massachusetts right now, so again I don't think that's going to happen. You know, we've seen this play out with George Bush, [though] there's no controlling authority like the Vatican or the prophet in the Mormon Church. But nonetheless, George Bush, in order to govern effectively a national audience, cannot wear his evangelical Christianity on his sleeve. That's just a requirement for the office if you have to govern all the people. Romney's smart enough to know that. We know that for a fact because he's governed Massachusetts.

HH: But are you concerned, John Mark Reynolds, that, of course, the Church is going to lay off if there's not much to be gained if you have a governor taking orders from Salt Lake City, but the fact that the president could expect the prophet from Salt Lake to call up major issues of life and death and war and peace.?

JMR: I think there are two possible answers to that question. Let me say the controversial thing first. I hope Romney takes his Mormonism seriously when he's in office and he uses his religion to guide him on major policy issues. The reason I don't think a Mormon is disqualified from political office in the United States is that Mormonism has become a mainstream part [of] the small "r" republican movement in the United States. Utah isn't governed as a banana republic.... Southern Idaho is dominantly Mormon yet the politics in those areas plays within the broad perimeters of republican values. So, I think to start with, I hope Romney takes his Mormonism seriously and uses it to guide culture of life issues when he makes a decision.

Secondly, I just think it's absurd to believe that an adult human being in such a responsible position would take direct orders from a religious figure at this point in the twenty-first century on non-religious issues. The Mormon Church doesn't have, to the best of my knowledge, a worked-out view on tax policy. So what in the world would the prophet call and tell Romney to do? Would the prophet call and have Romney impose Mormonism on the United States by dictate? That's just such an absurd possibility that I don't think it's worth refuting.

HH: The second perennial objection is that, as you write in *The New Mormon Challenge*, Craig Hazen, there are 60,000 Mormon missionaries at work at this very moment, maybe even higher since the book came out in 2002, and that their zeal would be increased and their message made more legitimate by the presence in the presidency of their co-religionist. Your response?

CH: I was wondering if you were going to bring it up because that's the thing that I've been thinking a lot about. As an evangelical Christian and a fellow who thinks that Mormonism, as it stands today, presents an errant view of Jesus and the saving Gospel . . . I don't believe that Joseph Smith was a prophet of God. I believe he was mistaken and that he led a whole group of people into a mistaken notion about the identity of God and the nature of salvation. But given that—if you're an evangelical with that on your plate—you need to wonder and I think take this question seriously: would a Mormon president, a candidate, a solid candidate, a guy who actually gets into the White House, would that further in some way the Church of Jesus Christ of Latter-day Saints? As an evangelical I don't want the Church of Jesus Christ of Latter-day Saints to be furthered. I think it actually leads many people away from God and not necessarily towards God.

It's a mixed bag, and I'll stick with some generalizations here. So here you've got: "If Romney is a candidate or he becomes the president, would that enhance the Church of Jesus Christ of Latter-day Saints? Would they bring more people into their Church roles? Would their faithful be more encouraged to do missionary work? Would they see this as some sort of fulfillment of prophecy or some end-times event?"

Mormons are very millennial in that respect. They are looking for the end of the world and have been since their own beginning. Those are questions that Christians are going to have to think through.

In my best thinking at this point, I don't think it's an issue. I just don't think that's going to happen and, in fact, it's going to be a mixed bag for Mormons in the exact same way it's been a mixed bag for evangelicals having one of our own in the White House.

HH: John Mark Reynolds?

JMR: I think it isn't a problem, and I think that one reason is that evangelicals are going to have to deal with the fact that Mormonism is no longer a tiny movement. It's already dominant in one state politically. It's going to be dominant in two or three states in terms of the Republican Party in any case. Mormonism is not a tiny group that's going to go away. It has a first-rate university to defend its point of view, so is it possible that this will be a coming-out party for Mormonism as a mainstream group?

Possibly, but it already is a mainstream group. It's already part of the American fabric and it has been for a hundred years. Mormonism isn't going to go away. Now, I don't agree with Mormonism. I don't think people should be Mormons, but we simply have to recognize that Mormonism is a player. We have to engage in dialogue. Just as my good friends who are Jewish don't agree with me about the status of Jesus Christ, yet I am able to make common cause with them and not pretend that if I vote for a Jewish candidate for president, I'm making more people become Jewish.... I don't think in the case of voting for a Mormon I'm doing anything other than recognizing the fact that Mormonism is here to stay as part of the fabric of [the] American nation.

HH: The third objection and perhaps the most pervasive, I have summed up under the heading "It's Just Too Weird," and by that I mean [the objection] that people of serious intellectual accomplishment cannot buy into the Mormon narrative. I [heard] this on a number of points and the governor does love and believes his faith and we have to take it at face value that he accepts the claims made by his denomination. Does [it concern] you [that he] would believe a story this outside of the mainstream of the Christian narrative? We'll start with you, Professor Reynolds.

JMR: Well, I think traditional Christians—and I'm certainly a traditional evangelical Christian—should always be hesitant about using the "it's too weird" argument. After all, my church believes that when we approach communion, it's the very body and blood of Christ and that a mysterious thing happens. I have secular friends who think that's "just too weird." How can you be rational and believe in it? When I've written about this, I've suggested that the "it's too weird" argument is only legitimate if the "it's too weird" belief has political overtones, if [the particular belief] is going to cause me to have some strange notion that will have political ramifications.

For example, I think a Mormon would have been disqualified for running for president in the 1970s because of [the church's] views about African Americans that have since changed. And that Romney is now on the record as saying that he was opposed to [them] and was very glad when they were changed.

I think the second thing is: Do Mormons defend their "weird beliefs" using standard rational arguments and traditional philosophical apologetics? And the answer is, whether they are successful or not, they try. They have a first-rate university. They run apologetics programs. They try and make rational arguments defending their point of view. Now I personally think those arguments fail, but then my atheist friends think that my arguments for the Christian faith fail. So, I think in the open public square, if you're trying to play the game, if you're trying to be rational and your beliefs have policy implications within the mainstream of, let's say, the Republican and Democratic parties, your religion should cease to be "weird" and we give you a pass.

HH: Professor Hazen.

CH: I think it's going to be a problem for a small group of evangelicals who study these things and think "how can anybody believe that?" I think by and large for Americans it's not going to be a problem because, unfortunately, Americans in the big picture approach religion in a very different way. It's all something internal, [and] the objectivity of a particular religious view just doesn't come into play for them. They think everybody's got a religious view and it's their personal view and I think that's how they are going to look at it at the end of the day with somebody like Romney.

So, in other words, they are not going to [be] critiquing it—"[H]ow can you possibly believe that there were literal gold plates with some language called 'Reformed Egyptian' etched on them?" I'd actually like to see Romney answer that question, to see if he actually tackles those kinds of things. On the other hand, I'd like to see George Bush defend the resurrection too, and I'm not sure he could.

HH: You lead me very nicely into the ultimate of our subject matters which is what is appropriate to ask a political candidate about their practices. Governor Romney has been asked if he wears the sacred undergarments of the faith. I cringed at that. I cringe actually at the whole conversation. It strikes me as [going against] the civic religion of America to probe too deeply into somebody's religious practices.

Mark Halperin of ABC News told me that he's got to answer these questions. He's a secularist, but they are fascinated. I think they're fascinated because they want to embarrass religious believers about the particulars of faith. What is appropriate, Craig Hazen? That he ought to draw a line on and say, "Beyond this I shall not answer"?

CH: I agree about the sacred underwear issue. That ought to be off limits. But it seems to me that it is fair game. If you're a faithful LDS man, and you're going into the public square, there are a lot of curious people out there who want to know about this religion you're drawing to their attention for the first time. All along they've put it in kind of the "offbeat religion of Utah" column, and you're bringing it right into the center of the nation. So he's going to have to be prepared to answer some fairly in-depth questions about Mormonism, and he's probably going to have to do it on his own as best he can. So in other words, he can't be turning to BYU because that actually digs him deeper in the LDS trough.

HH: This is fascinating. John Mark Reynolds, we did not ask Jack Kennedy—even at the height of the questions and scrutiny—to discuss with us the Vatican Council.

JMR: Or transubstantiation, or his belief about Our Lady of Fatima, or whether the Virgin of Guadalupe really appeared.

If we start down this road of probing—I think here if I [were] talking to reporters as a philosopher—I [would argue] that you have to make distinctions between what matters in the public square and what doesn't. And what matters in the public square is what's going to have public policy implications. What kind of underwear a man wears, so far as I can tell, has no public policy implications whatsoever. My own beliefs about the Mass or the Eucharist—where I do have views that aren't in the mainstream of, let's say, Christianity in the United States orthodoxy—is a minority movement inside of traditional Christianity. They are just not relevant because, as far as I can tell, they have no public policy implications.

Now, suppose Mormonism still believed in polygamy, which plainly [the Church] does not. That would have a public policy implication in an era when marriage is being defined, when the definition of marriage is under assault, and Romney would have to answer how his church's views of marriage play out. But since the Church now has adopted—and has for a hundred years—a traditional view of marriage, I don't think it [or similar questions] are relevant questions to ask a Mormon about their more unusual or esoteric religious beliefs, if they don't have public policy implications.

HH: Do you think the MSM has a different agenda at work when they pursue Romney on issues related to his LDS practice and beliefs other than curiosity?

JMR: Yes. I think if I were Romney I wouldn't do those. But what I would be tempted to do is ask a secularist in the MSM, "Are you asking these questions to embarrass a religious believer or do you really want to know the answer? In which case, here are a series of books you can go read. Why haven't you read them to start with?"

And then the second thing I think he should say is, "Look, I know I'm running for public office, so my life's a bit of fair game for everyone. But you also have a public microphone, so let me ask you as a secularist, do you believe in free will and if you don't, how come you're cashing your paycheck and taking credit for something that you didn't really do?"

Now I know that Romney can't do that because you can't get into that kind of interaction with the media. But I do think there is a secularist agenda to pick on things in each religious group—whether it is Orthodoxy or Roman Catholicism or evangelical Christianity—that the other groups will think that are odd about the Orthodox or odd about Roman Catholics or odd about Pentecostal Christians [such as] "Do you speak in tongues?"

I was once at a meeting where the head of one of the Gannett Newspapers—in Rochester, New York—told my Pentecostal high school students that she believed they were disqualified from office if they spoke in tongues because it was just too strange. I called the ACLU and the City of Rochester and said, "Gosh that seems like such an odd thing for this woman to be saying who's writing editorials about Pentecostal candidates for office. What do you think of this?" (Of course the ACLU said, "Well, we don't like it but we're not going to touch it," because it wasn't the favored group that they like to defend.)

I think we want to be very careful with religious believers to not let secularists divide the united, while they themselves dislike each other, they have their own internal "atheists vs. agnostics" wars, and only unite when they are talking to religious people. So we have to be careful not to let them—like slicing baloney—slice off strange beliefs we have from everybody else's point of view and make every religious believer look absurd in the pubic square. What they do to Romney today, they might do to a Pentecostal who prays in a prayer language tomorrow, to a Catholic on the Virgin of Guadalupe the next day, and to an Orthodox Christian about weeping icons the next week. So we want to stay out of that game.

HH: Craig Hazen?

CH: Just thinking politically, I don't think Romney's particular religious views or practices are going to cause him a lot of trouble except for a couple of big blocs. For example, the Southern Baptist Convention. I can image the SBC coming out and being fairly firm against having a Mormon in that office. It's just been the way that they've approached the Mormons. When the SBC had their convention in Salt Lake City, they kind of stormed into some offices at BYU and made films and asked tough questions. It did not really warm the Mormons' hearts with regard to [the SBC's] outreach. They just have a particular stance. It's not done well in bringing the Southern Baptists and the Mormons together for mutual evangelism or anything else.

Another group might be the Evangelical Free Churches of America and some of the reformed churches who have a tougher stand. Beyond that, by and large I think that Americans have a very favorable attitude towards Mormons. If you ask a guy on the street about the Mormons, they go, "I don't know much about them. I know most of them are in Utah, but you know, the ones I've met are really good. They really take care of each other. They are good folks. If I was going to live next door to somebody, I'd like it to be a Mormon family."

HH: Last question. Call on your theological training. You are both theologians, you're both skilled apologists and you spend a lot of time training people [in Christian apologetics], so this is a theological question. For a "mere Christian," is it sinful to not vote for a Mormon because of their Mormon belief?

JMR: I believe it is sinful to not vote for a Mormon in the American political system solely on the grounds of their Mormon beliefs because it is irrational. If you began to examine why you wouldn't vote for a Mormon, it's very difficult to come up with non-bigoted or informed reasons for doing so. The only exception to that that I've ever been presented is your earlier argument that it might advance the Church of Latter-day Saints, but I don't feel that that's a probable account. I think that bigotry is always a sin, and that most of the people that I've talked to who won't vote for a Mormon are simply basing their non-vote on a prejudice and a misunderstanding of the open public square in a republic and the function of civic religion inside the United States.

HH: Craig Hazen?

CH: Given the complexities of what goes into a person's voting choice: who they are running against, what state they live in, and all these things, I don't know that I could land on the "I know it would be sinful" side. But here is a scenario under which it could be sinful to vote *for* Romney: if [the voter] believed in their heart that by voting for Romney they were somehow going to push forward the Church of Jesus Christ of Latter-day Saints that preaches a false Jesus and a false Gospel—if they believed in their heart that that might be a result of voting for Romney, it could be a sin to vote for Romney.

HH: Interesting. Concluding thoughts for this roundtable. I just want to make sure that I give you an open opportunity.

CH: I would vote for Romney in a heartbeat and primarily because I'm looking for a candidate that has a set of values [that resonates with me], and I think he's the guy. Because he's been governor of Massachusetts, that takes away all the angst that I might have if he were more politically inexperienced and from, say, a state like Utah.

HH: John Mark Reynolds?

JMR: I'm very close to the signing on to vote for Romney in the primary, though I haven't made a decision yet. But I'm very close to deciding to vote for Romney, and this is for four reasons.

First of all, I think that in the post-Bush era we need an articulate defender of both the war in Iraq, and general republican values— small "r"—towards government and family values. Up to this point both Reagan and Bush have, in my opinion, been fantastic presidents, but they haven't been skillful defenders of our perspective. They've been congenial and they've been supportive.

We need someone with the intellectual horsepower that can connect. I don't think either Bush or Reagan were foolish, but none were connected to strong rhetorical skills as defenders of our perspectives, and I think Romney has had to be in a tough situation in Massachusetts with a tough religious perspective and has been a skillful defender [of our values].

Secondly, I think that in the case of Romney we have a person who is also helping mainstream Mormonism. To the person with the concern that Craig Hazen so eloquently talked about, which I think is a legitimate concern, I would say this: my Mormon friends better be concerned that having someone [such as] this in the public eye will tend to mainstream their own beliefs. In other words, when you're hiding, it's easier to have strange, or what we would call "aberrant," Christian beliefs. When they are out in the public square, when Romney's out defending their point of view, when BYU is going to be called on to explain what's going on, I think this will have a mainstreaming effect on Mormonism far more than it will have an effect on Christian views about Mormonism. So actually, if I were Mormon, I would be more concerned about this than as an evangelical.

CH: I agree with that. I think it's entirely possible that a successful Romney presidency could actually open the door for deeper talks and engagement with evangelical Christians. And any time that happens—if evangelicals go in with a loving spirit, presenting the true gospel of Jesus—I've discovered Mormons move in our direction. It could actually help to mainstream them in a very positive way from the standpoint of an evangelical Christian.

JMR: Yes, I think that's right. I think that's exactly right.

Third, I think evangelicals—and again I include myself in that—traditional Roman Catholics, traditional Orthodox, and traditional evangelicals have often been accused of being intolerant, unable to separate theology from civil religion, believing in some sort of weird Constantinism or theocracy.

This is an excellent opportunity for evangelicals to show their political maturity—just as evangelical maturity in supporting Lieberman in a race where Lieberman is the best of the choices offered to Connecticut voters has shown a maturity and puts a lie to those slanders—so an evangelical ability to consider Romney. I didn't say support, that will have to be made on political grounds, but to consider Romney, will show critics the coming maturity of the "religious right."

And then finally, I think, the final positive about a Romney candidacy is that we are all talking about religion and the public square and we're not pretending that religion can be separated from the public square. People care about their religion. Romney cares. Bush cares. Barack Obama cares. Hillary Clinton cares about her religious beliefs. And the more we can dialogue about this in open ways—not in ways where we are playing "gotcha" about Mormon underwear, but trying to understand how people's religion interplays with their reason—then that's going to be a positive and Mitt Romney forces us to do that.

HH: John Mark Reynolds and Craig Hazen, fascinating. Thank you very much. I appreciate it.

NOTE: I provided a copy of the transcript of this conversation to two members of the General Authorities of the LDS Church, as well as to its spokesman, Michael Otterson, along with the invitation to provide one or two responses to any or all of the points discussed within it. Mr. Otterson declined the invitation on behalf of the Church.

Acknowledgments

Many people assisted me in the writing of this book. I appreciate the willingness of Governor Romney and many of his staff to be interviewed for the book, and especially the cooperation provided to me by Peter Flaherty, Eric Kress, Beth Myers, and Spencer Zwick. Dr. Jim Davies has been a wonderful guide to many aspects of the book, Tagg and Josh Romney allowed me to ask about their dad, and Bob White about Bain Capital. Stephen Studdert contributed much insight on Mormons in D.C. and government as well.

The team at Regnery Gateway and Eagle Publishing took a deep breath and okayed the project despite the publishing world's experience that "horserace" books don't sell and the difficulty of conveying through marketing that this is not such a book. Jeffrey Carneal, Marji Ross, and Harry Crocker all encouraged the project, and Tim Carney provided great editorial assistance.

Sealy and Curtis Yates remain the best of friends and agents.

As she has for seven of my eight books, Lynne Chapman oversaw the compilation of the manuscript and kept many of the interview transcripts from vanishing forever. Lynne has been my assistant since 1989, and she hasn't once complained about an absentminded-ness that manifests itself in misplaced books, tickets, and even com-puters. She is an astonishingly talented jack and master of many trades.

Mike Stefani helped us recover those bits of manuscript and tran-script that would vanish into the virtual depths. Snow Philip cast her practiced proofreading eye across the pages. Sealy and Curtis Yates remain the best of friends and agents.

I began the book eight months ago when a Romney run and a dis-cussion of his faith became certain. I asked a number of young folks to help with the research, and each provided superb assistance. Thanks to Jessica Bowlin, Diana Day, Michael Gordin, Robbie Haglund, and Parisa Sadoughianzadeh.

The radio team threw in as well, and Duane Patterson worked his magic in arranging interviews that were crucial to the book but which would simply not have happened had Duane not been behind the wheel. Adam Ramsey is another fine radio producer who assisted in the work, as did Michael Nolf and Anthony Ochoa. The parade of interns each contributed as well, as the demand for a fact, a quote, or a footnote interspersed with answering calls was done by each with real enthusiasm, so thanks to Katie Cervantes, Michael Germain, Mitch Neubert, Aabria Lipscomb, Austin Swaim, and Patrick Ahearn.

For the decade I have taught at Chapman University Law School, where Dean Parham Williams has presided over a young, dynamic, and growing school. All of the faculty appreciate his enormous gifts, and I especially his support for nontraditional contributions to schol-arship and his support for faculty—Left and Right—who believe that law is often most influenced through public debate and argument about its many facets. My colleague John Eastman has contributed much to my understanding of the Constitution and especially its care-ful embrace of religious liberty. Barbara Babcock and Gloria Davis have always been ready to help marry the demands of teaching, writing, and journalism. My students have been gracious about sudden departures when an interview became available. I thank them all.

Salem Communications is the home of my radio show and of Townhall.com, where I am the executive editor. Before any other major media company understood the synergy between the radio and the Web, Salem's founders Edward Atsinger and Stuart Epperson had, and they acted on it. The new media infrastructure that has liberated American politics from the handicap of a deep Left bias, which still permeates the now very far fallen titans of old media, owes much to these two gentlemen and their colleagues within the management of Salem. David Evans, Greg Anderson, Joe Davis, and Jim Cumby have led the transition from a radio company to a new media company that includes radio stations, and in so doing have significantly altered the face of American media and continue to do so.

I have been especially grateful to Russ Hauth, David Spady, Russ Shubin, and Chuck DeFeo, all of whom love politics and public policy as much as I do, and who keep the business of broadcasting focused on the product and its purpose. My colleagues behind microphones—Bill Bennett, Dennis Prager, Michael Medved, and Albert Mohler—are great friends as well as communicators, and the many other hosts within the Salem network have always been eager to publicize my books, even when they did not agree with my points of view. It is an extraordinary company, and people who work within it do so because they view the mission of attracting, informing, and activating America's citizens as crucial to the future of the country. Whether it is Tom Tradup and the Dallas team, a GM in a local market, or a sales staffer making the pitch that keeps us all on the air, Salem's people distinguish it among the media companies scrambling for eyeballs and ears.

Mary Katharine Ham and Dean Barnett have helped keep Hugh-Hewitt.com full of posts through a year when I was often obliged to post only to my word processor. They are both exceptional observers of American politics, and I very much appreciate the thoughtfulness of their writing, and their great, good humor. Dean gets great thanks from me as he repeatedly reviewed the manuscript and provided me with a number of crucial observations, suggestions, and corrections. He has brought a lot of style to the project, and the errors, omissions, or imperfections that remain are the result of my stubbornness, not his unwillingness to try to provide the right touch.

As with every other book, the most important person in its completion and success, even as she is to my life, is Betsy, without whom nothing would get done and nothing would be nearly as sweet.

Index

A

ABC, 127, 150, 251, 281

abortion, 128; Catholic Church and, 115–16, 227; Giuliani, Rudy and, 3, 104, 105, 107, 112, 154, 260; judicial nominations and, 103–7; Kerry, John and, 227; McCain, John and, 104, 105, 112, 165; partial birth, 3; Romney, Mitt and, 103–17. *See also* pro-life movement

Abraham, Spence, 181

Acheson, Dean, 1

ACLU. *See* American Civil Liberties Union

Adams, John, 122, 238

Adams, John Quincy, 241

Afghanistan, 2

African Americans, Campaign 2008 and, 170

African embassy bombings, 15

Ahmadinejad, Mahmoud, 157, 158

Alaska, 40

Alexander, Lamar, 181

Alito, Samuel, 102, 104, 154, 155, 254, 260

Allen, George, 4, 250, 262

AMC. *See* American Motors Corporation

America Alone (Steyn), 185

American Civil Liberties Union (ACLU), 243, 283

American Conservative Union, 164

American Gospel: God, the Founding Fathers, and the Making of a Nation (Meacham), 228

American Motors Corporation (AMC), 74

Amorello, Matthew, 156

Ampad Corp., 202

Angel, D. Duane, 74, 210

Anna Karenina (Tolstoy), 97

Areeda, Phillip, 46

Arizona, marriage in, 119–20, 121

Article6Blog (www.article6blog.com), 185–86, 245

Aspen Institute, 239

The Assassins (Lewis), 185

Atlantic Monthly, 225, 226, 253

Automobile Council for War Production, 73

Automobile Manufacturers Association, 73

B

Bailey, John, 34

Bain, Bill, 47–48, 53

Bain & Company: approach of, 50–51; "Bain way" and, 56–59; data and analysis and, 51–52; founding of, 47–48; recruitment and, 52; rescue of, 55–56; Romney, Mitt at, 45–59, 86, 201–2; strategic audit and, 51–53

Bain Capital, 50, 51, 54; founding of, 40; success of, 57. *See also* Bain & Company

Baker, James, 5

Bakhash, Shaul, 159

Bandy, Lee, 172

Barbour, Haley, 145, 261

Barnett, Dean, 9–10

The Battle for Peace (Zinni and Koltz), 185

BCCI, 202

Begala, Paul, 250

Bennett, Bill, 185

Bennett, Bob, 86

Bethany House, 218

Bible, 219

Biden, Joe, 229, 261–62

"The Big Dig" (Central Artery/Tunnel Project), 155–57

Big Love, 220

Biola University, 258–59, 273

biological weapons, 2

Bird, Rose, 147

Black, Conrad, 202

Blanco, Kathleen, 145

Blomberg, Craig, 89

Boggs, Lilburn, 21–22

Bond, Rich, 179

Book of Mormon, 25, 213, 214, 217, 219, 223

border security, 3, 5
Boston Consulting Group, 48
Boston Globe, 5, 83, 87, 108,
  113, 124, 134, 139, 159, 169,
  178, 179, 187, 202
Boston Globe magazine, 38
Boston Phoenix, 197
Boyer Company, 182
Bradley, Gerard V., 235
Branch Davidians, 218
Bremer, Paul, 184
Breyer, Stephen, 46
Brigham and Women's Hospital,
  85
Brigham Young University
  (BYU), 40, 45, 206, 209
Broder, David, 23–26, 39–41, 221
Brown, Jerry, 147
Brown, Lowell, 185–86, 245
Brown, Pat, 147
Brownback, Sam, 112, 197, 262
Brzezinski, Zbigniew, 184
Buddhism, 218–19
Bush, George H. W., 11–12, 42,
  105, 177, 183; judicial nomi-
  nations and, 106, 153
Bush, George W., 2, 16, 23, 42,
  59, 105, 170, 182; education
  and, 150; faith of, 231, 242;
  judicial nominations and,
  101–2; Khatami, Mohammed
  and, 157; as MBA president,
  61; media management and,

177–78; military service of,
  199; pro-life movement and,
  112; Romney, Mitt and, 61;
  Salt Lake City Olympics and,
  69; stem cell research and,
  114; as Texas governor, 150;
  War on Terror and, 190, 263,
  264–65
Bush, Jeb, 3, 145, 181, 261
BYU. *See* Brigham Young
  University

C
California, 146–47
campaign finance reform, 2,
  106, 164, 252
Campaign 2008: African Americans and, 170; anti-Mormon
  literature and, 217–21; calendar for, 167–74; campaign
  management and, 180–89;
  fundraising and, 178–80;
  media and, 70; Mormonism
  and, 167–70; MSM and,
  170, 174–78, 249; religious
  bigotry and, 43; Romney,
  Mitt, advantages in, 163–93;
  Romney, Mitt, as Massachusetts governor and, 148–65;
  Romney, Mitt, criticism of
  and, 195–204; Romney,
  Mitt, faith of and, 6–14,
  42–43, 96–97, 205–48;

Campaign 2008: *(cont'd)* Romney, Mitt, family of and, 96–97, 174; Salt Lake City Olympics and, 63–64, 69–72; War on Terror and, 189–93, 263–68

Campbell, John, 5–6

Canfield, Sally, 183

Carter, Jimmy, 2, 150, 241

Carville, James, 250

Case, Mary Irene, 82

Castellanos, Alex, 183

Catholic Church, 170; abortion and, 115–16, 227; Communion and, 227; renewal of, 232

Cato Institute, 12

Center for Security Policy, 189

Central Artery/Tunnel Project ("The Big Dig"), 155–57

Chappell, Jenifer Marie, 82

Chaput, Charles, 115–16, 232–35

Cheney, Dick, 104, 254

The Christian and the Cults (Martin), 217

Christianity, 7; Mormonism vs., 96, 215–17, 225, 230–31

The Christian Science Myth (Martin), 217

Chrysler Corporation, 57

Church of Jesus Christ of Latter-day Saints (LDS). *See* Mormonism

Cillizza, Chris, 179

civic religion, 9, 11, 237, 259

Clarion-Ledger, 221

Clinton, Bill, 2, 229, 244, 250

Clinton, Hillary, 15, 43, 60; Campaign 2008 and, 43, 72, 169–70, 250, 260–61; MSM and, 175; Salt Lake City Olympics and, 64

cloning, 112, 113, 128

Cobra II (Gordon and Trainor), 185

The Colbert Report, 268

Cold War, 192

Cole, USS, 15

Colson, Chuck, 229–31

Commonwealth PAC, 135, 149, 169, 171, 178, 179, 182, 183

Communism, 29, 33

Congressional Quarterly, 180

Congressional Research Service, 159

Connecticut, 145

conservatives: America, preservation of and, 1; Giuliani, Rudy and, 3, 260; judiciary and, 101; life, value of and, 1; McCain, John and, 2–3, 259–60; Supreme Court, U.S. and, 101; War on Terrorism and, 2

Constitution, U.S.: Article VI of, 9, 11, 235–37; Establishment

Clause of, 237; First Amendment, 2, 237; Fourteenth Amendment, 9, 237–38; Free Exercise of Religion Clause of, 237; Full Faith and Credit Clause of, 125; judicial nominations and, 2, 102, 104, 104–5, 154; majoritarianism in, 1, 5; marriage and, 125, 131, 133, 135; Religious Test Clause of, 9, 235–37; Second Amendment, 4

Consulting magazine, 49

"The Corner," 108

Corporate America, 49

Costa, Cindi, 173

Cowdery, Oliver, 213–14

Coxe, Tench, 237

Cranbrook School for Boys, 75–76

D

DailyKos, 60

Davies, Ann. *See* Romney, Ann

Davies, James, 14, 82, 87–88

Davies, Rod, 82

Davis, Gray, 147

Davis, Mitch, 172, 245–46

Dawson, Katon, 173

Dean, Howard, 42, 60, 171

Defense of Marriage Act (DOMA), 120

Del Valle, Milena, 155, 156

DeMint, Jim, 115–16, 172, 187

Democratic National Convention (2004), 146, 183

Democratic Party, Democrats: judicial nominations and, 104, 105; marriage, defense of and, 120; War on Terror and, 14–15; War on Terrorism and, 2

Detroit Free Press, 38

Detroit News, 34, 38

Detroit Victory Council, 73

Deukmejian, George, 147

Dobson, James, 211, 221

Doctrine and Covenants, 214, 219

DOMA. *See* Defense of Marriage Act

Domenech, Ben, 108, 110

Dominos, 51

Dowd, Matthew, 184

Downing, Joe, 8–9

Dukakis, Michael, 171, 177

Duscha, Julius, 25

Dutko Worldwide, 183

E

Eastland, Terry, 229, 244

Edwards, John, 72

Eisenhower, Dwight, 38, 43, 70

Election 2000, 59, 180, 181, 196

Ellsworth, Oliver, 236–37

Engler, John, 181

Enron, 202
Establishment Clause, 237
euthanasia, 112
Evangelical Free Churches of
   America, 284
EvangelicalsForMitt.com, 186
*An Examination of the Constitu-
   tion* (Coxe), 237

F
Falwell, Jerry, 165–66, 221
family: marriage and, 130; Mor-
   monism and, 78–79, 89, 226
Farrakhan, Louis, 165
fascism, Islamist, 14–15
Federal Marriage Amendment,
   116–17, 135–39, 257
Fehrnstrom, Eric, 183
Felli, Jesse, 240
Feltus, Will, 183
Financial Times, 7
Finney, Charles, 272
First Amendment, 2, 237
Flaherty, Peter, 111, 183
Flint, Jerry, 33
Ford, Gerald, 16
Ford, Thomas, 22
Fortune magazine, 180
Fourteenth Amendment, 9,
   237–38
Framers of the Constitution:
   faith of, 228, 237–39; religion
   and, 10; values of, 101

Franklin, Benjamin, 238–39
Free Exercise of Religion
   Clause, 237
free market, 1
Frist, Bill, 104, 105, 187
Frist, George, 4
Full Faith and Credit Clause, 125
Future Jihad (Phares), 185
The Future of Democracy
   (Zakaria), 185

G
Gaffney, Frank, 189
Gallup, 220
Gang of 14 fiasco, 2–3, 104, 112,
   154, 166, 196, 254
Gardner, Kem, 86–87, 181–82
Garff, Robert, 86
Gay and Lesbian Alliance
   (GLA), 142
George III, King, 238
George Washington University,
   178, 179
Gephardt, Richard, 109, 171
Gigot, Paul, 157
Gingrich, Newt, 109, 262
Ginsberg, Ben, 183
Giuliani, Rudy, 5, 259; abortion
   and, 3, 104, 105, 107, 112,
   154, 260; background of, 197,
   258; campaign management
   and, 185; Campaign 2008 and,
   72, 167; conservatives and,

2–3, 260; judicial nominations and, 154; marriage and, 3, 124, 260; MSM and, 175; Vietnam War and, 199; War on Terror and, 107, 190, 260
GLA. *See* Gay and Lesbian Alliance
God, 60, 124; Mormonism and, 215–16, 219
The Godfather: Part II, 175
Goldwater, Barry, 22–23, 27, 29, 171
Good Morning America, 127
Goodridge v. *Massachusetts Department of Health*, 125, 126
Goodwin, Doris Kearns, 13, 58
Gordon, Lou, 31
Gordon, Michael, 185
Gore, Al, 59, 109, 177–78, 261, 266
Graham, R. Malcolm, 154
Grainger, Andrew, 154, 155
Greenwald, Mandy, 250
Ground Zero, 68–69

H

Hale-Bopp hitchhiker-suicides, 218
Halperin, Mark, 251–54, 281
Hannity, Sean, 185
Hanson, Victor Davis, 184
Hardball, 105, 175

Harper's magazine, 26
Harris, John, 251
Harvard Business School (HBS), 46, 47–48, 49, 56, 95, 206
Harvard Stem Cell Institute, 60, 113, 114
Harvard University, 4, 40, 46
Hatch, Orrin, 23, 86
Hazen, Craig, 259; interview with, 271–87
HBS. *See* Harvard Business School
health care: Medicare and Medicaid spending and, 266; Romney, Mitt and, 150–53; universal medical insurance plan and, 12, 150–53
Heaven's Gate cult, 218
Helman, Scott, 187
Heritage Foundation, 150–51, 152
The Heritage Guide to the Constitution, 235
Hess, Stephen, 23–26, 39–41, 221
Hezbollah, 157, 158
Hill, Anita, 203
Hinderaker, John, 257, 258
A History of Christianity in the United States and Canada (Noll), 239
Hitchens, Christopher, 205, 208, 224–25, 239

Holland, Jeffrey, 169
homosexuality: Iran and, 159;
    Islam and, 159; Romney, Mitt
    and, 5, 151–52, 159–60
Houseman, John, 46
Huckabee, Mike, 112, 262
Hughes, Sarah, 69
HughHewitt.com, 9
Hunter, Duncan, 262
Hurlbut, William, 114
Hurricane Katrina, 145
Hussein, Saddam, 261

I
Ickes, Harold, 164, 250
immigration: Kennedy, Edward
    and, 106, 165; McCain, John
    and, 164–65, 196
Ingraham, Laura, 185, 211
Inside the Olympic Industry
    (Lenskyj), 65
Instapundit.com, 188
International Olympic Commit-
    tee (IOC), 40, 65, 71
"In 2008, Will It Be Mormon in
    America?" (Eastland), 229
IOC. See International Olympic
    Committee
Iowa, 42, 97, 112; Campaign
    2008 and, 167–69
Iran, 4, 5; homosexuality and,
    159; Islamic Republic in, 2;
    nuclear weapons and, 157, 189

Iraq Study Group, 5
Iraq War. See War on Terror
Isaacson, Arlene, 139–40
Isaacson, Walter, 239
Islam, 159, 223
Islamist fascism, 14–15, 219
Israel, 158, 189

J
Jackson, Andrew, 238
Jay, John, 238
Jefferson, Thomas, 206, 227,
    239, 241, 247
Jeffords, Jim, 254
Jeffs, Warren, 220
Jehovah of the Watchtower
    (Martin), 217
Jehovah's Witnesses, 218
Jerusalem Post, 6
Jesus Christ, 212, 217, 218,
    226
jihadism, 267–68
John Birch Society, 29
JohnMarkReynolds.info, 275
Johnson, Paul, 238–39
Johnson, Scott, 257
Johnston, Phil, 199–200
John the Baptist, 213, 214
Jones, Jim, 218
Judaism, 7
judicial nominations: abortion
    and, 103–7; Bush, George H.
    W. and, 106, 153; Bush,

George W. and, 101–2; Constitution, U.S. and, 2, 102, 104, 104–5, 154; Democratic Party, Democrats and, 104, 105; filibustering and, 104, 106; Gang of 14 fiasco and, 2–3, 104, 112, 154, 166, 196, 254; Giuliani, Rudy and, 154; McCain, John and, 104, 105–6, 154, 166; Republican Party, Republicans and, 105, 154; Right vs. Left and, 102; Romney, Mitt and, 101–6, 153–55, 260. *See also* Supreme Court, U.S.

judiciary. *See* judicial nominations; Supreme Court, U.S.

K

Katrina, Hurricane, 145
Katzman, Kenneth, 159
Katzmann, Gary, 154–55
Kaufman, Ron, 183
Keating Five scandal, 196
Keenan, Lynn Romney, 82
Kempthorne, Dirk, 181
Kennedy, Anthony, 106
Kennedy, Edward, 3, 5, 40; 1994 Senate campaign of, 86, 87, 107, 108, 141, 188, 202, 244; immigration and, 106, 165, 196
Kennedy, Joe, 244

Kennedy, John F., 12, 13, 25–26, 169, 170, 221, 247, 259
Keough, Bruce, 171
Kerry, John, 171, 178, 203, 261–62; abortion and, 227; Campaign 2008 and, 72; faith of, 226–27; MSM and, 200–201; wealth of, 200–201
Kerry, Teresa Heinz, 199
Khan, A. Q., 264
Khatami, Mohammed, 157–60, 263
Khobar Towers bombing, 15
The Kingdom of the Cults (Martin), 217–18
Kingdoms in Conflict (Colson), 232
"King Follett Discourse" (Smith), 215
Kissinger, Henry, 70, 184
Koltz, Tony, 185
Korean War, 1
Koresh, David, 218
Krimsky, John, 64–65
Kristol, Bill, 184
Ku Klux Klan, 9

L

Lamont, Ned, 60
LDS. *See* Church of Jesus Christ of Latter-day Saints
Leahy, Patrick, 254
Leavitt, Mike, 71

Ledeen, Michael, 184

Lee, Rex, 211–14, 225

Lenskyj, Helen Jefferson, 65

"The Lessons of the Father" (Swidey), 38

Lewis, Bernard, 185

Lieberman, Joseph, 59, 227, 229, 248

Lileks, James, 266

Liljenquist, 82

Limbaugh, Rush, 185

Lincoln, Abraham, 58, 122, 140, 264, 265, 269; faith of, 239–41, 247

Linker, Damon, 8

Lodge, Henry Cabot, 34, 171

London Times, 135

The Looming Tower (Wright), 185

Lopez, Kathryn Jean, 108

Los Angeles Dodgers, 82

Los Angeles Times, 220

Louisiana, 145

Luther, Martin, 232

M

MacArthur, Douglas, 2

McCain, John, 5, 23, 229; abortion and, 104, 105, 112, 165; border security and, 3; campaign finance reform and, 2, 164, 196, 252; campaign management and, 185; Campaign 2008 and, 72, 167, 170, 249–50; Christian conservatives and, 165–66; conservatives and, 2–3, 259–60; Election 2000 and, 180, 181, 196; fundraising and, 179, 196; Gang of 14 fiasco and, 2–3, 104, 112, 154, 166, 196; immigration and, 164–65, 196; judicial nominations and, 2–3, 104, 105–6, 154, 166; Keating Five scandal and, 196; marriage, defense of and, 120–21, 124, 135, 139; military service of, 196, 198, 199; MSM and, 175, 250; Republican Party, Republicans and, 163–66; Romney, Mitt vs., 163–66; Salt Lake City Olympics and, 71; temper of, 197; War on Terror and, 3, 190, 192, 259

McCain-Feingold campaign finance reform bill, 2, 164, 252

McCullough, David, 1, 75

McCurry, Mike, 244–45

McKay, David O., 221

McKinsey & Company, 49

McNamara, Robert, 34, 192

Madison, James, 238

mainstream media (MSM): 1968 presidential campaign and,

28–30; Campaign 2008 and, 70, 170, 249; Clinton, Hillary and, 175; Giuliani, Rudy and, 175; Kerry, John and, 200–201; marriage, defense of and, 120, 124, 135; McCain, John and, 175, 250; Mormonism and, 234, 281–83; Obama, Barack and, 175; politics and, 28–30; pro-life movement and, 110; Republican Party, Republicans and, 163–64; Romney, Mitt and, 70, 174–78, 249–54, 262; Salt Lake City Olympics and, 176–77

majoritarianism, 1, 5

The Making of the President, 1968 (White), 23, 27

Malone, Joe, 182

marriage: in Arizona, 119–20, 121; Constitution, U.S. and, 125, 131, 133; defense of, 5, 116–17; definition of, 132–34; family and, 130; Federal Marriage Amendment and, 116–17, 135–39, 257; Giuliani, Rudy and, 3, 124, 260; judicial assault on, 3; in Massachusetts, 116, 119, 121, 121–29, 146; McCain, John and, 120–21, 124; Mormonism and, 209,

210, 216, 221, 282; MSM and, 124, 135, a; Romney, Mitt and, 5, 116–17, 146, 148, 257, 260; Supreme Court, U.S. and, 125; traditional definition of, 5, 119; in Vermont, 125

Marshall, Margaret J., 126

Martin, Walter, 217–20

Mary, 225

Mason, George W., 74

Massachusetts: Central Artery/Tunnel Project in, 155–57; marriage in, 116, 119, 121–29, 146; Romney, Mitt as governor of, 5, 61, 72, 110, 115, 116, 121–29, 147–65, 256

Massachusetts Constitution, 121, 123, 126, 127, 128

Massachusetts Gay and Lesbian Political Caucus, 139

Massachusetts Supreme Judicial Court, 116–17, 119, 123, 126, 127, 131, 134, 135, 140

Massachusetts Turnpike Authority (MTA), 155–57

Matthews, Chris, 105, 163

Maxwell, Neal, 14, 216–17

The Maze of Mormonism (Martin), 217

Meacham, Jon, 228–29, 238, 247

Meade, William J., 154, 155
media. *See* mainstream media
(MSM)
Meese, Ed, 16, 211
Meet the Press, 175, 200
Mehlman, Ken, 183, 184
Melton, Douglas A., 60, 113
Mexico, 210
Michigan, 97, 112; Campaign
2008 and, 167, 174; Romney,
George as governor of, 4;
state constitution of, 75
Miers, Harriet, 102, 263
Miller, William, 273
Mirengoff, Paul, 257
MittRomney.com, 187
Mohler, Albert, 251, 255–57
Mondale, Walter, 177
Mormon America (Ostling and
Ostling), 21, 215
Mormonism: anti-Mormon liter-
ature and, 217–21; baptism
and, 207, 213–14; Campaign
2008 and, 167–70; Christian-
ity, orthodox vs., 96, 215–17,
225, 230–31; confession and
forgiveness and, 207–8; doctrine of, 23–26; family and,
78–79, 89, 226; founding narrative of, 208–9; God, doctrine of and, 215–16, 219;
marriage and, 209, 210, 216,
221, 282; missionary work

and, 25, 205–6, 223–24,
278–79; MSM and, 8, 234,
281–83; origins of, 23,
212–14; patriotism and, 30,
226; polygamy and, 210, 216,
221, 282; presidency, influence on of, 221–22, 255–56,
277–78; presidential cam-
paigns and, 21–23; priesthood
in, 225; Salt Lake City
Olympics and, 66–67; salva-
tion and, 219–20; scriptures
of, 214, 219; as "weird,"
224–30, 280–81; women in,
225. *See also* Church of Jesus
Christ of Latter-day Saints
(LDS)
Mormonism (Martin), 217
Morris, Dick, 109, 110
Morrissey, Ed, 257–58
Mosser, Carl, 168
Mosteller, Cyndi, 172–73
MoveOn.org, 60
Mr. Smith Goes to Washington,
64
MTA. *See* Massachusetts Turn-
pike Authority
Mullen, Robert, 25
Multiple Sclerosis Society, 83
Murkowski, Frank, 145
Murphy, Michael, 180
MyDD, 60
Myers, Beth, 149, 182

N

Nash-Kelvinator Corporation, 74
National Catholic Bioethics Center, 114
National Governors' Conference (1967), 34
National Media, Inc., 183
National Review Online, 108
national security, 15
Nauvoo, Ill., 22, 209
NBC, 127
Neuhaus, Richard John, 8
New England Legal Foundation, 155
New Hampshire, 42, 97, 112; Campaign 2008 and, 167, 170–72
New Hampshire Federation of Republican Women, 135
New Jersey, marriage in, 125
The New Mormon Challenge, 168, 223, 272, 278
The New Republic, 7, 8
Newsweek, 25, 180, 228
New Testament, 213, 239
New York Times, 33, 106
Nixon, Richard, 4, 16, 25, 27, 28, 35, 164, 212, 230
Noll, Mark, 239–40
Noonan, Peggy, 266–67
North Korea, 2, 264
"The Note," 251

nuclear weapons, 2, 157, 189, 264

O

Obama, Barack, 43; Campaign 2008 and, 169–70, 250, 261
O'Connor, Sandra Day, 106
O'Donnell, Rosie, 243
Oliver, Jack, 182
"One Man, One Woman: A Citizen's Guide to Protecting Marriage" (Romney), 129
Ostling, Richard and Joan, 21–22, 215–16
The Other Side of Heaven (Davis), 245
Otterson, Michael R., 169, 287

P

P2008, 178, 179
Pacholczyk, Tadeusz, 114
Paine, Thomas, 239
Painting the Map Red (Hewitt), 170
The Paper Chase, 46
Pappu, Sridhar, 225–27, 229
Parkinson's disease, 113
Parra, Derek, 69
Patrick, Deval, 124
PBS. *See* Public Broadcasting Service
"The Pearl of Great Price," 214, 219

Pelosi, Nancy, 58
"People's Temple," 218
Pearson, Drew, 31
Phares, Walid, 185
polygamy, 210, 216, 221, 282
pornography, 128
Pratt, Orson, 272
President's Council on
    Bioethics, 114, 115
Prestap, Kim, 141–42
Prison Fellowship, 229
pro-life movement: Bush,
    George W. and, 112; McCain,
    John and, 105; MSM and,
    110; primary goal of, 103;
    Romney, Mitt and, 103–17;
    stem cell research and, 111.
    See also abortion
property rights, 1
Pryor, William, 254
Public Broadcasting Service
    (PBS), 14, 66

Q
Quadrennial Defense Review,
    191
Quorum of the Twelve Apostles,
    21, 216

R
Rapoza, Phillip, 154, 155
Rasmussen Reports, 10, 220
Rath, Tom, 171

Reagan, Ronald, 16, 34, 69, 105,
    177, 266, 269; as California
    governor, 146, 147; Cold War
    and, 192; judicial nominations
    and, 106; MSM and, 164
Reid, Harry, 58, 224
Reilly, Adam, 197
religion, 257; civic, 9, 11, 237,
    257, 259; freedom of, 1, 13,
    128
Religious Right, 8, 243, 287
Religious Test Clause, 9, 235–37
The Republican Establishment
    (Hess and Broder), 23, 221
Republican Log Cabin Club of
    Massachusetts, 141
Republican National Conven-
    tion (2004), 135, 146
Republican Party, Republicans:
    judicial nominations and, 105,
    154; marriage, defense of
    and, 120; McCain, John and,
    163–66; MSM and, 163–64
Reuther, Walter, 73
Reynolds, Glenn, 188
Reynolds, Helen, 188
Reynolds, John Mark, 259;
    interview with, 271–87; Mor-
    monism and, 272–73; politics
    and faith and, 275–76
Rhodes, James, 27
Rice, Condoleezza, 184, 248, 261
Ridge, Tom, 183

Right, Religious, 8, 243, 287

Roberts, B. H., 215–16, 219–20

Roberts, David, 56

Roberts, John, 102, 104, 154, 155, 254, 260

Roberts, Robin, 183

Robertson, Pat, 165–66

Robinson, Jane Romney, 82

Robinson, Tim, 63

Rockefeller, Nelson, 27, 31, 34–37

Rockwell, Norman, 93

Roe v. Wade, 3, 103, 104, 106, 125

Rogge, Jacques, 69

Roman Catholic Church. *See* Catholic Church

Romney, Ann, 4, 14, 75; character of, 88–89; conversion to Mormonism of, 13, 88, 209; family of, 78–86; marriage of, 79–81, 209; multiple sclerosis of, 60–61, 83–85, 112–13; Romney, Mitt career and, 79, 83, 86–89, 181–82; stem cell research and, 112–13

Romney, Benjamin Pratt ("Ben"), 82, 91–92, 209

Romney, Craig Edward, 78, 81, 82, 92, 209

Romney, Gaskell, 210

Romney, George: 1968 presidential campaign of, 22–23, 26–27, 27–37, 74, 221–22; background of, 73–75; "brainwashing" statement of, 31–35; character of, 38; faith of, 25, 209–10; marriage of, 78; as Michigan governor, 4; Rockefeller, Nelson betrayal of, 31, 34–37; Romney, Mitt and, 39–43

Romney, Joshua James ("Josh"), 82, 84–85, 91, 92–93, 95, 169, 209

Romney, Lenore, 37, 40–41, 75–76, 78

Romney, Matthew Scott ("Matt"), 82, 91, 209

Romney, Miles, 209–10

Romney, Mitt: 1994 Senate campaign of, 5, 40, 83, 86, 87–88, 107, 108, 141, 188, 202, 244; 2002 gubernatorial campaign of, 108–9, 180, 181; background of, 4, 73–81; at Bain & Company, 40, 45–59, 86; border security and, 5; Bush, George W. and, 61; as businessman, 4, 45–59, 201–4; Campaign 2008 and, 6–14; criticism of, 195–204; economy and, 4; education of, 40, 45–46, 76–78, 206; faith of, 4, 6–14, 96–97, 205–48; family of, 72, 78–97, 174,

Romney, Mitt: *(cont'd)* 262;
     health care and, 12, 150–53;
     homosexuality and, 5, 141–42,
     159–60; judicial nominations
     and, 101–6, 153–55, 260;
     Khatami, Mohammed and,
     157–60; marriage and, 4, 5,
     116–17, 121–43, 146, 148,
     257, 260; as Massachusetts
     governor, 5, 61, 72, 86, 110,
     115, 116, 121–29, 147–65,
     256; McCain, John vs.,
     163–66; MSM and, 70,
     174–78, 262; pro-life views of,
     4, 103–17, 188–89; Romney,
     Ann, multiple sclerosis and,
     60–61, 83–85; Salt Lake City
     Olympics and, 3, 40, 63–72,
     86–87; Second Amendment
     and, 4; stem cell research
     and, 60–61, 111–16, 146, 148;
     Vietnam War and, 198–99;
     War on Terror and, 4,
     184–85, 189–93, 260, 267;
     wealth of, 199–201
Romney, Scott, 75
Romney, Taggart ("Tagg"),
     75–76, 78, 81, 84–85, 89–91,
     92–93, 209
Romney: A Political Biography
     (Angel), 74
RomneyForPresident.com, 185
Roosevelt, Franklin D., 265, 269

Roosevelt, Theodore, 37–38
Roth, Hyman, 175
Rove, Karl, 183
Rubin, Michael, 159
rule of law, 2
Rumsfeld, Donald, 191, 263
RunMittRun.org, 245
Rush, Benjamin, 236
Russert, Tim, 200

S
Salmon, Matt, 243–44
Salt Lake City Olympics, 3;
     "Bain way" and, 56, 61, 65;
     Campaign 2008 and, 63–64,
     69–72; Clinton, Hillary and,
     64; financial problems and,
     65–67, 68, 149; "games for
     bribes" scandal and, 65; gay
     and lesbian community and,
     141–42; LDS and, 66–67;
     McCain, John and, 71; MSM
     and, 176–77; Romney, Mitt
     and, 40, 63–72, 86–87; Sep-
     tember 11 and, 68–69
Salt Lake City Tribune, 65
Salt Lake Olympic Committee
     (SLOC), 64, 65, 71, 149, 176
same-sex marriage: Constitution,
     U.S. and, 135; in Massachu-
     setts, 119, 121–29; Social
     Security and, 120. *See also*
     marriage

SBC. *See* Southern Baptist Convention

Scalia, Antonin, 154

Schmidt, Steven, 184

Scholle, August (Gus), 26

Schroeder, John, 186, 245

Schumer, Charles, 254

Schwarzenegger, Arnold, 6, 10–12, 145, 147, 181, 184

Scientology, 6, 7, 219

Scowcroft, Brent, 184

Searching for God in America (PBS), 14

Second Amendment, 4

Seed, Deeda, 66

September 11, 15, 68–69, 72, 107, 192

Sessions, Jeff, 181

Shakley Products, 49–50

Sharpton, Al, 165

Sherman, Roger, 236

Shields, Lynn Moon, 75, 76, 78, 83

Slate, 7

SLOC. *See* Salt Lake Olympic Committee

Smith, Al, 221

Smith, Joseph, 7, 209, 225, 268; God, doctrine of and, 215; Mormonism, founding of and, 212–14; presidential candidacy of, 21–23

Smith, Stephen, 187

Smith, William French, 16, 211, 212

Social Security, 57–58, 120, 266

Soros, George, 60, 164, 261

Souter, David, 106, 107, 153

South Carolina, 97, 112; Campaign 2008 and, 167, 172–73

Southern Baptist Convention (SBC), 284

Stanford, 56, 79, 206

Staples, 51, 69

The State, 172

stem cell research: Bush, George W. and, 114; multiple sclerosis and, 60–61; Romney, Mitt and, 111–16, 146, 148

Stephens, Bret, 6

Stevenson, Adlai, 43

Stewart, Jon, 268

Steyn, Mark, 185

Stirling, Don, 169

Straight Talk America PAC, 179

Sullivan, Amy, 227, 229

Sullivan, Andrew, 135, 243

Sununu, John, 172

Supreme Court, U.S.: campaign finance reform and, 164; conservatives and, 101; Election 2000 and, 59; marriage and, 125; War on Terror, detainees of and, 3. *See also* judicial nominations; judiciary

Swainson, John, 25

Swidey, Neil, 38–49
Swift Boat Veterans for Truth, 203
Syria, 5

T
Taft, Bob, 145
Taft-Hartley Act, 221
Taliban, 2
Tancredo, Tom, 262, 266
Team of Rivals (Goodwin), 58
Texas, 210
Thomas, Clarence, 154, 203
Thomas, Jennifer Dyan, 82
Thompson, Tommy, 181, 183, 262
Time magazine, 34, 74
Today Show, 70, 127
Tolstoy, Leo, 97
Torcaso, Roy, 237
Torcaso v. *Watkins*, 237
Trainor, Bernard, 185
Travaglini, Robert E., 114
Treer, Julie, 183
Truman, Harry S., 25, 70, 75, 269
Truman (McCullough), 1
Turnaround (Romney), 50, 63, 68, 72, 87, 142, 148, 174, 175, 176

U
UN. *See* United Nations

Under the Banner of Heaven (Krakauer), 220
Unification Church, 219
Union Leader (New Hampshire), 171
United Auto Workers, 73
United Nations (UN), 155
United States Dressage Federation, 83
United Way, 83
USA Today, 49, 150
U.S. Olympic Committee, 64–65, 71

V
The Vault, 47
Vennochi, Joan, 134–35, 140
Vermont, marriage in, 125
Vietnam War, 32–34, 199
The Village Enlightenment in America (Hazen), 272
VOLPAC, 187
Vuono, Ariane, 154–55

W
Wallace, Mike, 31
Wall Street Journal, 6, 129, 157, 246
Walrath, Allen, 74–75
War Footing (ed. Gaffney), 189
Warner, Mark, 145
War on Terror: Bush, George W. and, 190, 263, 264–65; Cam-

paign 2008 and, 189–93, 263–68; conservatives, American and, 2; Democratic Party, Democrats and, 2, 14–15; Giuliani, Rudy and, 107, 260; McCain, John and, 190, 192, 259; Romney, Mitt and, 4, 184–85, 189–93, 260, 267; treatment of detainees of, 3

Warren, Earl, 146, 147

Washington, George, 200, 238–39, 241

Washington Monthly, 227

Washington Post, 25, 106, 110, 179, 251

Washington Post Company, 7

Watergate, 16, 230

The Way to Win: Taking the White House in 2008 (Harris), 251, 252

weapons of mass destruction (WMD), 2, 157, 189, 264

Webb, James, 250

Weekly Standard, 229

Weisberg, Jacob, 7, 9, 10, 13

Westmoreland, William, 34

What Do Mormons Believe? (Lee), 212

White, Bob, 51–52, 148, 181

White, Theodore, 23, 26, 27–32, 39

Whitman, Christie, 181

Will, George, 191

Wilson, Pete, 147

Wilson, Woodrow, 241–42

WMD. *See* weapons of mass destruction

Wolfson, Howard, 250

World Trade Center bombing (1993), 15

World War I, 265

Wright, Lawrence, 185

Y

Young, Brigham, 14, 22, 209, 221

"Youth for Ford" campaign, 16

Z

Zakaria, Fareed, 185

Zinni, Anthony, 185

Zwick, Spencer, 182